'Fearful Realities'
New Perspectives on the Famine

EDITED BY

Chris Morash & Richard Hayes

IRISH ACADEMIC PRESS

This book was set in 10.5 on 12 point Bembo for
IRISH ACADEMIC PRESS
Kill Lane, Blackrock, Co. Dublin, Ireland
and in North America for
IRISH ACADEMIC PRESS
5804 NE Hassalo St, Portland, Oregon 97213.

A catalogue record for this title
is available from the British Library.

ISBN 0-7165-2565-8 cased
0-7165-2566-6 pbk

Printed in Ireland
by ColourBooks Ltd, Dublin

Contents

Preface

This collection of essays originated at a conference on the Famine organised by the Society for the Study of Nineteenth-Century Ireland, held in St Patrick's College, Maynooth in July of 1994. Consequently, this volume would not have come into being were it not for the continued work, guidance, and financial assistance of the Society for the Study of Nineteenth-Century Ireland, and in particular its executive officers. Similarly, St Patrick's College, Maynooth has been instrumental in helping the editors in their work in many ways. Bill Tinley and the Conference Centre were invaluable in the organisation of the initial conference; Brian Cosgrove, Peter Denman and the Department of English have provided financial and other assistance at all stages of the project; the Publications Committee generously provided financial support; and the Office of the Master co-sponsored the launch of the book. The editors would also like to thank Michael Adams and the staff at Irish Academic Press, as well as all the contributors, for making our work so light.

Individual contributors also have debts that require acknowledgment.

Charles Orser wishes to acknowledge the assistance of Luke Dodd, administrator of the Famine Museum, Strokestown; Farrell O'Gara, owner of Gorttoose; Lionel Pilkington and Angela Savage, UCG; Kevin Whelan, of the Royal Irish Academy; Terry Barry and Ronald Cox, Trinity College; Michael Ryan of the Chester Beatty Library; Conleth Manning, Office of Public Works; Collette O'Daly, National Library of Ireland; Don Mullan and the staff of Strokestown Park House. He also wishes to acknowledge the field support and editing skills of Janice L. Orser. The field research for 'Can there be an Archaeology of the Great Famine?' was conducted as part of an Illinois State University archaeological field course, administered by the Office of International Studies and Programmes, and the students were Leah Bottger, Ranan Chatterjea, Neil Cole, Katherine Hull, David Ryder, Jeanne Schultz, and Scott Wagers.

Matthew Stout wishes to record his thanks to Ms Geraldine Stout, Archaeologist, Archaeological Survey, Office of Public Works; Kevin Whelan, Royal Irish Academy; Dr William E. Vaughan, Trinity College.

Sean Ryder wishes to thank Áine Ní Léime and Niall Ó Ciosáin for their help and encouragement.

Larry Geary would like to acknowledge his indebtedness to the Wellcome Trust, whose support facilitated the research on which his article is based.

Donal Jordan wishes to thank William Davies of Cambridge University Press, and David Miller of Carnegie Mellon Univeristy. Neil Buttimer would like to acknowledge the assistance of Professor Séan Ó Coileáin and of Kenneth Nicholls.

'Fearful Realities': An Introduction

CHRIS MORASH & RICHARD HAYES

> The reader of these pages should be told that, if strange things are re-
> corded, it was because strange things were seen; ... And now, while looking
> at them calmly at a distance, they appear, even to myself, more like a
> dream than reality, because they appear out of *common course*, and out of
> the order of even nature itself. But they *are* realities, and many of them
> fearful ones – realities which none but eye-witnesses can understand, and
> none but those who passed through them can *feel*.[1]

It may well be no coincidence that two of the more respected and widely-read
modern studies of the Irish Famine – R.D. Edwards and T.D. Williams's *The
Great Famine* and Cathal Póirtéir's *The Great Irish Famine* – are interdisciplinary
collections of essays. There is something about the Famine which seems to
invoke what might almost be called a humility in historians, an unwillingness to
venture into one of the largest and darkest areas of Irish history without a strong
complement of colleagues bearing an arsenal of varied disciplinary weapons.
'Fearful' is probably the wrong word here, even if it was the word used by one
eyewitness of the period, the American traveller, Asenath Nicholson, when she
wrote of the condition of Ireland in 1848 as a series of 'fearful realities'. 'The
famine', she writes when recording what she calls 'the superstitions of the peasantry', 'changed their poetical romance into such fearful realities that no time
was left to bestow on imagination'.[2]

The two words which recur in Nicholson's work from the late 1840s and
early 1850s – 'realities' and 'imagination' – and the third term with disrupts
them – 'fearful' – anticipate in many ways the focus of debate which emerged at
a conference dealing with the Famine held a century and a half later. In July of
1994, the Society for the Study of Nineteenth-Century Ireland's conference on
the Famine brought together at St Patrick's College, Maynooth an archeolo-
gist, a medical historian, literary and cultural critics, a church historian, as well as
historians with interests in population change, class allegiances, and relief administration.

For some of the scholars at this conference, particularly those we have included in the opening section entitled 'Realities: Responses and Implications',

---

1 Asenath Nicholson, *Lights and Shades of Ireland* (New York, 1851), v. iii, p. 229.
2 Nicholson, *Lights and Shades*, v. iii, p. 427.

the Famine is a presence to be invoked, conjured into existence as a physical, tangible reality. In the opening essay, Matthew Stout examines the realities of depopulation and consolidation in the Smith estate in Baltyboys, county Wicklow, through a combination of statistical sources and an eyewitness account – the diaries of Elizabeth Smith, the wife of the landlord of the estate. Following Stout's essay, Donald Jordan considers the demographic and economic changes which occured during and after the Famine in county Mayo. In spite of the fact that both these papers deal with different parts of the country, however, they do reach similar conclusions: that, at the expense of small farmers, large grazier farmers were among those to benefit from the Famine.

The next essay in the section, by Laurence Geary of the Royal College of Surgeons in Ireland, begins where perhaps any study of the Famine should begin: with the body. As well as drawing attention to the variety and malignity of diseases which appeared as 'famine's shadow' during the Great Famine, his essay gives an account of what in one sense were the most real responses to the suffering, those of medical institutions to the disease and the hunger.

The 'Realities' section moves to a close with an essay by James S. Donnelly, Jr., which opens up the question of interpretation. Where earlier papers in this section address themselves to those aspects of the Famine which can be measured – incidence of disease, changes in landholding, mechanisms of relief – Donnelly examines the ways in which we can ascribe meaning to these factual realities. The final paper in the section moves the question of establishing the physical reality of the Famine into a new arena, as Charles Orser, Jr., one of the pioneers in the field of slave archeology in the United States, poses the question: 'can there be an archeology of the Great Famine?'. In his account of his preliminary excavations on the Strokestown estate in County Roscommon, the answer would appear to be 'yes'. While some of the earlier essays in the collection, particularly Matthew Stout's work on the Baltyboys estate in County Wicklow, locate traces of the past in the landscape in ways which recall, for instance, the work of Kevin Whelan, Orser digs more deeply into the soil to unearth those physical objects whose tangible physicality brings the reality of the Famine into our own age.

Orser's move beyond the written word brings us into the territory marked out by the second section, 'Representations'. While none of the literary, cultural or theological historians and critics in this section would deny the physical reality of the Famine, many of them are troubled by its elusiveness while simultaneously attesting to the wide range of relatively unknown written representations which do exist. Neil Buttimer's pioneering work on the Famine in Gaelic manuscripts, for instance, alerts English-language readers for the first time to the wealth of Irish-langauge material on the Famine which remains unpublished, concluding that the Gaelic culture which the Famine did so much to destroy 'did not depart in unbroken silence'. Other essays in this section make reference to a comparably wide range of materials, from poems to novels to travel narratives to newspapers to political pamphlets and religious tracts. Nonetheless, many of these critics share a common late twentieth-century concern that the relationship between representation and the reality it replaces is far from direct or simply. 'We can't take language, even the language of journalism, at "face value",' Sean Ryder reminds us in his essay, 'since "obvious meanings" and "face values" are not immutable.' 'The point is,' he indicates, 'we can't assess discourse and representation apart from its material contexts'. Indeed, Tom Boylan and Timothy Foley's reading of the discourse of political economy as it was applied to the Famine demonstrates all too clearly that the relationship between what we are calling 'Realities' and 'Representations' is an active one, which can be compared to that 'circular relation' which Michel Foucault discerns linking 'truth' 'with systems of power which produce and sustain it, and to effects of power which it induces and which extends it'.[3]

In this respect, the essays in the second half of the book depend upon the material contexts established by the writers in the first half, just as the material in the 'Realities' section is problematised and challenged by that which follows it. Chris Morash's essay, for instance, takes certain images whose origin is in the physical, bodily suffering which Laurence Geary's essay recounts in the opening pages, and traces their genealogy as forms of language whose claims to truth ultimately become self-contained, referring primarily to other representations rather than to a prior physical reality. Similarly, Margaret Kelleher's study of the 'female gaze' reminds us of the ways in which any form of representation is necessarily gender inflected; we may think we are seeing things 'as they are', but, as feminist theory reminds us, our ways of seeing are never completely neutral. Who we are determines what we see as much as what we happen to be looking at. Nor is this identification of the Famine as a site of controversy and discursive jousting a recent phenomena, as Robert Mahony's essay on John Mitchel's influential writing of the Famine points out, demonstrating the ways in which the residue of earlier attempts to inscribe the Famine in a meaningful historical context continue to have an afterlife which outlives their political usefulness. Indeed, this is also the basic point of the collection's final essay, in which the Revd Robert Dunlop attempts to redress the Famine's continuing bitter sectarian aftertaste.

It well may be objected that there is something just a bit too tidy, too binary in the arrangement of these essays into the neatly opposed categories of 'Realities' and 'Representations'. If that is so, it is because there is a missing third term, a ghostly Other which haunts these pages, something which 'seemed more like a dream than reality' to Asenath Nicholson in the late 1840s. This third, 'fearful'

3 Michel Foucault, 'Truth and Power' in *The Foucault Reader*, ed. Paul Rabinow (New York, 1984), p. 74

element, might be named as the Famine dead, whose numbers and suffering was, for Nicholson and so many others of the period, 'out of the order of even nature itself'. Essays such as those which follow attempt to weave a net of discourses, practices, words, and artifacts which will define just what that 'order of nature' was perceived to have been by those who experienced that which we so inadequately call 'the Famine'. It is neither to romanticise nor to mystify the Famine, however, to claim that the meaning of suffering and death on the scale which occured during those years slips through our nets, no matter how carefully woven. On the contrary, to assert that such suffering has a reality, even if it resists both empirical analysis and representation – 'perhaps more than any other human experience'[4] – is to identify that point at which the scholarly enterprise becomes a moral imperative. To admit the full adequacy of any analysis or representation of the Famine would be to perform an act of closure which is analogous to forgetting insofar as it consigns the past to the past. Instead, suspended in the 'fearful' position of proclaiming the reality of the Famine while simultaneously problematising its representation, we perform that act which T.W. Adorno urges in 'Commitment', a secularising of Pascal's 'theological saying, *On ne doit plus dormir.*' 'The abundance of real suffering', Adorno writes, 'tolerates no forgetting.'[5] So too in their combined attempts to keep both the reality and the representation of the Famine before us, do the contributors to this volume challenge us to tolerate no forgetting.

4 Elaine Scarry, *Resisting Representation* (Oxford, 1994), p. 20.
5 T.W. Adorno, 'Commitment' in *The Frankfurt School Reader* (New York, 1982), p. 312.

I 'Realities': Responses and Implications

The Geography and Implications of Post-Famine Population Decline in Baltyboys, County Wicklow

MATTHEW STOUT

The Famine was the key turning point in the social history of modern Ireland. The death of over one million people and emigration of an equal number were only the beginning of a process of depopulation which followed the loss of the staple diet of three million Irish men and women.[1] This decline in population facilitated the consolidation of land holdings and led to an increase in prosperity and security amongst the tenants who survived this cataclysm. Three key sources are available with which to examine the dramatic landscape and population changes in Ireland in the mid-nineteenth century. The population decline is enumerated in the decennial censuses from 1841. Specific information on land holdings is provided for pre-Famine Ireland by the *Tithe Applotment Books*, and from 1851 by *Griffiths' Valuation* and subsequent records held in the valuation office.[2] An analysis of these records provides the results of a process of depopulation and consolidation but does not deal with the process itself. To understand these processes we must refer to contemporary accounts and, where possible, marry the qualitative and quantitative sources.

Such a combination of sources is available for the Smith estate in Baltyboys, county Wicklow. Here we are fortunate in having the published diaries of Elizabeth Smith, the wife of the landlord of a small estate.[3] In this paper I will examine the statistical sources for population and land tenure using the Smith diaries as a means of interpreting the changes recorded in those sources. It will be seen that the consolidation of land holdings on the Baltyboys estate was the long-term policy of the residential landlord, facilitated by, but not initiated by or solely the result of, the Famine. As a micro study, examining only one of the *c*.62,000 townlands in Ireland (0.006% of the total land area in Ireland), it is possible to focus on the human tragedy subsumed in the statistical sources. The

---

1 J. Mokyr, *Why Ireland Starved: a Quantitative and Analytical History of the Irish Economy, 1800-1850* (London, 1983), table 9.1, pp. 230, 266.

2 For an introduction to these sources see W. Nolan, *Tracing the Past: Sources for Local Studies in the Republic of Ireland* (Dublin, 1982).

3 E. Grant (Smith), *The Highland Lady in Ireland: Journals 1840-50*, eds P. Pelly and A. Tod (Edinburgh, 1991). E. Smith (*née* Grant), *The Irish Journals of Elizabeth Smith, 1840-50*, eds D. Thomson and M. McGusty (Oxford, 1980).

study also focuses on an eastern region while most Famine studies have looked
to the west of Ireland.

Elizabeth Smith, who left us her diaries, was born in Edinburgh in 1797.[4]
She came to Ireland in 1830 after her husband, in her own words 'a poor sad
Orangeman', inherited a small county Wicklow estate.[5] She was an accomplished writer who earned substantial sums for articles published in Scottish
magazines and is most famous for her book *Memoirs of a Highland Lady*, first
published in 1898.[6] Her diaries, begun in 1840, provide a detailed description of
the greater part of the population on her Wicklow estate, so detailed that it is
possible to combine her writings with statistical sources to present an accurate
picture of the distribution of population and changing land-holding patterns in
pre- and post-Famine Baltyboys. By comparing this material with statistical
sources three decades later, it is possible to demonstrate how, in the post-Famine period, steady population decline stands in stark contrast to the continuity of
land tenure.

The Smith estate of Baltyboys corresponded to the townland of Baltyboys
Lower in the parish of Boystown, in the barony of Lower Talbotstown, within
two miles (3km) of Blessington, in west county Wicklow (figure 1). The large
townland of 1142 acres (462ha) is a roughly triangular-shaped ridge with the
Kings River and Liffey River forming its north-east and north-west sides, respectively. The 'base' of the triangle is demarcated by a straight townland boundary unassociated with any natural features. The ridge bounded by the rivers rises
sharply from below the 600 foot (183m) contour (the level of the Poulaphouca
Reservoir) to 993 feet (303m) in as little as one-half mile (800m). Due to the
steep gradient, most of the individual holdings displayed a typical environmen-
tal egalitarianism by running down the hill to include both rough upland pasture and waterlogged lowlands. Baltyboys House stands near the apex of the
triangle; nonetheless, it stood no more than two miles (3.2km) from all the
Smith's tenants, which is to say it was a very tight estate unit, unusual in that it
was possible for the landlord to know all the tenants.

Pre-Famine Population and Land Tenure

The *Tithe Applotment Books*, compiled between 1823 and 1838, survive in manuscript form in the National Archives in Dublin. On the Baltyboys estate, the
area for each holding is given in statute acres and the accuracy of the report is
certified in a document signed and sealed by Col. Henry Smith, husband of

4 Grant (Smith), *The Highland Lady*, p. vii.
5 Smith (*née* Grant), *The Irish Journals*, pp. xiii-xv.
6 E. Grant (Smith), *Memoirs of a Highland Lady*, ed. A. Tod (Edinburgh, 1988).

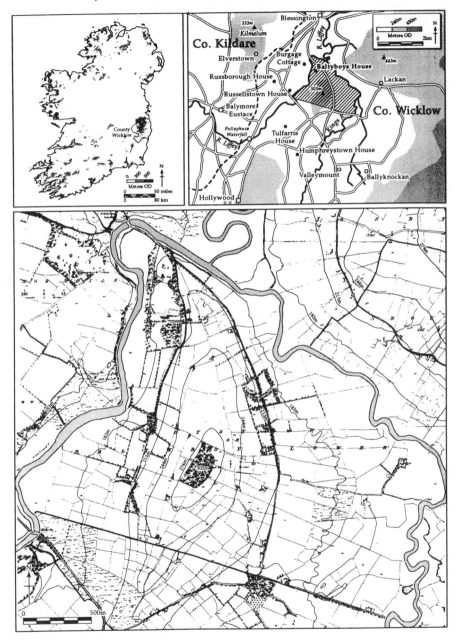

Figure 1 The location of the Smith estate, Baltyboys Lower townland, north-west county Wicklow.

Elizabeth.[7] In itself, this indicates the interest the Smiths had in their newly inherited estate, a marked change from the absentee administration of Henry Smith's brother. Because of the accuracy of information in this source it is possible to relate most holdings to those recorded in the Primary Valuation and draw a plan of the tenancies for pre-Famine Baltyboys (figure 2). The *Tithe Applotment Books* record thirty separate holdings held by twenty-eight individuals. This made the average holding forty acres (16ha) per tenant. That figure obscures the diversity in holding size, however. Four men, John and Thomas Darker, and Thomas and Hugh Kelly held almost half of the estate. In contrast eleven holdings were under 15 acres (6ha).

The land assessment preserved in the *Applotment Books* offers us a glimpse of an estate in transition. John and Thomas Darker still held the 'demesne' land surrounding Baltyboys house before the completion of the Smiths' homecoming (figure 2, plot 4). The Smiths' influence is to be seen in the case of the southern holding of Thomas Kelly (figure 2, plot 9). This was land taken from George Kearns in an effort to consolidate and increase the Kelly's farm. Henry Smith had one holding in his own name at this stage, having been lately taken over from a tenant named Quinn (figure 2, plot 27). The concentration of dwellings in this and adjacent holdings suggests that Quinn had rented landless dwellings to sub tenants, a practise Smith would have stopped in order to maximise his rents.

In examining the population on the Baltyboys estate we are fortunate in that the first reliable census for Ireland was taken four years before the Famine in 1841. We can rely on the accuracy of these figures for Baltyboys Lower because the census data was collected by the Smiths with the same care taken in the compilation of the *Tithe Applotment Books*. In June 1841 Elizabeth Smith wrote:

> Busy filling up the Census papers which are very complete as to information, the use of which I don't exactly know, the poor people here are all terrified that they were to have been kidnapped or pressed or murdered on the night of the 6th. Half of them were not to go to bed and had barricaded their doors.[8]

The 1841 census gives a population of 260 persons on the Baltyboys estate. From the detailed descriptions provided in the diaries it is possible to locate the individual families and ascribe a probable number for each household. Used in combination with the map sources, it is possible to construct a fairly accurate distribution map marking the high watermark in the townland's population just prior to the Famine (figure 2). Approximately one-fifth of the population was

7 N.A.I., TAB 32/4, Boystown.
8 Grant (Smith), *The Highland Lady*, p. 64.

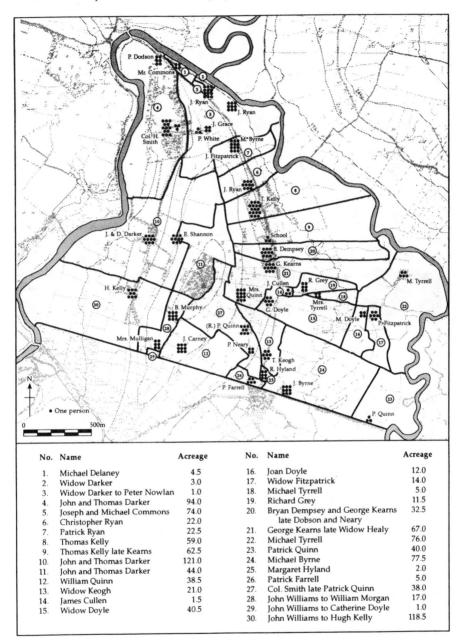

No.	Name	Acreage	No.	Name	Acreage
1.	Michael Delaney	4.5	16.	Joan Doyle	12.0
2.	Widow Darker	3.0	17.	Widow Fitzpatrick	14.0
3.	Widow Darker to Peter Nowlan	1.0	18.	Michael Tyrrell	5.0
4.	John and Thomas Darker	94.0	19.	Richard Grey	11.5
5.	Joseph and Michael Commons	74.0	20.	Bryan Dempsey and George Kearns	32.5
6.	Christopher Ryan	22.0		late Dobson and Neary	
7.	Patrick Ryan	22.5	21.	George Kearns late Widow Healy	67.0
8.	Thomas Kelly	59.0	22.	Michael Tyrrell	76.0
9.	Thomas Kelly late Kearns	62.5	23.	Patrick Quinn	40.0
10.	John and Thomas Darker	121.0	24.	Michael Byrne	77.5
11.	John and Thomas Darker	44.0	25.	Margaret Hyland	2.0
12.	William Quinn	38.5	26.	Patrick Farrell	5.0
13.	Widow Keogh	21.0	27.	Col. Smith late Patrick Quinn	38.0
14.	James Cullen	1.5	28.	John Williams to William Morgan	17.0
15.	Widow Doyle	40.5	29.	John Williams to Catherine Doyle	1.0
			30.	John Williams to Hugh Kelly	118.5

Figure 2 Pre famine Baltyboys (based on the 1841 census, the tithe applotment books and the Smith diaries).

Plate 1   Baltyboys house which has been recently restored (photo B. Fitzgerald).

located on or near Baltyboys house (plate 1) and gained a livelihood from working on the Smith estate. This includes the Smiths, their household servants, live-in outdoor farm labourers, and the Darkers, who administered the Smith estate, and who also held lands of their own.

> Past the Darker's excellent house where I did not call knowing well that all there was as one could wish. Northerns, protestants, well-educated, industrious, they are a credit to the country. Of the two bachelor brothers John manages the good farm of ninety-six acres; Tom is the Colonel's steward and bailiff at a salary of fifty pounds. Two maiden sisters take charge of the house, etc. Amongst them they have brought up five orphan nephews and nieces.[9]

On the demesne lands, there were five dwellings which housed the remainder of the Smith retinue and their families: a retired nurse maid, the gardener, herd, stableman and a general labourer.

The major population group was made up of the large tenants, their families and labourers. On the east side of the hill these tenants' houses were located at

9 Ibid., pp. 294-5.

the western, or uphill, side of their holdings. Many of these farm houses still survive and are substantial buildings, often of two storeys, with an extensive cluster of out buildings, often forming an enclosed yard. As large as these buildings are, the size of the population they supported is impressive. The diaries tell us that the ten largest land holdings accounted for as many as eighty-seven persons, over one-third of the townland's population. Tom Kelly, for instance, had a wife and seven children. In addition, he employed as many as seven people, most of whom resided either in the house or the farm buildings which overlooked his 120 acre (49ha) holding. His house, which still survives, was thatched within living memory. The outbuildings, in contrast, were always slated (plate 2). Mrs Smith's description of the Kelly household is typical in its detail as it is in its begrudging attitude towards her larger, more independent tenants. She wrote in January 1847:

> Tom Kelly, an old man now, with old untidy ways, married at fifty, a
> girl with a hundred pounds who has made him an excellent wife. They
> have a large yard, new good offices, a garden, house of three large rooms,
> and seven children, four boys and three girls; the four elder ones at school;
> plenty here but in an uncomfortable manner and the worst farming though

Plate 2   The modest farmhouse of Tom Kelly, originally thatched, overlooked his 121 acre farm. Seventeen persons were accommodated within the house and its well-built slated farm buildings.

the rent is never behind; no draining, no turnips, not sufficient stock. Hal means to resume about twenty acres of the low ground to reclaim himself as this stupid old creature can't be moved to exertion and we shall have a world of plague to get back the possession, both husband and wife acting tragedy when informed of it although they got this addition to their old holding on the express understanding of improving it.

    ... Tom Kelly will manage fewer acres better as he will not diminish his labourers and they are too few for the size of the present farm – two old half-useless men and a little boy, all of whom he gets at half wages, with a niece as maid-servant. His little daughter, one of my pets, manages her younger brothers and sisters.[10]

A third grouping in the Baltyboys population is made up of a few craftsmen on small holdings; a mason and two carpenters. Their families and apprentices made up about ten per cent of the townland's total population. Mrs Smith described the mason in January 1847:

James Carney...he is doing well on his farm of twenty-three acres; has it well stocked, lives in a good three roomed slated house with a pretty wife and four children, two of them at school; his trade has hitherto kept him easy, but no one is building this year, so he has had to part with his men, his wife with her maid, to leave enough food behind.[11]

We must assume that they were able to survive the Famine years due to their trades, rather than their small holdings.

    The remainder of the populations was made up of the smaller tenant farmers, former tenants who still held houses from which the land had been dispossessed, and sub-tenants, those who had a house through one of the Smith's larger tenants. For the most part, these were the very poor who survived on their plot of potatoes and acted as casual agricultural labourers. Few of their homes survive (plates 3–4):

five acres of this leased ground are let to Bartle Murphy up at the top of the hill close by the moat which once defended one of Cromwell's watch towers. The Colonel has planted all these furzy fields and Murphy has the charge of them at a small salary without which he must have been begging, the five acres having ruined him: his potatoes gone, his two cows dead of the murrain, nothing left of all his labour but a cwt. and a half of oatmeal. There are six children, four at school, one at the breast.[12]

10 Ibid., p. 287.
11 Ibid., p. 296.
12 Ibid., p. 295.

Plate 3   The remains of the home of Bartholomew Murphy lies on the 274m contour above the Poulaphouca Reservoir. Murphy, who farmed only 8.5 acres, was an employee of the Smiths in charge of the nearby plantation.

Plate 4   The small house belonging to the Hylands was associated with only two acres of land.

Nearly two-fifths of the population in Baltyboys lived in conditions which could not have been much better that those described in the following diary entry of January 1847:

> I went up the hill again first calling on the Widow Quinn, who being left some years ago on her husband's death insolvent with a large and very young family and she an ailing woman, the Colonel relieved her of her land, forgave her seven years' rent, gave her the stock and crop to dispose of and left her the house and garden for her life. All her children were employed as they were fit for work and she has certainly done better than if she had retained her ill-managed farm. All her sons are in good places, one of them with us; her daughters married except one who lives with her and takes in washing. I put mother and daughter on the souplist, times being so hard. Two of the daughters are very well married; the third made a wretched one; she took a sickly labouring lad who is often laid up, but to whom she has brought seven children. They live in the mother's cowhouse where she had no right to put them and thus settle a whole family of beggars upon us, but we did not look after things then as we have learned to do now. It is the most wretched abode imaginable, without window or fire-place, mud for the floor, neither water or weather-tight, nor scarce a door, all black with smoke, no furniture scarcely. Yet times are brightening for the nearly naked inmates. A brother in America sent them at Christmas ten pounds which paid their debts, and bought them some meal and fuel, and their eldest son is to go out to this kind uncle in March.[13]

This extreme case illustrates the unimaginable poverty of those who lived on the margins of the estate system and highlights the exceptional vulnerability of older women within this system.

Baltyboys During the Famine

In a postscript to the journal, written near the end of her life, Mrs Smith refers to their policy of consolidation and the strategy they employed, which was the orthodox political economy of the day. She wrote:

> We determined to get rid of the little tenants and to increase the large farms – and we did it – but not at once – just watched for opportunities

---

13 Ibid., pp. 292-3.

and managed this delicate business without annoying anyone – or even causing a murmur.[14]

That a 'murmur' was caused is discussed below, but what is of key importance in the above statement, confirmed by the *Tithe Applotment Books*, is that consolidation and its corollary, depopulation, were the pre-Famine goals of at least one resident landlord.

Famine provided the greatest opportunity towards their aim of getting rid of the 'little tenants'. Even before the blight, bad harvests threatened the population of Baltyboys. In October 1841 Smith recorded:

> Bitter cold and dismal is the prospect before us, so early, so severe a winter, no fuel, no harvest, corn still out and malting, potato crop a failure, what will become of the improvident poor of this country, in the Poor House some must be driven to take refuge but it won't contain a fourth part of the starving population and many will die rather than enter it.[15]

She wrote of the need for a new agricultural system to replace the total reliance on the potato in November 1842 and at the same time recognised the harm caused by the programme of land consolidation:

> Our population is increasing, our means of providing for it not increasing in proportion, too much property seems to have got into too few hands, too many mouths have too little to fill them, there is a want of energy, a want of principle, a want of knowledge ... A better system of agriculture by which a greater supply of nourishment may be extracted from the ground seems indispensable.[16]

The first mention of the potato failure which caused the Great Irish Famine comes in October 1845.[17] In September 1846 she states simply: 'Here comes the famine ... so here we are, the peasantry starving.'[18] The famine diseases, dysentery, inflammatory attacks, influenza and fever,[19] are recorded in entries from September 1846, and from January and March 1847.[20] However, these diaries

14 Smith (*née* Grant), *The Irish Journals*, p. xviii.
15 Grant (Smith), *The Highland Lady*, p. 80.
16 Ibid., p. 150.
17 Ibid., p. 197.
18 Ibid., p. 261.
19 W.P. MacArthur, 'Medical History of the Famine' in R.D. Edwards and T.D. Williams (eds), *The Great Famine: Studies in Irish History* (2nd ed., Dublin, 1994), pp. 263-315.
20 Grant (Smith), *The Highland Lady*, pp. 258, 292, 307.

are a poor source for statistical information concerning the actual death toll in the townland. For example, in May 1847 she records the first death from the Famine in a family that had lost seven out of ten children:

> he desired me to have poor little Andy Ryan buried at once, the house fumigated etc. ... After dinner I walked to John Darker's and he wrote up to forbid any wake, to order the funeral this morning and then a general cleansing – all which was attended to by these unfortunate parents; they have now but three children left of ten, and their only girl will hardly long survive for she is a wretched looking little creature. Between constitutional delicacy, the great dung heap at their door, the mother's carelessness, and the father's aversion to go in time for the Doctor they have lost a fine clever family.[21]

The cumulative effects of death and emigration were so extensive that it led to the closure of her boys' school. In April 1850 she wrote:

> There are very few boys left on our side of the country; there will be few men soon for they are pouring out in shoals to America. Crowds upon crowds swarm along the roads, the bye roads, following carts with their trunks and other property. We have forty children as yet in the girls' school; but really I don't think there will be half that number by autumn.[22]

The progress made towards her stated goals of depopulation and farm consolidation is evident in the *Primary valuation* and their accompanying maps, compiled circa 1851. The recently published Ordnance Survey maps for County Wicklow added to their accuracy and permitted the preparation of annotated maps corresponding to the reference number in the first column of the valuation tables. This source indicates that the land of Baltyboys Lower was held by ten fewer (18) persons, in eight fewer holdings, in 1851 (figure 3). Only six of the 1851 holdings were under fifteen acres (6ha) opposed to eleven in 1836, and the average holding per tenant had risen from forty (16ha) to sixty acres (24ha). The most profound difference between 1836 and 1851 was in the demesne lands (figure 3, plot 2). These were consolidated, probably early in the 1840s, into one 182 acre block then in the name of James King (Mrs Smith's son-in-law). This was accomplished at the expense of the Commons', who were probably bachelors without direct heirs, and, to a lesser extent, the Darker Brothers.

21 Ibid., pp. 331-2.
22 Ibid., p. 507.

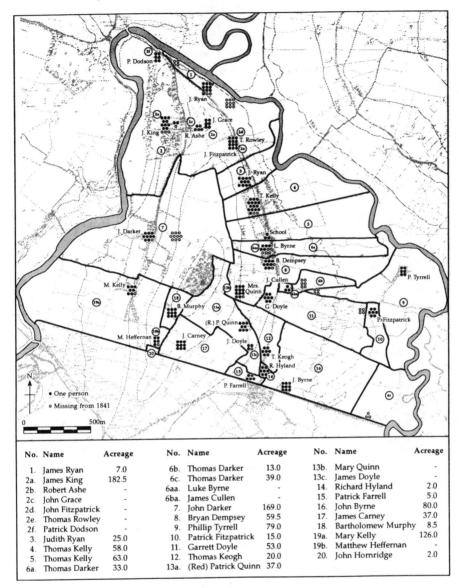

No.	Name	Acreage	No.	Name	Acreage	No.	Name	Acreage
1.	James Ryan	7.0	6b.	Thomas Darker	13.0	13b.	Mary Quinn	-
2a.	James King	182.5	6c.	Thomas Darker	39.0	13c.	James Doyle	-
2b.	Robert Ashe	-	6aa.	Luke Byrne	-	14.	Richard Hyland	2.0
2c.	John Grace	-	6ba.	James Cullen	-	15.	Patrick Farrell	5.0
2d.	John Fitzpatrick	-	7.	John Darker	169.0	16.	John Byrne	80.0
2e.	Thomas Rowley	-	8.	Bryan Dempsey	59.5	17.	James Carney	37.0
2f.	Patrick Dodson	-	9.	Phillip Tyrrell	79.0	18.	Bartholomew Murphy	8.5
3.	Judith Ryan	25.0	10.	Patrick Fitzpatrick	15.0	19a.	Mary Kelly	126.0
4.	Thomas Kelly	58.0	11.	Garrett Doyle	53.0	19b.	Matthew Heffernan	-
5.	Thomas Kelly	63.0	12.	Thomas Keogh	20.0	20.	John Hornridge	2.0
6a.	Thomas Darker	33.0	13a.	(Red) Patrick Quinn	37.0			

Figure 3   Baltyboys immediately after the famine (based on the 1851 census,
Griffiths' valuation, Valuations Office records and the Smith diaries).

Under Lord John Russell, the administration of famine relief shifted its emphasis from the straightforward provision of food to public work. The Poor Relief
Bill of 1847 facilitated the efforts to reduce both the population and the number
of small holdings on the Smith estate. In April Elizabeth Smith wrote in praise
of the notorious Gregory Clause:[23]

> there have been two clauses inserted by the Member for Dublin, Mr.
> Gregory, one of which precludes the holder of more than a rood of land
> from being in any way assisted ...The beggars are the small holders, enti-
> tled to no relief, and so we shall gradually get rid of them; they must give
> up their patches and take to labour.[24]

In November 1848 she describes the results of this policy:

> Driving about, the many unroofed cabins give additional desolation to
> the wet and dirty lanes. The moment the Poor House receives the in-
> mates the wretched dwelling is destroyed so that a return is impossible;
> quantities are still even at this season going off to America, many of them
> with plenty of money in their pockets! And we miss them not. This
> winter will surely make some room.[25]

The diaries of Mrs Smith describe in detail the consolidation process which
led to the transfer of lands to the Darker brothers just before the compilation of
Griffiths' Valuation. John Darker was given exclusive control over lands previously shared with his brother (figure 3, plot 7). To offset this, and in advance of
his marriage, Thomas Darker was given three holdings which had been the
property of George Kearns, Richard Grey and Patrick Quinn (figure 3, plots
6abc). It is useful to take a closer look at the history of the holding taken from
Pat Quinn, in the extreme south-east of the townland, as it illustrates the complex relationship between landlord and tenant, and provides an insight into the
meandering course of the Smith's consolidation policy. Pat Quinn held his farm
of forty acres (16ha) in 1840 when we hear of his defaulting on his rent in
September. Smith wrote:

> Tom Darker [their steward] has distrained the three bad Tenants, Kearns,
> Doyle and Quinn. John [Robinson, their solicitor and land agent] had
> no difficulty with the poor creatures whose crops he seized. He left them

23 For a passionate discussion of the effects of the Gregory Act see J.S. Donnelly, Jr., 'Mass
   Eviction and the Great Famine: The Clearances Revisited' in C. Póirtéir (ed.), *The
   Great Irish Famine* (Cork, 1995), pp. 155-73.
24 Grant (Smith), *The Highland Lady*, p. 313.
25 Ibid., p. 425.

all that they would require for the support of their families, merely took what they would have improperly disposed of, and before May comes, when they will be dispossessed, we must see to get something done for them. Farm they never will – Quinn from vice and Kearns from folly, and Doyle from something between the two.[26]

Quinn was a year behind in rent in June 1843,[27] but, despite the threats of dispossession, an entry from 1844 shows that he remained a tenant on the Smith estate, emphasising the point that notice of eviction cannot be taken as an index of actual dispossession:

Pat Quinn obdurate: he will neither pay his rent nor give up his land on the kind conditions proposed; so he must be put out; and with his vindictive disposition this will be a disagreeable business.[28]

In March 1846 this holding was in the hands of the Smiths.

Hal had an offer from Mr Hanks for Pat Quinn's ground, but has refused it, finding the management of land on his own account so profitable.[29]

In September, profits from the cattle raised on his land were such that Elizabeth Smith longed for the depopulation of Baltyboys. Further, she was fully aware of how famine facilitated this ambition:

Mr Darker sold ten of the young cattle off of Pat Quinn's farm, the fourth part of the stock on it, and on these ten he has made a profit equal to the half year's rent, rather more indeed. I wish there was not a tenant in Baltiboys, there will not be many by and by, no small holders at any rate. When potatoes are gone a few acres won't be worth a man's time to manage. What a revolution for good will this failure of cheap food cause.[30]

Nonetheless, Paddy Quinn may still have been in possession of this holding at the beginning of 1847, and in favour after paying his November rent.[31] Finally, in March 1850, we learn of the decision which is preserved in *Griffiths' Valuation*; Mrs Smith wrote: Tom Darker is to have fifty-one acres on the other side

26 Ibid., p. 39-40.
27 Ibid., p. 175.
28 Smith (*née* Grant), *The Irish Journals*, p. 69.
29 Grant (Smith), *The Highland Lady*, p. 214.
30 Ibid., p. 260.
31 Ibid., p. 307. The editors believe this to be a reference to (Red) Pat Quinn. Nonetheless, Pat Quinn still occupied a house on his land (or former land) in December 1847, p. 361.

of the hill – all the scattered bits we have purchased from different little tenants.[32]

Clearly Patrick Quinn's grip on this plot of land was tenuous. But what is
also made clear in the diaries is that his right to that holding went beyond legal
entitlements. Over a period of ten years he was clearly a bad tenant in his landlord's view, yet it took over six years to finally prise him from his holding. Six
months or more after his dispossession (prior to March 1846) it was still described as 'Pat Quinn's ground'. The use of patronyms in Ireland to describe
holdings is in stark contrast to the use of toponyms in English holdings, like
Grange Farm or Willow Farm that we hear about in the *Archers* radio serial on
BBC Radio 4. It demonstrates the insecure position of landlord towards tenant
and shows how, linguistically at least, the tenants had won the land war before
it was ever begun.

The imposition of the Protestant Tom Darker onto lands held by the long
established tenants Quinn, Grey and Kearns caused not just a murmur of discontent but, in Mrs Smith's words, 'a most unpleasant feeling among the people'. Threatening letters were sent to Thomas Darker and Col. Henry Smith, in
return, threatened to close the school. The following passages illustrate the tensions caused by the new allocation of lands as well as the power and confidence
of Mrs Smith in handling estate affairs in opposition to her husband:

> he will tell these gentry that one and all must quit should harm of any
> kind happen to any of the Darkers. They are a most odious people. They
> seem incapable of rising out of low vindictive evil feelings. Not a man in
> Baltiboys is the worse for Tom Darker cultivating these patches on his
> own account instead of on the Colonel's. What business is it then of
> theirs? ... I wish they were all in America, I know.
>
> The Colonel had terrified me to death about my school declaring he
> would close it and fill the house with police and he actually wrote and
> offered it to the magistrates so I should have been obliged to write also
> and say that I could not agree.[33]

What later occurred is not clear from the diaries which concentrate on the
marriage of her first daughter at this point. No subsequent intimidation is reported but Mrs Smith was very disillusioned by the threatening letters and a
spate of sheep stealing. We can only speculate on whether this ill feeling influenced the decision of the Smiths to quit Baltyboys in the same year. In July 1850
Elizabeth Smith refines a familiar theme:

32 Ibid., p. 506.
33 Ibid., pp. 512-13.

Envy, jealousy, malice, evil speaking, hatred, lying, and all uncharitableness, fill the minds of our wretched peasantry. Fancy that fine boy of Jack Byrne's having been used by his father as his instrument in this letter business – made to write the two threatening notices – it has almost been proved against them and the police expect to bring it quite home to that house. How I do wish we had not one tenant in Baltiboys. It will come to that probably. And if we do not live to carry it out, do you keep it in mind, dear Jack [her son], to get all your land into your own hands; graze it; till only what the cattle require; house and pay your few servants well; and grow flax to employ their women.[34]

The ten years between 1841 and 1851 saw a decline in population of fifty-three, from 260 to 207 persons. Naturally the population would have increased in the first half of the decade; nonetheless, the drop of twenty per cent compares favourably with the information extracted from the diaries and *Griffiths' Valuation* and is comparable to the decline in population for the barony and county as a whole.[35] Seven families seem to have disappeared in those years. Mrs Smith provides us with an account of one large scale emigration and there are numerous references to the assisted emigration of individuals:

Cairns [Kearns] is off today, begging to the last. Cousin Charles goes with them – unable to part from the children particularly from one boy by some strange accident the perfect image of himself ...Such a set – 'tis worth all they have cost to rid of them.

We must be careful in our expenditure as probably the few small tenants we have may be induced to emigrate if assisted. Lachlin and Mary Ryan are gone – to New Orleans – with a large party of friends, Mary under the charge of Kiogh [Keogh] the tailor's son and wife. We paid all her expenses and most of her brother's ... Even in a business point of view this is a £10 profitably laid out. These orphans who have much plagued us will cost us no more, and they may act as pioneers for their numerous relations.[36]

If my interpretation of Mrs Smith's diary is correct, the assisted emigration of family units accounts for forty per cent of the population decline. Presumably

34 Ibid., pp. 514-15.
35 K. Hannigan, 'Wicklow before and after the famine' in K. Hannigan and W. Nolan (eds), *Wicklow, History and Society; Interdisciplinary Essays on the History of an Irish County* (Dublin, 1994), pp. 789-822. The population of Lower Talbotstown fell 22% between 1841 and 1851. County Wicklow's population fell 21.5% during the same period. See p. 813, table 20.8.
36 Grant (Smith), *The Highland Lady*, pp. 313-14, 499.

deaths and individual emigration made up the other sixty per cent. The failure to account for the drop in population is a large gap in the normally detailed memoirs. The omission is probably best explained by the fact that many of those missing were from the ranks of the farm labourers. This group rarely received mention by name in the Smith diaries – a fact mirrored by their exclusion from the debate surrounding the land question. Unexpectedly, many of the very poor landless householders seem to have survived the Famine years if not the subsequent decades.

Post-Famine Population Decline and Consolidation

To understand the long term effects of the Famine it is necessary to examine the Baltyboys estate nearly four decades after the potato crop first failed. We learn from the valuation records that the same large tenants, or their heirs, were still *in situ* (figure 4). Eleven of the fifteen major tenants – those with over thirty-five acres of land – or their descendants, survived the period 1836-83. Of the four who failed to survive, two seem to have been bachelors with no direct descendants. Indeed, most of the changes which occurred during the 1840s became a permanent part of post-Famine Baltyboys. Only minor alterations were made in the farm holdings between 1851 and 1883, probably at the instigation of Elizabeth Smith who, incredibly, re-occupied Baltyboys House in 1882 at the age of eighty-five. Twenty-three acres (9ha) were taken from the Darker holdings. Twelve of these (5ha) were added to the Tyrrell lands (figure 3, plot 6b – figure 4, plot 9), and eleven (4ha) were added to the demesne lands, once more in the name of Smith.

More profound was the drop in population. The 1881 census records only 136 persons living in the townland, down by 48% from 260 four decades earlier, one third fewer persons than in 1851. In 1841 4.4 acres (1.8ha) had supported one person, forty years later the figure was 8.4 acres (3.4ha). The valuation records indicate where on the estate most of the decline in population came from (figure 4). Although the 'big house' had been re-occupied, the other dwellings on the demesne were empty or gone. The lodge occupied by the Dodsons up until 1871 (figure 3, house 2f) is now in the name of Mrs Smith, as is the dwelling occupied by Robert Ashe between 1851 and 1863 (figure 3, house 2c). There is no mention of the house occupied by John Grace from 1851 to 1879 (figure 3, house 2a). The 'joint tenement' of T. Rowley and J. Fitzpatrick is 'down' from 1875 (figure 3, house 2de). These five dwellings housed in the region of twenty-nine persons in 1851. It is evident, therefore, that the withdrawal of patronage on the part of the resident landlord had accounted for as much as forty-one per cent of the decline in population at Baltyboys. Five other dwellings were abandoned prior to 1883. The most notable departure was that

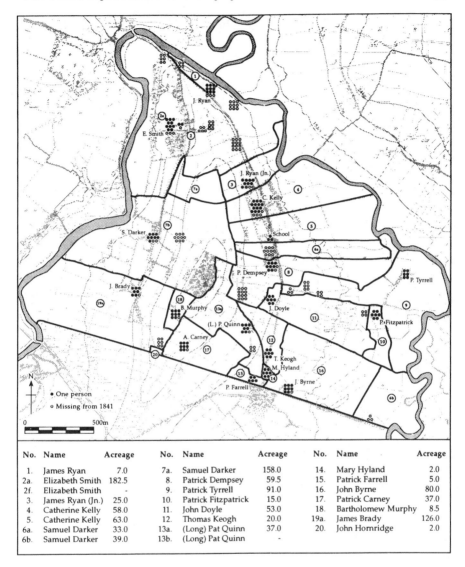

No.	Name	Acreage	No.	Name	Acreage	No.	Name	Acreage
1.	James Ryan	7.0	7a.	Samuel Darker	158.0	14.	Mary Hyland	2.0
2a.	Elizabeth Smith	182.5	8.	Patrick Dempsey	59.5	15.	Patrick Farrell	5.0
2f.	Elizabeth Smith	-	9.	Patrick Tyrrell	91.0	16.	John Byrne	80.0
3.	James Ryan (Jn.)	25.0	10.	Patrick Fitzpatrick	15.0	17.	Patrick Carney	37.0
4.	Catherine Kelly	58.0	11.	John Doyle	53.0	18.	Bartholomew Murphy	8.5
5.	Catherine Kelly	63.0	12.	Thomas Keogh	20.0	19a.	James Brady	126.0
6a.	Samuel Darker	33.0	13a.	(Long) Pat Quinn	37.0	20.	John Hornridge	2.0
6b.	Samuel Darker	39.0	13b.	(Long) Pat Quinn	-			

Figure 4   Post-famine Baltyboys in 1883 (based on the 1881 census and Valuations Office records).

of the extended family housed at the Widow Quinn's. This house passed into the vacant possession of Long Pat Quinn in 1882. Four other landless dwellings also disappeared.

Conclusion

The aspects of population and land tenure discussed in this paper highlight the major dichotomy in post-Famine Ireland; the contrast between profound population change on the one hand and continuity in land tenure on the other. The consolidation of some holdings did lead to a decline in their overall number, but the basic layout of farms was unchanged, a feature also noted in Smith's analysis of Clogheen-Burncourt parish in south county Tipperary.[37] Throughout our period, Baltyboys remains an area dominated by the established tenant farmer and it was this element of society which shaped the ethos of post-Famine Ireland. In contrast, the sources testify to decay at either extreme of the Baltyboys social pyramid. The pyramidal structure of society had a very narrow top and a very wide base. These are the elements which were carved out of the Irish landscape as a result of the changes brought about by the Great Irish Famine. The landless cottier and the smaller tenants could not survive the loss of their staple food and the decreased demand for their labour. On the Smith estate, largely due to the efforts of the resident landlord and his remarkable wife, this population emigrated rather than died. Nonetheless, the population was greatly reduced. We have also seen how the drop in the numbers employed on the Baltyboys estate accounted for a large proportion of that decline. This probably mirrored a similar drop in output and profitability of the demesne farm. Mrs Smith did not foresee how the policy of consolidation and depopulation would lead, ultimately, to the decline in prominence of her own position. More broadly, it may suggest that the Famine and post-Famine policies removed the large labour force which supported and were supported by the landed gentry, an unlikely coalition which could have provided a bulwark against the rising power of the tenant farmer.

---

37 W. Smyth, 'Land Holding Changes, Kinship Networks and Class Transformation in Rural Ireland: A Case Study from County Tipperary' in *Irish Geography*, xvi (1983), pp. 16-35.

The Famine and Its Aftermath in County Mayo[1]

DONALD JORDAN

The Famine of 1846-50 marks a major turning point in the economic and social development of modern Ireland. Famine depopulation and post-Famine land clearances and emigration accelerated a trend, established before the Famine, of consolidation of holdings into larger, more profitable ones. The reduction in the number of subsistence producers that the Famine brought about allowed for a larger market surplus for those who survived the blight with their land holdings intact or enlarged, and cleared the way for the fuller commercialisation of Irish agriculture. A rise in livestock prices, stimulated by a growing British beef market, further encouraged the consolidation of holdings and a switch from tillage to livestock farming. These demographic and economic changes brought new wealth and prominence to those with sizable holdings of good pasture land. Within the agrarian community the balance between the various classes of farmers shifted markedly to the advantage of the larger farmers, whose agricultural, inheritance and marriage practices became the norm for Irish society.

These structural changes occurred more slowly in Mayo than they did in the more prosperous counties of Ireland. There were proportionally fewer large farm families in Mayo to lead the way by taking full advantage of the dynamic post-Famine economy. The county, and especially its eastern and western peripheries, remained peopled with small farmers who married early and worked tillage farms that were regularly subdivided to meet the land hunger of the next generation. Nonetheless, the process of the consolidation of holdings and the shift from labour-intensive tillage farming to labour-extensive grazing did occur, bringing with it conflicts over land and tensions within the farming community. While the lines of division between larger and more prosperous farmers, concentrated in central Mayo, and the smaller, impoverished farmers increasingly relegated to the peripheral regions cannot be precisely drawn, following the Famine, and largely as a consequence of it, Mayo developed more fully than previously into a county that contained two economies and two social systems:

1 This article is extracted to a large degree from my *Land and Popular Politics in Ireland: County Mayo from the Plantation to the Land War* (Cambridge, 1994), which contains a fuller treatment of the Famine in County Mayo. Preparing this article has given me a welcome opportunity to revise and update the argument as well as to recalculate the data. I wish to thank William Davies of Cambridge University Press for his permission to publish this article

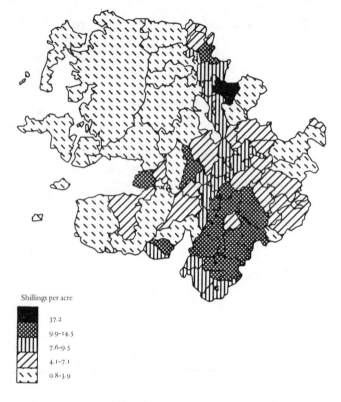

Shillings per acre

37.2
9.9-14.5
7.6-9.5
4.1-7.1
0.8-3.9

Map 1   Valuation of land, 1881, by parish, County mayo (shillings per acre).
Source: *The census of Ireland for the year 1881, pt. 1: area, houses and
population, vol. iii, province of Connaught, no. 3, county of Mayo,*
pp. 285-353, H. C. 1882 [c. 3268-III], lxxix, 273.

one concentrated in but not confined to the central lowlands and one concentrated in but not confined to the periphery.[2] Map 1[3] illustrates the valuation of
the land by parish, clearly revealing that the best land was concentrated in a
central corridor that begins at Killala Bay in north Mayo, widens out in mid-
Mayo to include the land between Castlebar and Westport, and then continues
south and east to the Galway and Roscommon borders.

As was the case throughout Ireland, the Famine inaugurated a period of
population decline in County Mayo that saw the population drop 51 per cent
between 1841 and 1911.

2 The core-periphery thesis is developed in ibid., pp. 5-7, 13-17.
3 Maps 1-3 were prepared by David Miller of Carnegie Mellon University for *Land and
  Popular Politics in Ireland*. Again, I wish to express my gratitude to him.

Table 1: Population of County Mayo 1841-1911

Year	Males	Females	Total	Percentage Change
1841	194,198	194,689	388,887	
1851	133,264	141,235	274,499	-29.41
1861	125,636	129,160	254,796	-7.18
1871	120,877	125,153	246,030	-3.44
1881	119,421	125,791	245,212	-0.33
1891	107,498	111,536	219,034	-10.68
1901	97,564	101,602	199,166	-9.07
1911	96,345	95,832	192,177	-3.51

Source: W.E. Vaughan and A. J. Fitzpatrick (eds), *Irish Historical Statistics: Population 1821-1971* (Dublin, 1978), p. 14.

This population loss was not distributed evenly throughout the county. The massive population loss during the Famine was heavier in central Mayo than in the peripheral regions, especially the eastern periphery, where one parish, Kilmovee, actually experienced a six per cent increase in population between 1841 and 1851. In a pattern that was to continue until the 1880s, the poorest regions of the county suffered less depopulation than did the more prosperous central lowlands, as can be seen from a comparison of Maps 2 and 3.

Between 1851 and 1881 many parishes that experienced the least population loss between 1841 and 1851 gained in population, despite a ten per cent drop for the county as a whole. All of the five parishes that lost fifteen per cent or less of their population between 1841 and 1851 gained population during the subsequent thirty years. Of the ten parishes that lost fifteen to twenty-five per cent of their population between 1841 and 1851, eight experienced a population gain by 1881. At the other extreme, all the parishes that experienced a depopulation in excess of forty per cent between 1841 and 1851 continued afterwards to decline in population, often at very high rates.

The salient components of Famine depopulation – death and emigration – were present throughout the county.[4] It is impossible to isolate statistically one or the other of these factors on a parish basis, but it seems safe to assume that Famine mortality was the least likely of the two to contribute significantly to the regional variation in depopulation within the county. At the time of the Famine all regions of Mayo contained a considerable number of people who

---

4 Estimates of the total Famine-driven depopulation in County Mayo range from 114,000 (S.H. Cousens) to 170,000 (J. Mokyr), with excess mortality being credited with forty-four to sixty-six per cent of the total, respectively. See Jordan, *Land and Popular Politics in Ireland*, pp. 107-9.

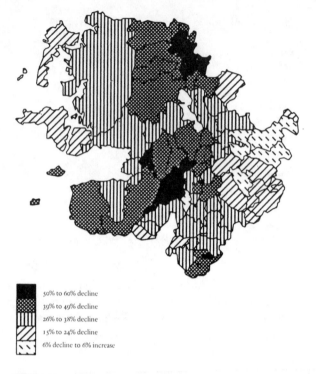

50% to 60% decline
39% to 49% decline
26% to 38% decline
15% to 24% decline
6% decline to 6% increase

Map 2   Rural Population change, 1841-51, by parish, County Mayo.
Source: *The census of Ireland for the year 1851, pt. i: showing the area,
population and the number of houses, by townlands, and electoral divisions,* vol.
iv, pp. 455-514, H. C. 1852-3 (1542), xcii, 453. Populations of the
towns of Ballina, Killala, Westport, Hollymount, Cong, Castlebar and
Ballinrobe excluded.

were heavily dependent on the potato and who suffered severely when it failed.
On the other hand, emigration, at least that forced by eviction, may have accounted for the heavy depopulation from the fertile lowlands. This was the area
where there was the greatest incentive for landlords to clear the land of tenants
and amalgamate holdings into large grazing farms. Although none of the poor
law unions for which statistics on farm sizes were compiled in 1847 consisted
entirely of good quality lowland, Ballinrobe had a larger share than any other
union in Mayo. During the Famine the union was ravaged by death and evictions, especially in 1848, compelling *The Telegraph or Connaught Ranger* to compare its fate to that of Skibereen in County Cork.[5] The effect of Famine evictions
in the union is evident when comparing farm size in 1847 and in 1851. Between

5   7 June 1848, 3 Jan. 1849.

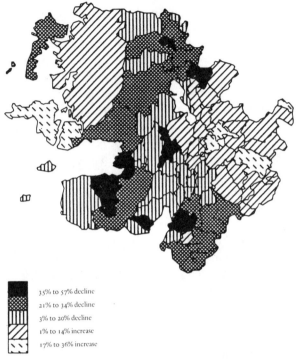

35% to 57% decline
21% to 34% decline
3% to 20% decline
1% to 14% increase
17% to 36% increase

Map 3   Rural Population change, 1851-81, by parish, County Mayo.
Source: *The census of Ireland for the year 1881, area, houses and population,*
vol. iii, province of Connaught, no. 3, county of Mayo, pp. 285-353, H. C.
1882 [C.3268-III], lxxix, 273. Note: Populations of the towns of
Ballina, Killala, Westport, Hollymount, Cong, Castlebar and Ballinrobe
excluded.

those years the number of farms of fifteen acres or less fell from seventy-five to
sixty-one per cent, while the median size of farms rose from seventeen to twenty-
six acres.[6] This was the pattern in all poor law unions whose territory included
portions of the central lowlands. It appears that many of the families displaced
by the evictions that made the amalgamation of holdings possible took to the
emigrant ships or migrated elsewhere in Ireland.

6 Jordan, *Land and Popular Politics in Ireland,* pp. 136-7. In order to create four new unions
for County Mayo, the poor law unions were reorganized in 1850. The eastern portion
of the Ballinrobe union was separated off to form the Claremorris union. For purposes
of comparison, the figures for 1851 include both the Ballinrobe and Claremorris unions. The 1851 figure for the Ballinrobe union as it was constituted in 1851 show
holdings of fifteen acres or less to represent sixty-four per cent of the total and the
median size of holdings to be thirty acres.

Famine depopulation was lowest in the eastern periphery, especially in the Swinford union, which comprised much of the eastern portion of the county. S.H. Cousens has argued that regions such as that comprising the Swinford union were spared excessive Famine depopulation and experienced population growth after 1851 due in large part to the availability of wasteland that could be reclaimed and converted into small holdings for people who would otherwise be compelled to emigrate.[7] According to the commissioners of the 1851 census, Mayo had the largest area of unclaimed wasteland of any county in Ireland. The commissioners estimated that between 1841 and 1851, 10.9 per cent of that wasteland had been reclaimed, lowering the proportion of such land in the county from 58.8 per cent to 47.68 per cent.[8] In 1845 Richard Griffith, the General Valuation Commissioner for Ireland, estimated for the Devon Commission that 58.7 per cent of the land of Mayo was unclaimed. Comparing Griffith's estimate with that contained in the 1841 census would indicate that little reclamation had gone on between 1841 and 1845, when the population of the county was rising.[9] Rather, the bulk of the decennial reclamation appears to have occurred during the Famine, when it would seem improbable that a starving population would have much time or energy for clearing and draining new lands. This was the assumption of K.H. Connell in his study of the reclamation of waste land in Ireland:

> When starvation was almost universal, it can hardly be supposed that the peasants had either the resources or the incentive to drain mountain and bog as never before. And, moreover, when death and emigration caused neighbours to vacate their holdings it is unlikely that the need to clear fresh land seemed as urgent as in former years.[10]

Yet, in eastern Mayo land was reclaimed during the Famine and it seems reasonable to suggest that the people doing the reclamation had been evicted from land in the more fertile lowlands. In eastern Mayo they found land of marginal quality that held little incentive for landlord-initiated consolidation. The result was low Famine depopulation and rapid repopulation during the following decades.[11]

---

7 S.H. Cousens, 'Emigration and Demographic Change in Ireland, 1851-1861' in *Econ. Hist. Rev.*, second series, xiv, 2 (Dec. 1961), pp. 278-88.

8 *The Census of Ireland for the Year 1851*, part vi: general report, pp. x-xii, H. C. 1856 (2134). xxxi, I.

9 *Report from Her Majesty's Commissioners of Inquiry into the State of Law and Practice in Respect to the Occupation of Land in Ireland*, p. 51, H. C. 1845 (605), xix, I.

10 K.H. Connell, 'The Colonization of Waste Land in Ireland, 1780-1845' in *Econ. Hist. Rev.*, second series, ii, 1 (1950), p. 48.

11 Cousens, 'Emigration and Demographic Change', p. 280.

The regional variations in levels of population growth and decline in post-Famine Mayo were further reinforced by differing levels of natural increase (i.e., excess births over deaths) within the county. Between 1861 and 1871 the rate of natural increase in Mayo, when calculated by poor law union, varied from twelve to fifteen per cent in the central and northwestern sections of the county to sixteen to nineteen per cent in the east and in the parishes of Achill and Burrishoole in the west. Between 1871 and 1881 all of eastern and western Mayo had rates of twelve to fifteen per cent, while the rate in the central strip fell to between eight and eleven per cent.[12] By 1901 the division was even sharper. Between 1891 and 1901 the poor law unions that included portions of central Mayo had levels of natural increase ranging from 5.1 per cent in the Ballinrobe union to 7.5 per cent in the Ballina union, while the Belmullet and Westport unions had rates of 11.3 per cent and 9.5 per cent respectively. In the unions of east Mayo, Swinford had a rate of 9.3 per cent and Claremorris a rate of 9 per cent.[13]

The decline in the number of births that characterised post-Famine Ireland is generally attributed to a rise in the age of marriage, an increase in the number of people not marrying, and the high rate of emigration of potential parents.[14] Prior to the Famine, marriage patterns tended to be conditioned by the ease with which land on many estates could be subdivided among all heirs and by the potato, which enabled a large family to be fed on a small parcel of land. In impoverished counties such as Mayo, where land was easily subdivided and where the practice of impartible inheritance of land had not yet found acceptance, there were few restraints to early marriages since the new couple would have little difficulty obtaining a potato patch. Stemming from the work of K.H. Connell, it has long been accepted by Irish historians that the practice of early and frequent marriages was the norm throughout pre-Famine Ireland.[15] How-

12 S.H. Cousens, 'The Regional Variations in Population Changes in Ireland, 1861-1881' in *Econ. Hist. Rev.*, second series, xvii, 2 (Dec. 1964), pp. 306, 314.

13 *The Census of Ireland for the Year 1901*, part I: area, houses and population: also the ages, civil or conjugal condition, occupations, birthplaces, religion and education of the people, vol. iv, province of Connaught, no. 3, county of Mayo, p. 104, H. C. 1902 [Cd. 1059-II], cxviii, 365.

14 For discussions of Irish demographic history during the nineteenth century, see B.M. Walsh, 'A Perspective on Irish Population Patterns' in *Éire-Ireland*, iv, 3 (Autumn, 1969), pp. 3-21; K.H. Connell, 'Land and Population in Ireland, 1780-1845', *Econ. Hist. Rev.*, second series, ii, 3 (1950), pp. 278-89; K.H. Connell, 'Peasant Marriage in Ireland: Its Structure and Development since the Famine', *Econ. Hist. Rev.*, second series, xiv, 3 (April 1962), pp. 502-23; J. Lee, *The Modernisation of Irish Society* (Dublin 1973), pp. 1-9. For a brief discussion of regional differences in depopulation in Mayo, see: E. Almquist, 'Mayo and Beyond: Land, Domestic Industry and Rural Transformation in the Irish West' (unpublished Ph.D. thesis: Boston University 1977), pp. 239-42.

15 *The Population of Ireland, 1750-1845* (Oxford, 1950).

ever, recent research has demonstrated that O'Connell's analysis of pre-Famine marriages failed to account for the complexity of a rapidly changing set of practices. It now seems certain that many farmers, especially the more substantial ones who tended to be clustered in the wealthier eastern and central regions of Ireland, were engaged in complex and carefully calculated marriage and inheritance practices prior to the Famine that established stringent terms over the possibility and the timing of marriage. S.J. Connolly suggests that future research on pre-Famine marriage in Ireland might:

> reveal the existence of two groups within the farming community: a minority of larger occupiers, among whom marriage was postponed almost or entirely as long as it was to be in post-Famine Ireland, and a larger group of small farmers, deeply concerned with the implications of marriage for the orderly transfer of property from one generation to the next, but nevertheless willing to subdivide the family holding in order to allow their sons to marry while still in their twenties.[16]

Such a division of marriage practices was noted in pre-Famine Mayo in 1825 by the Catholic archbishop of Tuam. In testimony before a parliamentary committee examining the state of Ireland, Archbishop Oliver Kelly reported that among the more prosperous farmer/weavers in the vicinity of Westport and Newport there was 'an indisposition ... to contract improvident marriages'. He continued:

> I did observe that in those prosperous districts the marriages were not so frequent as I found them in the more impoverished districts ... I have perfectly on my recollection that the circumstance [in the prosperous districts] struck me at the time, and that I did inquire amongst the people how it happened; and the reply I received was that they had no idea of entering into the matrimonial state until they could acquire a competency for their own support, and the support of a family. In other parts of the country, where I observed very considerable poverty, I found a greater indifference about their future comforts than among persons in a more prosperous situation in life.[17]

For the majority of Mayo's small farmers the lack of hope for an improved future combined with few restraints on the subdivision of holdings and the survival of the rundale system, meant there was little incentive to limit marriage

16 S.J. Connolly, 'Marriage in Pre-Famine Ireland' in A. Cosgrove (ed.), *Marriage in Ireland* (Dublin, 1985), pp. 117-20.
17 *Second Report from the Select Committee on the State of Ireland*, p. 247, H. C. 1825 (129 continued), viii, 173.

or to impose lofty financial expectations on it. A Catholic curate, speaking in 1836 before the royal commission appointed to inquire into the condition of Ireland's poor, summed up the beliefs of many of the county's small holders when he reported that they were 'induced to marry by feeling that their condition cannot be made much worse, or, rather, they know they can lose nothing, and they promise themselves some pleasure in the society of a wife'.[18]

The near elimination of rundale and the gradual increase in the median size of holdings following the Famine brought a slow transformation of marriage practices in rural Mayo, although as David Fitzpatrick has recently noted, farmers in the west tended to marry younger and in larger numbers than their counterparts in the east until the last third of the nineteenth century.[19] One consequence of the Famine, in Mayo as elsewhere, was that there was a greater proportion of larger farmers who were more likely to practice restrictive marriage practices. As Lee has noted, 'a disproportionate number of Famine survivors belonged to classes with above average age at marriage ... Even had age at marriage remained unchanged within social groups, the reduction in the proportion of earlier marrying strata would have raised average age at marriage'.[20]

In this new environment it became increasingly the norm for the timing of marriage and the choice of a partner to be controlled by parents who were concerned above all with the commercial advantages of the marriage. Encouraged by the unwillingness of many post-Famine landlords to countenance the further subdivision of the land and by their own heightened expectations, the prime concern of many parents was to preserve the farm intact by leaving it in its entirety to one heir and to provide a dowry to allow at least one daughter to marry well. To the male heir, not necessarily the eldest son, fell the privilege of marrying. The landless sons were left either to emigrate or to remain celibate since, without land, marriage was improbable. Even the inheriting son was often prevented from marrying until he came into the land on or near the death of his parents. The pattern was similar for daughters, with the one chosen or willing to marry into a neighbouring farm family being provided with a suitable dowry while her sisters were left to emigrate or remain unmarried. Marriage negotiations were protracted, parents of potential brides being concerned primarily with assurances of when and under what circumstances their prospective son-in-law would come into the land. Parents of potential grooms were equally concerned with the amount of cash, stock and/or land that their prospective

18 *Poor Inquiry (Ireland): Appendix (F) Containing Baronial Examinations Relative to Con-acre, Quarter or Score Ground, Small Tenantry, Consolidation of Farms and Dislodged Tenantry, Emigration, Landlord and Tenant, Nature and State of Agriculture, Taxation, Roads, Observations on the Nature and State of Agriculture: and Supplement*, p. 43, H. C. 1836 (38), xxxiii, I.

19 Connolly, 'Marriage in Post-Famine Ireland' in Cosgrove (ed.), *Marriage in Ireland*, pp. 117-20.

20 Lee, *Modernisation of Irish Society*, p. 4.

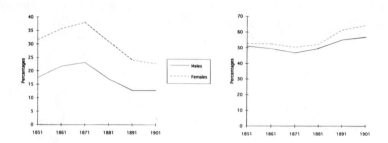

Figure 1   *(left)* Proportion of those between 15 and 34 years of age who were
              married or widowed. Source: *The census of Ireland for the year 1851, pt. i:*
              showing the area, population and the number of houses, by townlands, and
              electoral divisions, vol. iv, pp. 577, H. C. 1852-3 (1542), xcii, 453.
Figure 2   *(right)* Proportion of men between 15 and 64 and women between 15
              and 64 who never married. Source: *The census of Ireland for the year 1861,*
              pt. v: general report, p. 419, H. C. 1863 (3204-IV), lxi, I.

daughter-in-law's dowry contained. Frequently, the couple had little or no say
in these matters.[21]

   One consequence of these restrictive marriage practices was an increase in
celibacy, especially after 1881, although its spread was slower in the west than in
the east.[22] Two frequently employed indices of late and infrequent marriage are
the proportion of young men and women who are married and the proportion
of fertile adults who never marry.[23] As can be seen from Figures 1 and 2, the
proportion of married young men and women fell in Mayo from 1871, while
the percentage of fertile adults who never married rose steadily.

   The figures indicate that the restrictive marriage practices associated with
the post-Famine period began to have a significant impact in Mayo after 1871.
Brendan Walsh has calculated that the marriage rate per 1000 single women fell
more rapidly in Mayo after 1871 than in any county in Ireland. At the same
time, according to Walsh's figures the fertility rate (children under one year of
age per 1000 women aged fifteen to forty-five) in the west remained high despite a national downward trend. Walsh charts a demographic transition between 1871 and 1911 in which the west of Ireland was transformed from a

21   D. Fitzpatrick, 'Marriage in Post-Famine Ireland', pp. 116-29; also see C. O'Gráda,
     Ireland Before and After the Famine: Explorations in Economic History, 1800-1925 (rev. ed.,
     Manchester, 1993), pp. 180-94.
22   Fitzpatrick, 'Marriage in Post-Famine Ireland', pp. 117-18.
23   S.H. Cousens, 'The Regional Variations in Population ...', pp. 315-8; B.M. Walsh,
     'Marriage Rates and Population Pressure: Ireland, 1871 and 1911' in *Econ. Hist. Rev.*,
     second series, xxiii, 1 (April 1970), pp. 148, 151.

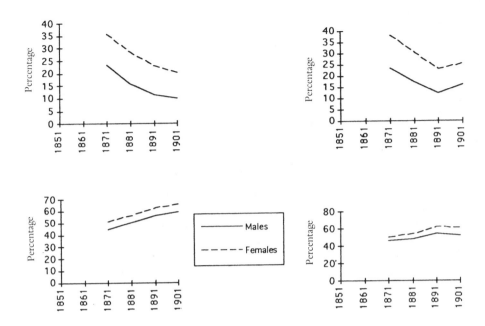

Figure 3a   (top left) Proportion of those between 15 and 34 years of age who were married or widowed, Ballinrobe Poor Law Union. Source: *The census of Ireland for the year 1871, pt. i: area, houses and population, vol. iv, province of Connaught, no. 3, county of Mayo*, pp. 361-2.

Figure 3b   (top right) Proportion of those between 15 and 34 years of age who were married or widowed, Swinford Poor Law Union. Source: *The census of Ireland for the year 1881, pt. 1: area, houses and population, vol. iii, province of Connaught, no. 3, county of Mayo*, pp. 261-2, H. C. 1882 [C.3268-III], lxxix, 273.

Figure 4a   (bottom left) Proportion of men between 15 and 64 and women between 15 and 44 who never married, Ballinrobe Poor Law Union. Source: *The census of Ireland for the year 1891, pt. i: area, houses and population, vol. iv, province of Connaught, no. 3, county of Mayo*, pp. 361-2, H. C. 1892 [C 6685-II], xciii, 277.

Figure 4b   (bottom right) Proportion of men between 15 and 64 and women between 15 and 44 who never married, Swinford Poor Law Union. Source: *The census of Ireland for the year 1901, pt. i: area, houses and population, vol. iv, province of Connaught, no. 3, county of Mayo*, pp. 108-9, H. C. 1902 [Cd 1059-ii], cxxciii, 365.

region with high marriage and fertility rates to one with a low marriage level but continued high fertility. He argues that a primary cause of this transformation was the desire on the part of Mayo's farmers to secure higher living standards by reducing the population pressure on the land. With fertility within marriage remaining high, Walsh argues that restraining from marriage was an accepted means of controlling the population.[24]

Surprisingly, the indices of age and frequency of marriage do not show a wide diversity between central Mayo and the peripheral areas of the county. As indicated in Figures 3 and 4, in 1871, when the census first contains breakdowns of age and conjugal status by poor law union, the Ballinrobe and Swinford unions were roughly equivalent in both the proportion of young men and women who were married and the proportion of fertile adults who were not married. Until 1891 both unions followed similar paths in the decline in the number of young adults who were married and the rise in the number of celibates. Yet, by 1901 the two unions were experiencing different marriage patterns as the Swinford union reversed course with an increased proportion of its population being married and a levelling off of the number of celibates.

From these indices it would appear that there was very little difference between the marriage patterns in the centre and the periphery during the last third of the nineteenth century. However, when the marriage rate (marriages per 1000 population) of the two unions is compared a wide divergence appears. In 1864, at the time of the first registration of marriages, births and deaths, the Swinford union had a marriage rate of 6.3 while the Ballinrobe union had one of 3.0. These were respectively the highest and lowest rates in the county with the county average being 4.6. However, by the beginning of the twentieth century the marriage rate in the two unions had converged. In 1901 the rates were 4.5 for the Swinford union, 3.5 for the Ballinrobe union, and 3.9 for the county of Mayo.[25]

The explanation for the seeming disparity between the two indices is most probably found in differences in the rate of emigration between the core and the periphery within County Mayo. While the emigration statistics do not reveal the districts within the county from which emigrants departed, it seems probable that by the 1870s, if not earlier, Mayo's high number of emigrants came to a large degree from the poorest regions of the county, in contrast to the situation during the Famine. Walsh theorises that by the 1870s population growth had resulted in a scarcity of land in those regions that experienced growth during the thirty years following the Famine.[26] As a consequence of this new land shortage, subdivision of holdings was slowed and many people who would have stayed in Mayo had land been available, opted to emigrate.

24 Walsh, 'Marriage Rates and Population Pressure', pp. 148–62.
25 *First Annual Report of the Registrar General of Marriages, Births, and Deaths in Ireland, 1864,* pp. 40, 46, H. C. 1868–9 (4137), xvi, 665; *Thirty-eighth Detailed Annual Report of the Registrar General (Ireland), Containing a General Astract of the Number of Marriages, Births and Deaths Registered in Ireland during the year 1901,* pp. 40, 46, H. C. 1902 [Cd. 1225], xviii, 501.
26 Walsh, 'Marriage Rates and Population Pressure', pp. 158–9.

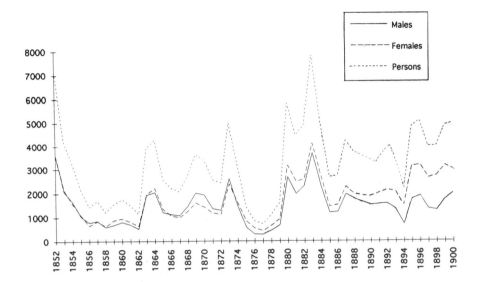

Figure 5 Emigration, County Mayo, 1852-1900. Source: W.E. Vaughan and A.J. Fitzpatrick (eds), *Irish Historical Statistics: Population 1821-1971* (Dublin, 1978), pp. 337-9.

In the Swinford union the number of men aged between fifteen and thirty-four, which had risen steadily from 1851 to 1881, fell from 6909 in 1881 to 6562 in 1901. Over the same period the number of women in this age bracket fell more sharply from 8893 to 7823 due to the substantially higher rate of emigration among women.[27] The growing divergence in the emigration rate of men and women after 1888, illustrated in Figure 5, no doubt contributed to the sharp upswing in the percentage of women aged between fifteen and thirty-four in 1901 who were married, as fewer young women were available to marry. Similarly, the slight rise in the proportion of married men can also be attributed to emigration, since with the departure of the landless young men the proportion of men with access to land and thus to marriage would increase.

In the Ballinrobe union the gradual decline in the proportion of young men and women who were married and the gradual rise in the number of celibates continued unabated from 1871 to 1901. This occurred less from a scarcity of land due to overpopulation, as was the case in the Swinford union, than from the slow but steady consolidation of holdings in the Ballinrobe union. These consolidations limited the amount of land available for new families as market-

27 *The Census of Ireland for the Year 1881, Part I: Area, Houses, and Population, vol. iii, Province of Connaught, No. 3, County of Mayo*, p. 362, H. C. 1882 [C 3268-III], lxxix, 273; *Census of Ireland, 1901*, part i, vol. iv, no. 3, p. 109.

oriented and aggressive farmers took up the farms of their less fortunate or less resolute neighbours.

Although by the end of the century marriage patterns in the two unions, representing Mayo's core and periphery, had coalesced to a large degree and conformed to the national pattern of late and infrequent marriages with many left celibate, the reasons for this change were significantly different in the two regions. Among small farmers, concentrated in but not exclusive to the periphery, the demographic transformation began during the 1870s as a result of population pressure on the small holdings that limited land available to new families and compelled many to emigrate. It is significant that small farmers were driven to abandon their marriage traditions in order to preserve a share of the small farm economy for the fortunate few who could secure land. In contrast, the more prosperous farmers clustered on the good land of central Mayo adopted prudent marriage practices that were calculated to increase the size of their holdings and to capitalize better on the dynamic post-Famine livestock economy. In both instances, the stage was set by the Famine, which had left large portions of the county densely populated, while initiating a dramatic depopulation in the county's more fertile centre.

'The Late Disastrous Epidemic': Medical Relief and the Great Famine

LAURENCE M. GEARY

'Famine, pinching famine, is around'.
Richard Long, MD, 'Report of the Arthurstown dispensary and fever hospital for 1846', *Dublin Medical Press*, 24 February 1847, p. 125.

During famine, two factors, often working in tandem, facilitate the occurrence of epidemics. These are the impairment of the individual immune system by starvation and the loss of community resistance to the spread of disease. Several phenomena contribute to the latter, among them population movements, neglect of personal and domestic hygiene, and overcrowding of public institutions, such as hospitals, workhouses and jails. Almost any endemic illness has the potential to become epidemic during famine.[1] In Ireland, for hundreds of years, fever, dysentery and smallpox had been the most notorious and destructive diseases and all three reappeared with increased malignity during the Great Famine. The terrifying mortality caused by these scourges was compounded by the presence of other epidemic infections, notably tuberculosis, rheumatic fever, bronchitis, influenza, pneumonia, diarrhoea and measles,[2] and was further exacerbated by the appearance of Asiatic cholera as a pandemic in 1848-9.[3]

'Famine fever', the term employed by contemporaries to designate the great despoiler of these years, embraced two distinct but symptomatically related infections, typhus fever and relapsing fever. Eighteenth- and nineteenth-century doctors did not know how these diseases were caused and assigned a whole host of reasons to their generation and diffusion. Some contended that famine was the sole or paramount cause,[4] an explanation that left many unconvinced. The latter claimed that food shortage was only one of several social issues involved. There was also poverty, the wretched housing of the poor, the paucity and inferior quality of their diet, their lack of clothing and fuel, dirt, depression, and

1 Robert Dirks, 'Famine and Disease' in *The Cambridge World History of Human Disease* (Cambridge, 1993), pp. 160-1.
2 'Report upon the recent epidemic fever in Ireland', *Dublin Quarterly Journal of Medical Science*, vii (1849), pp. 64-126, 340-404; viii (1849), pp. 1-86, 270-339.
3 *Report of the Commissioners of Health, Ireland, on the Epidemics of 1846 to 1850* (Dublin, 1852), pp. 28-42.
4 See, for instance, D.J. Corrigan, *On Famine and Fever as Cause and Effect in Ireland; with Observations on Hospital Location, and the Dispensation in Outdoor Relief of Food and Medicine* (Dublin, 1846), pp. 1-33.

intoxication, not to mention the pig in the kitchen and the middens at the front door.[5] The strongly opinionated William Kingsley, physician to the Roscrea fever hospital in County Tipperary, complained to the Board of Health in June 1847 that the ubiquitous cess-pools which disfigured the cabins of the poor were 'a constant, fertile and permanent source of typhus fever, in consequence of the putrid effluvia exhaled from them and blown by the wind into the interior of those filthy habitations'. They were also a national disgrace, he said.[6] Some Irish medical practitioners traced the country's recurring outbreaks of fever to what earlier writers termed 'the epidemic constitution', some unspecified connection between atmospheric or electrical phenomena and the generation of disease.[7]

It is now known that the vector of typhus fever and relapsing fever was not famine, nor social distress, still less atmospheric peculiarities, but *pediculus humanus*, the human body louse. The social disruption and squalor caused by famine favoured lice infestation. The lice feasted on the unwashed and susceptible skin of the poor, multiplied in their filthy and tattered clothing, and went forth, carried the length and breadth of the country by a population who had taken to the roads, vagrants, beggars and the evicted, as well as those who had abandoned their homes voluntarily. The mushrooming lice population found new and unresisting hosts at food depots and relief works, at social and religious gatherings, and in many public institutions which proved to be veritable breeding grounds.

The character of 'the late disastrous epidemic', to use William Wilde's term of late 1848, varied considerably.[8] Typhus fever prevailed in some parts of the country, relapsing fever in others. In certain districts the primary disease changed from typhus to relapsing fever and back again to typhus. Elsewhere, the two conspired together as 'famine fever'. No part of the country was immune, although some areas were more seriously affected than others. Relapsing fever was the prevalent disease among the destitute and the starving. As its name indicates, the disease is characterised by recurring bouts of fever. High temperature, generalised aches and pains, nausea, vomiting, nose bleeding and jaundice are features of the disease. The first attack ends after five or six days with a sharp

5 See, for instance, *First Report of the General Board of Health* (Dublin, 1822), p. 118; *Poor Inquiry (Ireland). Appendix B, Containing General Reports upon the Existing System of Public Medical Relief in Ireland; Local Reports upon Dispensaries, Fever Hospitals, County Infirmaries and Lunatic Asylums; with Supplement, Parts 1 and 2, Containing Answers to Questions from the Officers etc. of Medical Institutions*, British Parliamentary Papers, 1835 (369) xxxii, part 2, supplement, pp. 1-262.
6 *Dublin Medical Press*, 16 June 1847, p. 382.
7 Henry Kennedy, *Observations on the Connexion between Famine and Fever in Ireland, and Elsewhere* (Dublin, 1847), pp. 43-8; *Dublin Quarterly Journal of Medical Science*, vii (1849), p. 92; R.J. Graves, *A System of Clinical Medicine* (Dublin, 1843), pp. 41-2, 45.
8 'Report upon the recent epidemic fever in Ireland', *Dublin Quarterly Journal of Medical Science*, vii (1849), pp. 64-126, 340-404; viii (1849), pp. 1-86, 270-339.

crisis attended by profuse sweating and exhaustion. The symptoms return after about a week and there may be several such relapses before the disease runs its course. Such a progression was described by one midlands doctor as 'the fever being lighted up three or four times'.[9] These recurring attacks further weakened an already debilitated population and left them very vulnerable to a host of other infections, notably dysentery and diarrhoea.

Fever and other epidemic infections appeared as famine's shadow during the winter and spring of 1846-7, following the general failure of the potato crop. Government officials in Dublin were inundated with reports of the distress and social dislocation that prevailed. In late December 1846, Dr Henry J. Smith, Mountrath, informed the Lord Lieutenant that the ill effects of bad and insufficient food were already apparent in the gaunt features and emaciated frames of the great majority of the poor.[10] In mid-January 1847, fever and dysentery 'of an alarming and malignant character' were reported from Carlingford, County Louth. The dispensary was fourteen miles from the union poorhouse and there was no other hospital in the county.[11] Similar reports were received from Nenagh, County Tipperary, Omagh, County Tyrone and Coolavin, County Sligo, where there was neither dispensary nor resident apothecary. It was thought that the workhouse fever hospital at Boyle, which was then under construction, would not be capable of accommodating more than one-tenth of the union's fever patients.[12] Thousands fleeing from famine and pestilence flocked into Galway in the opening weeks of 1847, all but submerging the fever hospital and workhouse hospital in the process.[13] Such an influx, there and elsewhere, greatly alarmed the residents, who feared that the migrants might be carriers of fever and other infectious diseases.[14]

The Central Board of Health, which had been established in March 1846 and disbanded in the following August due to a lack of demand for their services, were reappointed in the first week of February 1847. The Board consisted of the prominent Dublin medical practitioners, Dominic John Corrigan and Sir Philip Crampton, the chemist Sir Robert Kane, who was medically qualified but who had almost entirely ceased to practice by the time of the Famine, and two senior civil servants, Sir Randolph Routh and Edward Twistleton. In effect, Corrigan and Crampton were the Board of Health. At their first meeting, the Board instructed Dr Robert William Smith of Eccles Street, Dublin, to inspect the overcrowded and badly administered Lurgan workhouse. They considered a request for aid from the Tullamore board of guardians, and a report

9 *Dublin Quarterly Journal of Medical Science*, viii (1849), p. 42.
10 CSORP 1847 H 363, NAI.
11 CSORP 1847 H 802, NAI.
12 CSORP 1847 H 1410, CSORP 1847 H 1347, CSORP 1847 H 4126, NAI.
13 CSORP 1847 H 962, NAI.
14 CSORP 1847 H 1347, NAI.

from John H. Leahy, physician to the Drimoleague dispensary in County Cork, in which he stated that fever, dysentery and dropsy had increased to such an extent throughout the district that he was unable to cope.[15] Thereafter, correspondence of a similar nature poured into the office on a daily basis. Some communications referred to the complete absence of medical relief in many parts of the country and requested the establishment of temporary fever hospitals. Others commented on the overcrowding and indebtedness of county and district fever hospitals and expressed the fears of the community concerning the possible closure of these institutions through lack of funds. A report from Killarney in April 1847 stated that people were 'literally dropping in the streets and perishing in their miserable cabins'. The local workhouse was full, as was the fever hospital, which was the only one in an area of 144 square miles. The hospital had been built to accommodate fifty-four patients but now contained 130 and its funds were almost completely exhausted.[16] The managing committee of the Clonmel fever hospital found themselves in a similar situation. They appealed for government assistance in March 1847, claiming that their position was 'truly awful'. Like other committees, they found it impossible to raise funds locally, such were the demands on the charitable. The response in this instance, as it was in all such cases, was that the government did not have any funds at their disposal for the maintenance of fever hospitals or other charitable institutions.[17]

The government's persistent refusal to sanction emergency funding for the country's existing fever hospitals and dispensaries was a grave mistake. These institutions should have been the first line of defence against infection and their continued existence guaranteed. On at least two occasions in the spring of 1847, the Central Board of Health warned the government that the country was on the verge of a fever epidemic as severe and as widespread as any that had yet occurred. Corrigan and Crampton arrived at this conclusion after receiving a letter from Samuel Edge, MD, physician to the Doonane fever hospital in the barony of Slievemangue, Queen's County, in which he depicted the densely populated and impoverished district where he resided as 'one large hospital', a locality where starvation, fever, dysentery and diarrhoea were wreaking a terrible toll. Ten inquests had been held there during the previous week and a verdict of death by starvation returned in each case. The fever hospital was in debt, he said, and people were dying of disease in the shadow of an institution which should have been able to relieve them. The local board of Poor Law guardians refused to help, when asked. The Poor Law commissioners replied that they did not have the power, the Lord Lieutenant that he did not have the means.[18]

The Board of Health believed that the existing legislation relating to fever and other contagious diseases in Ireland was inadequate to meet the current

15 CSORP 1847 H 1704, NAI.   17 CSORP 1847 H 3513, NAI.
16 CSORP 1847 H 4789, NAI.   18 CSORP 1847 H 3420, NAI.

emergency. They informed the Lord Lieutenant that the fever act of 1818[19] had 'not worked well'. They and others were concerned about the way in which fever hospitals established under its provisions were funded and administered, and there had been rumours about peculation and jobbing. The amended Poor Law act of 1843,[20] which empowered boards of guardians to provide relief for the poor of the union afflicted with fever, was also defective. Experience had convinced Corrigan and Crampton that Poor Law guardians were 'not fitted for the sole superintendence of the care of the sick poor'. The Board claimed that this act and the temporary fever act of 1846[21] shared 'the same great funda-mental error'. The question of relieving the sick and of implementing precau-tionary or preventive measures was decided at local level and was bound to be influenced by local concerns. The result was often unnecessary expenditure or the opposite, a refusal to sanction aid for the sick. If a board of guardians adopted the latter course, the Board of Health was largely powerless to act, there being no other method of supplying the necessary funds.[22]

Defective legislation was compounded by the deficiencies of the country's existing medical institutions. The latter were considered by the Board of Health as 'peculiarly unfitted' to cope with the demands of the Famine.[23] The institu-tions to which they referred were the medical charities which had evolved during the eighteenth and early nineteenth centuries to provide free medical aid to the sick poor. There were approximately 650 in existence by the mid-1830s, consisting of 528 dispensaries, 64 fever hospitals, 38 county and other provincial infirmaries, 11 district lunatic asylums, and 7 voluntary hospitals in Dublin.[24] A decade later, when the Great Famine began, there were 664 dispensaries, 101 fever hospitals and 41 infirmaries catering for the many needs of the sick poor.[25] Those who were suffering from fever and other contagious diseases were largely debarred from the infirmaries and were tended, instead, by dispensary medical officers, or in fever hospitals, where such existed. The medical charities came under enormous pressure during the Famine. Writing in May 1847, Dr Stirling

19 58 Geo. III, c. 47, 'An act to establish fever hospitals, and to make other regulations for relief of the suffering poor, and for preventing the increase of infectious fevers in Ireland', 30 May 1818.

20 6 and 7 Vic., c. 92, 'An act for the further amendment of an act for the more effectual relief of the destitute poor in Ireland', 24 August 1843

21 9 and 10 Vic., c. 6, 'An act to make provision, until the first day of September one thousand eight hundred and forty-seven, for the treatment of poor persons afflicted with fever in Ireland', 24 March 1846

22 CSORP 1847 H 3420, NAI. See also, D.J. Corrigan to the Lord Lieutenant, 24 Febru-ary 1847, OP 1847/147, NAI.

23 Report of the Commissioners of Health, Ireland, on the Epidemics of 1846 to 1850, p. 2.

24 Denis Phelan, A Statistical Inquiry into the Present State of the Medical Charities of Ireland (Dublin, 1835), pp. 1-2.

25 Report from the Select Committee of the House of Lords on the Laws Relating to the Destitute Poor and into the Operation of the Medical Charities in Ireland; Together with the Minutes of

of Thomastown observed that he and his colleagues in the dispensary service were 'overwhelmed with work'.[26]

Dispensaries dated from an 1805 act of parliament and were the most important branch of the medical charities system. They were intended, as one parliamentary inquiry phrased it, to bring relief 'to the door of the sick'.[27] However, the entire dispensary system was grossly abused and its usefulness was further limited by a number of inherent defects. Dispensaries were not established on any set principle but could be opened anywhere, irrespective of need or demand. The only requirement was the procurement of local subscriptions, which the county grand jury was then obliged to match. The combined amount was placed at the disposal of a committee elected from among the subscribers, to be used at their discretion to provide medical relief for the sick poor. The method of funding, irregular and unreliable as it was, placed great strains on the system and resulted in a very uneven distribution of dispensaries. They were mainly concentrated in the towns and the better off areas, where subscriptions could more readily be raised, and were scarce in the poorer and remoter rural districts, where the need for them was greatest.

In general, the contract that was understood to exist between the medical officer and the subscribers was that the sick poor of the district who attended the dispensary would be supplied with medicine and advice, and that a limited domiciliary service would also be provided. Dispensaries generally opened for a couple of hours on two or three mornings of the week but there was great variation as it was left to each dispensary committee to determine the times at which the doctor would attend. All rural dispensaries and some urban ones had only one medical officer attached. Few had assistants, which meant that emergency aid was often unavailable, and the institution was unstaffed for lengthy periods. Assistants, where they were employed, were generally poorly paid and unqualified. There was no obligation on medical officers to reside in their dispensary districts. Some lived in towns several miles away, where they had their private practice.[28]

The contagiousness of fever was generally conceded, as was the necessity of isolating the infected. To this end, three different types of institutions, county, district and Poor Law union fever hospitals, evolved in the first half of the nineteenth century. The latter were the most recent, dating from 1843. They were supported out of the rates and were open to all who resided within the Poor Law union. County fever hospitals, which admitted the infected from all

Evidence taken before the said Committee, British Parliamentary Papers, 1846 (694) xi, part 1, pp. xxv–xxvi.

26 *Dublin Medical Press*, 2 June 1847, p. 342.

27 *Report from the Select Committee of the House of Lords on the Laws Relating to the Destitute Poor and into the Operation of the Medical Charities in Ireland*, p. xxvi.

28 Phelan, *A Statistical inquiry into the Present State of the Medical Charities of Ireland*, pp. 145–160

parts of the county, were entirely supported by local taxation. They evolved fitfully and not every county had one. In the 1830s, Monaghan, Donegal, Tyrone, Leitrim, Fermanagh, Roscommon, Mayo and Longford, were without a fever hospital of any description. In another five counties, the single fever hospital was so small and the funds so scarce that its use was extremely limited. District fever hospitals were the product of the 1816-19 fever epidemic, when as many as 1,500,000 people may have been infected. These institutions were supported by a combination of local philanthropy and local rates. Unlike county fever hospitals, there was no limit to the number which could be established. However, their method of funding, not least the necessity of raising local subscriptions on an annual basis, retarded their development.[29]

As the Board of Health feared, the medical charities, along with the country's other public institutions, such as jails, bridewells and workhouses, were swamped by the Famine's victims. The clamour, confusion and consternation attendant on a workhouse were graphically captured by a contemporary writer, Dr R.R. Madden. On a bitter February morning in 1851, men, women and children, conservatively estimated at 1000, sought admission to the Kilrush union workhouse in County Clare. The precincts of the workhouse resembled the suburbs of a town during a fair, according to Madden. Low backed cars, from which the horses had been removed, were ranged along the front wall of the building. The cars were occupied by the old and the young, the majority too listless, emaciated or diseased to stand or even sit upright. Those who had been unable to procure transport had crawled to the workhouse from distant parts and were to be seen squatting near the entrance, waiting their turn to be called. The courtyard was thronged with a dense mass of misery, 'clamouring and pressing forward, the less weak thrusting aside the more infirm, the young hustling the old, the women pulling back the children, larger children pushing back the smaller, uttering confused cries of pain, impatience, anger and despair'.[30]

This Hogarthian scene was simply a reflection and a repetition of those that had occurred throughout the country during the previous four years. The numbers admitted to hospitals and workhouses were often so great that overcrowding became a serious health problem. The Mitchelstown workhouse, originally intended for 900 inmates, contained 1533 paupers by the first week of February 1847. One hundred and seventy eight of these were in hospital, two, three and sometimes four to a bed, and the increasing morbidity and mortality figures

29 *Report from the Select Committee of the House of Lords on the Laws Relating to the Destitute Poor and into the Operation of the Medical Charities in Ireland*, pp. xxvii-xxviii. See also, Peter Froggatt, 'The Response of the Medical Profession to the Great Famine' in E.M. Crawford (ed.), *Famine, the Irish experience, 900-1900: Subsistence Crises and Famines in Ireland* (Edinburgh, 1989), pp. 134-56.
30 Kilrush union workhouses, CSORP 1851/03508, NAI.

were causing alarm. According to the workhouse doctor, those who could not be admitted were left to die on the highways or to linger on in their own hovels, 'a helpless mass of famine and disease'.[31] A few weeks later, it was reported that there were 418 patients in the Armagh workhouse hospital, which was originally designed to accommodate 100. Two hundred and fifty five were fever stricken, as were the medical officers.[32] Eight hundred and thirteen of the 960 inmates of Castlerea workhouse were sick on an April day in 1847.[33]

Elsewhere, the situation was even worse. In the opening months of 1847, the Cork, Bantry and Lurgan workhouses were investigated by the Poor Law commissioners and by the Board of Health, following reports of overcrowding, mismanagement, neglect and excessive mortality. Ninety-five of the 800 inmates of the Lurgan workhouse died during the week ending 6 February 1847. During the following week, 164 deaths were recorded in the Cork union workhouse, where the number of inmates exceeded the physicians' recommendations by 1000. They and Dr Stephens, the medical inspector of the Board of Health, attributed the alarming sickness and mortality in the institution to the debilitated or dying condition of the poor on admission, to overcrowding and to poor ventilation. The hospital attached to the Bantry union workhouse was found on inquiry to be in such a frightful state of filth and neglect that the Poor Law commissioners requested the medical officer's resignation and dismissed the master and matron from office.[34]

While mismanagement and negligence were a feature of some institutions and while the conditions in many were quite appalling it would be wrong to attach the entire blame to administrative indifference. The system was simply unable to cope with the demands made upon it by the Famine. Government response to the spread of disease was indecisive and inadequate. Medical officers, boards of guardians and local relief committees were presented with an appalling dilemma. They were often the arbiters of life and death and were generally loath to exclude the starving, the sick and the dying from relief and shelter. The Lurgan guardians, for instance, attributed the defects that were detected in their workhouse to the pressure of the times and to their own reluctance to reject any of the poor people who swarmed round the entrance, seeking admission.

Such a reaction was regarded as highly irresponsible by the Board of Health and the Poor Law commissioners. They were no less charitable or humane than hospital or workhouse administrators but were convinced that overcrowding was a major factor in generating disease and as such posed a grave threat to

31 CSORP 1847 H 1358, and CSORP 1847 H 1704, NAI.
32 CSORP 1847 H 3574, NAI.
33 CSORP 1847 H 5011, NAI.
34 CSORP 1847 H 6048, NAI. A similar situation prevailed in many of the country's prisons. See, for instance, *Dublin Quarterly Journal of Medical Science*, vii (1849), pp. 86-7, 365-6, and *Dublin Medical Press*, 16 June 1847, pp. 381-2.

public health. They contended that the indiscriminate institutionalisation of the sick and the hungry was a greater evil than allowing them to fend for themselves outside. The Board of Health were convinced that individuals, no matter how scanty and uncertain their resources, had a better chance of surviving famine than they had of avoiding death within a disease-ridden institution. In mid-April 1847, the Kilkenny guardians were instructed to reduce 'the fearful amount of sickness in the workhouse', which, the Board felt, posed an unacceptable risk to all classes in the city and its environs. 'Fever, once generated, will not be confined within the crowded camp hospital, the jail or the workhouse in which it may have originated', they observed. If unchecked, the disease would spread among rich and poor alike, involving all in a common danger. The Board of Health emphasised the way in which fever variously affected the different social classes. According to their reckoning, the mortality rate from the disease was one in thirty among the poor but one in two among their social superiors.[35]

To relieve the pressure on overcrowded institutions, emergency legislation, dating from 24 August 1846, enabled the Board of Health to provide temporary fever hospitals or dispensaries when and where required. Between February 1847 and August 1850, when the Board of Health was finally disbanded, 576 such applications were received, 373 of which were granted. The Board of Health demanded weekly hospital returns which showed that 332,462 patients were treated in these institutions, 173,723 females and 158,739 males. The overall death rate of slightly more than ten per cent masked the considerable variations that occurred in different institutions and at different times. During the six months ending 7 November 1849, the mortality rate at Carnacregg hospital in the Ballinasloe union was almost thirty per cent, which the medical officer, Dr Butler, attributed to overcrowding, the patients' poor general health on admission, and the fact that many endured successive attacks of fever, dysentery and cholera. His colleague in Killaloe, County Clare, assigned high institutional mortality 'to the debilitated condition of the patients, many of whom were brought to hospital in a hopeless state'. Deprivation and general debility left much of the general population vulnerable to a host of infections. In the Limerick union hospital, for instance, where 235 of the 817 patients died during a period of six months in 1849, dysentery and measles, which affected the old and deprived and very young children respectively, were responsible for the entire mortality. A contributory factor to the twenty-five per cent death rate in the Tulla hospital, according to the medical officer, was the poor condition of the building. The canvas roof left in both wind and rain. The floors were constantly wet and the wards full of smoke, 'from the necessity of lighting the fire on the floor'.[36]

35 CSORP 1847 H 5282, NAI.
36 Report of the Commissioners of Health, Ireland, on the Epidemics of 1846 to 1850, pp. 1-11.

Where temporary fever hospitals were sanctioned, the Board of Health recommended that an existing building be procured and adapted for the purpose.
If this were not feasible, or if additional accommodation were required in existing hospitals, the Board supplied the applicants with plans for the construction
of wooden fever sheds and bedsteads, of a simple and economical design, which
had been drawn up by architect of the Poor Law Commission.[37] These wooden
sheds were preferred by the Board of Health to tents belonging to the Ordnance department which were used in some places for part of 1847.[38] Three
different types of tents were employed, hospital tents, marquees and round tents,
which could accommodate 14, 4, and 3 fever patients respectively. Dominic
Corrigan considered that marquees and round tents were 'ill adapted for hospital purposes'.[39]

Where possible, temporary fever hospitals and dispensaries were staffed by
local doctors, who were paid five shillings a day in addition to their permanent
salaries. This was considered an insulting level of remuneration by many members of the profession, especially the Dublin based leadership, who had little or
no connection with the service. The ensuing controversy was simply another
feature of the struggle that had been going on between the government and the
medical profession for a decade to wrest control of the medical charities. A
petition, objecting to the level of payment, was organised and supported by the
leading lights of the profession and signed by some 1100 doctors nation-wide.[40]
It was unceremoniously rejected by the government on the advice of the Central Board of Health, who cited a number of precedents and reasons to support
their contention that the recommended salary was both just and adequate.[41]
Thereafter, Crampton and Corrigan were subjected to the grossest personal and
professional abuse. Their motives were questioned, their activities mercilessly
scrutinised.[42] The Central Board of Health ignored the profession's anger and
invective and persevered with their unenviable and unpaid task. They continued to give unstinting support to the doctors in their employ who manned the
emergency health institutions and sheltered them from the sniping, strictures
and meanness of boards of guardians and local committees of various hues.[43]

The medical profession emerged subdued and dejected from the Famine,
their numbers and morale severely depleted. Many doctors acknowledged their

37 Ibid., p. 26.
38 CSORP 1847 H 7867, NAI.
39 CSORP 1847 H 5970, NAI.
40 R.J. Graves, *A Letter Relative to the Proceedings of the Central Board of Health in Ireland*
    (Dublin, 1847), reprinted from *Dublin Quarterly Journal of Medical Science*, iv (1847), pp.
    513–44.
41 CSORP 1847 H 7888, NAI; see also, *Report of the Commissioners of Health, Ireland, on the
    Epidemics of 1846 to 1850*, pp. 45, 55–6.
42 See, for instance, *Dublin Medical Press*, 1 December 1847, pp. 345–6.
43 See, for instance, CSORP 1847 H 7794; 1847 H 8034, NAI

inability to contain the successive waves of disease that swept over the country. They were simply unable to cope with the sheer scale of the Famine, a disaster which almost completely overwhelmed the country's medical resources. In its wake, the Medical Charities Act of 1851 provided for the introduction of a state funded dispensary system, to provide free medical relief to the sick poor. The system was administered by the Poor Law Commission, who were also given responsibility for the fever and county hospitals, as well as the workhouse infirmaries. With some modifications, this system survived until relatively recent times.[44]

'Irish Property Must Pay for Irish Poverty': British Public Opinion and the Great Irish Famine

JAMES S. DONNELLY, JR.

Ever since the Great Famine people have debated the culpability of the British government in the mass deaths which marked and defined that horrendous social catastrophe. For those disposed to judge the British government harshly, its most serious sins have included its adamant refusal to stop the export of domestically produced grain, especially in the winter of 1846-7, its unwillingness to prevent or even to slow down the mass evictions, or clearances, of perhaps a half-million persons, and the implementation of a poor-law system that greatly facilitated clearances and was woefully inadequate in providing relief to the famine-stricken population. But even if we are inclined to censure the British government severely, we must seek to understand the political and ideological context in which such important government decisions were made. Though some considerable strides have recently been taken in this direction,[1] a great deal remains to be uncovered about British public opinion (especially middle-class opinion) and its shifting currents in relation to Ireland during the famine. In this essay I focus primarily on parliamentary and public attitudes to the Poor Law Amendment Act of June 1847 and to its disastrous consequences in Ireland thereafter. It was this law that radically shifted the burden of providing public relief away from the British treasury, placing it instead squarely on the shoulders of Irish landlords and tenants. It was also this same law which drastically increased the weight of that burden by authorising relief outside the workhouses in a broad array of circumstances. In so doing, this law powerfully contributed to the famine clearances, which were specifically facilitated by one of its provisions – the notorious Gregory or quarter-acre clause.[2]

It is generally recognised that the 1847 Poor Law Amendment Act embodied the principle popular in Britain that Irish property must support Irish poverty. But not sufficiently appreciated are the vehemence and the scope of the attacks made in Britain on Irish landlords and the Irish land system before, dur-

---

1 See especially the following articles by Dr Peter Gray: '*Punch* and the Great Famine' in *History Ireland*, i, 2 (Summer 1993), pp. 26-33; 'The Triumph of Dogma: Ideology and Famine Relief', ibid., iii, 2 (Summer 1995), pp. 26-34; 'Ideology and the Famine' in Cathal Póirtéir (ed.), *The Great Irish Famine* (Cork, 1995), pp. 86-103.
2 For discussions of the Poor Law Amendment Act of June 1847 and the Gregory or quarter-acre clause, see Christine Kinealy, *This Great Calamity: The Irish Famine, 1845-52* (Dublin, 1994), pp. 180-4, 216-27.

ing, and after the passage of this legislation. So neglectful of their duties and so oppressive had Irish landed proprietors allegedly been over several generations that they were widely held in Britain to have created the conditions that led to the famine. The *Illustrated London News* delivered a sweeping condemnation in March 1847:

> The tales of ejectments, clearings, and all the long list of legal but heartless practices that reach England from the other side of the channel have hardened Englishmen against those who have for centuries held the fate of Ireland in their hands. The plain fact is before us, too dreadfully evident to be overlooked: with the possession of the property of the island, an absolute monopoly of political power, patronage, and place − ... the dominant class in Ireland have reduced both England and Ireland to this.[3]

It was frequently asserted, however, that by pampering Irish landlords in the years since the Act of Union in 1800, the British parliament was at least partly to blame: 'There were no laws it would not pass at their request, and no abuse it would not defend for them', declared the *London News* in February.[4] Through its persistent neglect, confessed the *Times* in March, wealthy Britain had permitted in Ireland 'a mass of poverty, disaffection, and degradation without a parallel in the world. It allowed proprietors to suck the very life-blood of that wretched race.'[5] According to John Arthur Roebuck, the independent Radical MP for Bath, Irish landlords were 'very much like slaveholders, with white slaves' and 'had been made so very much by English legislation'.[6] By shamelessly exploiting their tenants, Irish landlords, insisted the *London News*, had reduced them to serfdom, 'and the Irish cotter is as much a serf as the Russian peasant, with the difference that he is worse fed ... '.[7] The *Times* too spoke of pre-famine Ireland as having displayed 'the worst symptoms of eastern despotism polluting the surface of a free empire', along with 'the worst privations of Turkish and Russian slavery'.[8]

The predatory character of Irish landlordism was widely attributed in England to the deep financial indebtedness of so many Irish landlords. 'As a body it appears in a thousand ways that the curse of need and embarrassment is upon them: they are obliged', commented the *London News* in February 1847, 'to screw and extort the utmost farthing that can be got in any possible way from

3 *I.L.N.*, 20 March 1847.
4 *I.L.N.*, 13 February 1847.
5 *Times*, 24 March 1847.
6 *Hansard's Parliamentary Debates*, 3rd series, xc (1847), col. 1030.
7 *I.L.N.*, 20 February 1847.
8 *Times*, 29 March 1847.

anybody ...'.[9] The *Times* sneered at the Irish landlord in March as 'the old original pauper of Ireland' and 'the grandfather of all destitute persons'. Among 'the things which disgrace Ireland and disgust Christendom', the paper declared, were 'the squalid destitution of the many' and 'the unscrupulous necessities of their needy masters'.[10] But the very condition that made predators of Irish land-lords in their own country turned them into greedy, clamouring supplicants at Westminster in Britain. Roebuck, one of their fiercest critics there, declared in January of the same year that 'he had no sympathy whatever for Irish landlords, whom he designated as beggars'.[11] Another Radical, Archibald Hastie, MP for Paisley, contemptuously dismissed Irish landlords in February as a body of men who 'had done nothing but sit down and howl for English money'.[12] In the press also the Irish landed elite was pictured with a begging bowl in its hands. However much Irish proprietors might differ in other respects, acidly remarked the *London News*, they 'are ready alike to hold out their hands for loans and grants' from the government.[13] 'Give, give,' was their constant cry to others. The *Times* posed as the protector of British working-class interests against the outright robbery 'deliberately planned' by Irish landlords – 'those shameless and importunate mendicants', 'the spoilt pets of the state'. English workers, the paper claimed, paid nine-tenths of all taxes, and thus of the £10 million now being spent on Irish famine relief, 'they pay nine [million]'. Were English workers 'to sink into a nation of overworked, underpaid drudges, slaves, helots, mere mechanic operative animals, for the sole purpose of maintaining the landlords of Ireland in disgraceful luxury'? In the inflammatory language of the *Times*, 'the Irish landlord was counting the millions he could extract from British industry, as coolly as the butcher anticipates in fancy the cutting up of his bullocks and sheep'.[14] From the landlords' past avoidance of various taxes and their current readiness 'to harass the government and impose upon the English public new burthens for the performance of duties which they neglect,' observed the Eng-lish rural writer Alexander Somerville in March 1847, 'it will be seen that as a class Irish landowners stand at the very bottom of the scale of honest and hon-ourable men'.[15] No reader of Somerville's recently republished *Letters from Ire-land during the Famine of 1847*, which appeared originally in the *Manchester Examiner*, could fail to perceive the depth of English middle-class hostility to Irish land-lords.[16]

9 *I.L.N.*, 20 February 1847.
10 *Times*, 2 April 1847.
11 *I.L.N.*, 23 January 1847.
12 *Hansard's Parliamentary Debates*, 3rd series, lxxxix (1847), col. 955.
13 *I.L.N.*, 6 February 1847.
14 *Times*, 10 March 1847.
15 Alexander Somerville, *Letters from Ireland during the Famine of 1847*, ed. K.D.M. Snell (Dublin, 1994), p. 118.
16 Ibid., p. 8.

Among the crimes charged against Irish landlords, none perhaps aroused more resentment in Britain early in 1847 than what was seen as their dumping of evicted pauper tenants on the shores of England, Scotland, and Wales. In the British press and in parliament a strong connection was drawn between Irish evictions and the swelling tide of Irish immigrants into Britain, most of them very poor and many of them diseased. Liverpool took the brunt of this so-called Irish 'invasion', with as many as 50,000 pouring into that port city during the month of March alone, and with many of the new arrivals dying in the streets or crowding into its hospitals and workhouses.[17] In driving their pauper tenants across the Irish Sea to Britain, Irish landlords were widely held to be capitalising on the knowledge that in extremities these destitute people would be supported there under the English poor law. Thus Irish immunity from a poor law which recognised even a limited right to outdoor relief became in British eyes another means by which Irish proprietors evaded their social responsibilities and shifted a burden which properly belonged to them onto the shoulders of British tax-payers. As the *Times* complained in April, 'Liverpool, Manchester, and Bristol pay with vicarious infliction the penalty of English indifference [to the inad-equacies of the Irish poor law] and Irish immunity'.[18] And the paper warned that unless the Irish poor law were amended to provide for substantial outdoor relief, 'every port, every city in this island, will atone for its political negligence by the actual presence of that [Irish] poverty' which it had not insisted that parliament direct to be relieved in Ireland.[19] It was not only a question of money but also one of physical and cultural degradation. 'No argument that pen ever writ or heart ever indited [about maintaining the Irish poor at home in Ireland] can match with the spectacle', declared the *Times*, 'of England positively in-vaded, overrun, devoured, infected, poisoned, and desolated by Irish pauper-ism.' Maliciously, the paper suggested that the classical economist Nassau Senior should try to proclaim the virtues of the workhouse test and the evils of outdoor relief in the Liverpool Exchange.[20] It was assumed that he would be about as popular there as evicting Irish landowners.

It was this badly soiled reputation that Irish landlord MPs and their parlia-mentary allies took into the lengthy debates that surrounded the relief policies of Lord John Russell's Whig government in the early months of 1847. What the parliamentary spokesmen for the Irish landlords wished above all to avoid was any change in the Irish poor law which would result in the general or widespread extension of outdoor relief. Even if filled to capacity and free of epidemic disease, the existing workhouses were capable of accommodating only a small fraction of the three million or more people who were destitute in the

17 *Times*, 5 April 1847.
18 *Times*, 20 April 1847.
19 *Times*, 16 April 1847.
20 Ibid.

spring and summer of 1847. The prospect of extending outdoor relief to these millions filled Irish landlords with dread. They claimed to be 'willing to submit to any charge' necessary to further extend workhouse accommodation, but they loudly clamoured for the retention of the workhouse test of destitution for the able-bodied poor. A petition to this effect was signed and presented to parliament by forty-three MPs and sixty-four peers who were said to have residences in both Ireland and Britain.[21]

But British public opinion was horrified at the apparent consequences of conceding what Irish landlords were seeking. They were pilloried and ridiculed for resisting the principle of outdoor relief at the very time, in March 1847, when over 700,000 Irish labourers were receiving it on the public works and would mostly have perished without it. In citing the arguments of such classical economists as Nassau Senior and George Cornewall Lewis against outdoor relief, Irish landlord MPs, said the *Times* dismissively, were citing 'names which, to all public purposes, not only are dead but stink'; their opinions the paper flatly labelled as 'putrid'. Against the landlords' clamour for the maintenance of the workhouse test, the *Times* declared without much exaggeration:

> The workhouses are all full and only hold 100,000, while 4,000,000 are starving. The workhouses too are mere charnel-houses ... Do they expect voluntary aid from the landlords? ... If those 4,000,000 were now left to the spontaneous benevolence of the landlords, they would be as Sennacherib's army before the 1st of May.[22]

Russell's government, however, had resolved to amend the Irish poor law in such a way as to allow outdoor relief in the form of food to be given not only to those disabled from labour but also to the able-bodied if the workhouse was full or otherwise incapable of receiving them. The cost of any relief given outside the workhouse was to be charged on the poor rates of the union as a whole, with the landlords paying the entire rate for holdings valued at £4 or less, and about half the rates for holdings valued at more than £4. Union rating and the £4-rating clause were bound to be contentious issues. There was of course a close correlation between districts with deep destitution and areas with a high percentage of holdings valued at £4 or less. The *locus classicus* for this phenomenon was Mayo, where a staggering 75 per cent of all occupiers had holdings in this category, and where destitution was a ubiquitous scourge throughout most of the county.[23] Along with landlords in similar circumstances elsewhere, a Mayo proprietor would now be afflicted not only with a mass of destitute tenants

21 *Hansard's Parliamentary Debates*, 3rd series, xc (1847), cols. 1249-50, 1414.
22 *Times*, 15 March 1847.
23 Donald E. Jordan, Jr., *Land and Popular Politics in Ireland: County Mayo from the Plantation to the Land War* (Cambridge, 1994), p. 110.

paying little or no rent but also with the heavy added drain arising from his total liability for the statutory relief of by far the greater number of them. What landlord would want to keep such tenants?

The government did not much concern itself with this question, but it certainly did worry that if poor rates were charged not on the union as a whole but rather on those chunks of it called electoral divisions, many landlords in particular electoral divisions would be strongly tempted to evict their pauper tenants in the hope that these destitute people would take refuge in some other electoral division, thus freeing the evicting proprietor from claims for their poor relief. As the *Times* was to put it with characteristic pungency, if electoral-division rating were conceded, it would allow estate-clearing landlords to create a multitude of 'traps for human vermin', a Skibbereen in every poor-law union, or '130 vast almshouses maintained from the public exchequer'.[24] Union rating, by contrast, would equalise burdens by removing the premium on dumping, and in theory it would provide an incentive for proprietors to create employment without their having to fear the imposition of a double burden – the relief of one's own tenants and of someone else's besides. But whatever the exact distribution, the landlord burden, especially with the £4-rating clause included, would be great. In fact, taken together, these proposals appeared to spell a staggering load of new taxation for the Irish landed interest.

In terror at this prospect, Irish landlord MPs tried to persuade their British colleagues that the Irish landed interest would be ruined by the proposed legislation. 'In fact,' declared William Gregory, the Galway landowner and Tory MP for Dublin city, 'the whole rental of Ireland would not suffice for the relief which must be required under this bill.' Apart altogether from demoralising much of the rural population, Gregory argued, the bill would absorb the capital of the country, diminish wages, reduce labourers to paupers, and thus in the end 'would be more prejudicial to the poor than the rich'.[25] Thomas Bateson, a Conservative MP for County Londonderry, employed essentially the same reasoning to draw an even more alarming picture. 'If once the right of outdoor relief to able-bodied paupers were established by law,' he declared,

> pauperism would be encouraged, the whole property of the country absorbed, and the population demoralised. Having brought the country into this state of insolvency and ruin, the whole of Ireland would be one monster union, and the prime minister of England the head relieving officer.[26]

24 *Times*, 8 May 1847.
25 *Hansard's Parliamentary Debates*, 3rd series, xc (1847), col. 1276.
26 Ibid., col. 1283.

But their dramatic portrayals of the financial disaster which Irish landlords saw ahead failed to elicit much sympathy from English or Scottish MPs or in the British press. The *Times* doubted that an amended poor law would 'swamp the landowners', as their friends alleged. But even if it did, 'we are not sure that the price is too great to pay for the regeneration of the people ...'.[27] The worst enemies of Irish landlords almost hoped for their destruction. Proclaimed Roebuck with implacable bitterness: 'He would apply the English poor law [with provision for outdoor relief] to Ireland, which, though it might sweep away two-thirds of the Irish landlords, he cared not for [them]'.[28] Apparently, Roebuck was not alone. The Irish MP William Gregory openly admitted in the House of Commons that it would not be enough for him to show that 'all the property in many parts of Ireland would be entirely swallowed up' by granting outdoor relief to the able-bodied poor, for 'he feared that, with many members of the house, that would be the chief recommendation of the measure'.[29] At least one British newspaper, the Catholic *Tablet*, happily embraced this extraordinary reasoning: 'When, therefore, we hear it urged as an objection to the poor laws that a compulsory system of outdoor relief will ruin the landlords, we answer that this is its best possible recommendation'.[30] Even much less hostile commentators ridiculed the 'lamentable stories' of landlord partisans, heard especially in the House of Lords, about the 'black and hideous ruin before them'. If Irish landlords 'could be believed,' declared the *London News*, 'one would think they were the class to be pitied, not the famine-stricken peasantry'. To hear the Irish landlords tell it, 'there cannot well be a greater affliction than the possession of a few thousands or tens of thousands a year of Irish property. Estates in Ireland are mere myths, fictions; rentals are fabulous; and returns from the land in [the] shape of money are matter of legend and tradition only ...'. But the predicted doom of Irish landlords was premature, in the opinion of the *London News*: 'Some remaining thousands will still flow in even after the rates are paid; and on the whole the affliction of an estate, even an Irish estate, may continue to be endured'.[31]

The Whig government easily turned back efforts by the Protectionist Tories and Irish landlord MPs to throw the entire burden of the poor rates on the occupying tenants. The attempt only exacerbated English middle-class revulsion for the Irish landlords' almost criminal avoidance of their social responsibilities. Even British peers generally failed to support them on this issue. Sensing his isolation, the Protectionist leader Lord Stanley 'did not venture even to divide' the House of Lords on his amendment for tenant payment of rates.

27 *Times*, 29 March 1847.
28 *I.L.N.*, 23 January 1847.
29 *Hansard's Parliamentary Debates*, 3rd series, xc (1847), col. 1273.
30 Quoted ibid., col. 1301.
31 *I.L.N.*, 22 May 1847.

'Never', crowed the *London News*, 'did a long-threatened and rather dreaded opposition end so innocently: it was a most lame and impotent conclusion.' Had the effort succeeded, its critics argued, it 'would have made the collection of any rate impossible', so great would have been the outrage among Irish tenants.[32]

Thus British government ministers, many British MPs, and a wide section of the British press were able to project the 1847 Poor Law Amendment Act as a long overdue measure of popular justice as well as a distinctive act of genuine benevolence toward Ireland on the part of the British parliament. The absence of such a measure since the beginning of the famine, asserted the *Times*, had cost England £10 million and Ireland 'probably a hundred thousand lives, not to mention the sufferings of the survivors'.[33] Almost all of the leading press organs would have agreed with Roebuck's description of the proposed law as 'a great act of justice due to the Irish people, due to them by England'.[34] For the *Times* the government's bill

> is the just extension to the Irish poor of the rights long guaranteed to the English poor. It is the chief and most desiderated fruit of the Union. Without this, any legislative connexion between the two countries was a fiction and a fraud. Without this, nine-tenths of the Irish nation were debarred from the privileges which the law and conscience of the state had awarded to their equals in Great Britain.[35]

The proposed law would end the scandalous injustice under which currently the property of Ireland, or so the *London News* claimed, was paying 'about five pence in the pound on its rental by law and, where there is no compulsion, giving little or nothing'.[36] Citing similar statistics showing how little Irish landlords contributed to poor relief, the *Times* contrasted their parsimony in this regard with their wild extravagance in other respects, such as their heavy outlay for hunting and hounds. Said the paper savagely: 'A class which pampers a population of dogs, and suffers a human population to perish, calls for the hardest terms that eloquent indignation can supply and the sternest treatment that legislation can devise'.[37]

In their justifications for a revamped Irish poor law British newspapers easily mixed arguments based on economic self-interest with others based on the injunctions of Christian charity. Responding to the Protestant archbishop of Dublin,

32 *I.L.N.*, 15 May 1847.
33 *Times*, 30 March 1847.
34 *Hansard's Parliamentary Debates*, 3rd series, xc (1847), col. 1408.
35 *Times*, 20 April 1847.
36 *I.L.N.*, 20 March 1847.
37 *Times*, 9 March 1847.

who protested against the imposition of a poor law permitting outdoor relief, the *London News* found his arguments to be 'singularly cold and hard, and if it be not presumption to say it of a prelate of the church, completely at variance with the doctrines and precepts of the Gospel'. Property was not, as the archbishop maintained, 'a citadel to be defended against the attacks of pauperism'; instead, Christians must recognise 'the duty of sharing our good things with our poorer brethren, to which "the Scripture moveth us in sundry places"'.[38] Of course, British self-interest would be well served by the new law, and with varying degrees of frankness this critical point was made frequently: Irish poverty, massive in its dimensions, could not permanently be allowed to siphon off English wealth. 'Pauperism in Ireland', moaned the *London News*,

> is now draining ten million [pounds] a year from the English exchequer; to that the Irish legislators make no objection; it is quite according to 'sound principles'. Englishmen think the drain can be stopped, and [want to] fix Irish property with a rate, as they themselves were saddled with one between two and three centuries ago.[39]

What is most remarkable, then, about the discussion of the Great Famine in Britain in early and mid-1847 is the extremely harsh and almost unanimous verdict given against Irish landlords, to the point of holding them primarily responsible for having allowed the country 'to sink to its present awful state'.[40] The Poor Law Amendment Act was partly intended as a heavy punishment for their grievous derelictions of duty in the past, and it was also designed to insure that they met their responsibilities in the future. This British fixation on the delinquencies of the Irish landed elite helped to blind much of the educated British public as to how the amended poor law would operate in practice. To judge from the extreme scarcity of comment in the British press at the time of its adoption, the significance of the Gregory clause was missed almost completely. If it was correct to say that melancholy tales of Irish evictions had hardened English hearts against the objections of Irish landlords to a 'real' poor law, it is bitterly ironic that such a poor law was itself so deeply implicated in the clearances and other horrors that followed its enactment.

Recognition of the tragic consequences of the amended poor law was slow to emerge among the British public and press. But an awareness of its devastating impact gradually took hold. The *London News* conceded early in March 1848 that 'its immediate revision' was 'absolutely necessary to prevent a large and aggravated augmentation of the social evils which afflict the unhappy sister country'. The paper condemned as an 'absurd resolve' the Whig government's

38 *I.L.N.*, 3 April 1847.
39 Ibid.
40 Ibid.

refusal to accede to a request from Irish MPs for a committee of inquiry into the operation of the poor law in Ireland.[41] And by November 1848 the *London News* seemed ready to recant its earlier faith in the amended poor law and to grant the Irish landlords' case against it. 'All argument' originally supported its introduction, but

> alas! such is the wide extent of the misery and destitution of that country that the poor law, so just in theory, so fair-sounding, so applicable else-where, has broken down ... Small farmers and great landed proprietors are equally pinched or crushed beneath the operation of the law. With-out the poor law the people would have died of famine; with a poor law the people are not elevated above habitual and constant pauperism, and the property of the landlords is all but confiscated.[42]

In fact, however, neither the *London News* nor the *Times* was ready to jetti-son the poor law, even if occasionally the language of their editorials suggested otherwise. As late as January 1849 the *Times* still pronounced itself in favour of 'giving effect to the provisions of the poor law': 'We urge its adoption now, in this season of gloom, despondence, and dismay, because we recognize this to be the only sure protection against the recurrence of other seasons as gloomy and as dismal as the present'.[43] Almost forgetting its past severe criticisms of the poor law, the *London News* had insisted a month earlier: 'The people of this country must listen to no representations or remonstrances intended to shake their faith in the efficacy of that enactment'.[44] What these quotations suggest is the exist-ence in Britain of a widespread public ambivalence about the real and perceived practical consequences of strictly administering the poor law, an ambivalence that contributed heavily to a paralysis of the moral and political will to take effective countermeasures.

What was true of British attitudes toward the amended poor law in general was also true of British reactions to the clearances. On the one hand, prior to the widespread availability of outdoor relief, British commentators invariably con-demned the clearances and their perpetrators out of hand for driving the unrelieved rural poor into the country towns and port cities of Ireland. These 'sinks and cesspools of destitution', declared the *Times* in May 1847, 'are a crea-tion of landlordism – the work of a class without social humanity, without legal obligation, without natural shame'.[45] To some extent, moral outrage of this kind persisted in the midst of outdoor relief as clearances mushroomed under

41 *I.L.N.*, 4 March 1848.
42 *I.L.N.*, 25 November 1848.
43 *Times*, 13 January 1849.
44 *I.L.N.*, 16 December 1848.
45 *Times*, 1 May 1847.

the spur of the Gregory clause and heavy poor rates. Mass evictions, such as the especially cruel ejectments on the Blake estate in County Galway, prompted the *London News* in April 1848 to declare sternly:

> In November [1847] a coercion act was most properly passed through parliament to defend the Irish landlords from the murderous revenge of their exasperated tenants. Justice demands that with equal celerity a bill should now be passed to protect defenceless tenants from the equally murderous clearances of tyrannical landlords.[46]

The British response to the clearances, however, was by no means unambiguously disapproving. How could it be? One of the principal aims of the new poor law adopted in mid-1847 was, in the words of the *Times*, 'to compass indirectly the destruction of very small holdings and to convert the cottier, who is nicknamed a farmer and who starves on a *cow's grass*, into a labourer subsisting on competent wages'. If this aim could only be accomplished, the *Times* dared to hope, 'We shall also cease to witness the insane competition for land ..., degrading men to the appetite and food of beasts and peopling the land with a race savage, reckless, and irreconcilable'.[47] Part of the theory of the amended poor law was that Irish landlords would spend a great deal of money giving large-scale employment to their former tenants as labourers in the improvement of their estates. And if they did not employ them, they would at least have to support them in or out of the workhouse. Thus the mere passage of the amended poor law had the potential to shift British attitudes about the clearances, and this is partly what happened. Before its passage, asserted the *London News* in December 1848, clearances were 'cruel and unjust in the extreme', but now, with outdoor relief widely available, 'we have no right, how great soever the apparent or real hardship may be, to find fault with the landlord'. Indeed, claimed this editorial writer with a breathtaking leap into unreality, ejectment in Ireland, 'which was horrible before the poor law came into operation, has now become harmless'.[48]

Repeatedly after 1847 attitudes that were much less critical of clearances, or even mildly approving, found a definite place in the British press. Alongside reports lifted from Irish newspapers that condemned evictions and their perpetrators in the harshest terms were other reports or editorials which palliated, excused, or justified landlord actions. A resigned tone of inevitability suffused an account in the *London News* in April 1849 about the impending clearance of 731 persons from Toomyvara in north Tipperary ('nearly the entire village'), which was part of the Massy-Dawson estate. The landlords, remarked the *Lon-*

46 *I.L.N.*, 1 April 1848.
47 *Times*, 1 May 1847.
48 *I.L.N.*, 16 December 1848.

don News indulgently, 'are abused in the popular journals, but it is not suggested what [else] they should do. The more stringent the poor law, the more surely will the clearance system continue.'[49] When Massy-Dawson later carried out the mass eviction of at least 500 persons and levelled the whole village, it was said in exculpation that he 'got no rent lately' from Toomyvara, and that 'the village was a receptacle for all the evicted tenantry of the neighbouring estates'.[50] And in an editorial devoted exclusively to the subject of clearances in October 1849, the *London News* offered the classic defence of the political economists:

> The truth is that these evictions ... are not merely a legal but a natural process; and however much we may deplore the misery from which they spring, and which they so dreadfully aggravate, we cannot compel the Irish proprietors to continue in their miserable holdings the wretched swarms of people who pay no rent, and who prevent the improvement of property as long as they remain upon it.[51]

Lastly, there was a growing readiness in Britain to accept that, given their precarious financial condition, many Irish proprietors simply could not afford the kind of costly estate improvements, such as thorough drainage, which might have enabled them to transform cottiers into wage labourers. Earlier, this point had been conceded only grudgingly, as in the sneering remark of the *Times* in May 1847 that 'human drainage' was 'the only drainage an Irish landlord will ever think of doing at his own expense'.[52] But later, at the end of 1848, the *London News* portrayed clearances and the consolidation of evicted holdings as 'the easiest mode of improvement, and therefore,' it said excusingly, 'poor landlords are compelled to resort' to them.[53]

Even so humane an English politician and friend of the Irish poor as George Poulett Scrope, who had roundly denounced the Gregory clause before its adoption, was prepared to place the blame for the clearances elsewhere than on the landlords, whom he saw as generally acting under compulsion and out of an instinct for self-preservation:

> It sounds very well to English ears to preach forbearance and generosity to the landowners. But it should be remembered that few of them have it in their power to be merciful or generous to their poorer tenantry ... They are themselves engaged in a life and death struggle with their credi-

49 *I.L.N.*, 14 April 1849.
50 *I.L.N.*, 2 June 1849.
51 *I.L.N.*, 20 October 1849.
52 *Times*, 8 May 1847.
53 *I.L.N.*, 16 December 1848.

tors. Moreover, the greater number of the depopulators are mere agents for absent landlords or for the law-receivers under the courts acting for creditors ... Those landlords who have yet some voice in the management of their estates ... think themselves justified – most of them, indeed, are compelled by the overwhelming pressure of their own difficulties –to follow the example [of the receivers for estates under Court of Chancery jurisdiction].[54]

Though Scrope considered it 'absurd' to blame 'a few [*sic*] reckless, bankrupt, wretched landlords', he did not hesitate to accuse the Russell government of the 'crime' of refusing to mitigate the 'ferocity' of the amended poor law. In strident language of which even the revolutionary nationalist John Mitchel would have approved, Scrope thundered that the government would 'be held responsible for it by history, by posterity – aye, and perhaps before long, by the retributive justice of God and the vengeance of a people infuriated by a barbarous oppression, and brought at last to bay by their destroyers'.[55] A similar verdict was rendered by a special correspondent of the *London News* whose articles in late 1849 and early 1850 sought to illustrate the heartless severities of the amended poor law, especially in relation to the clearances. With the Gregory clause particularly in mind, this correspondent declared bluntly:

> The poor law, said to be for the relief of the people and the means of their salvation, was the instrument of their destruction. Calmly and quietly ... from Westminster itself, which is the centre of civilization, did the decree go forth which has made the temporary but terrible visitation of a potato rot the means of exterminating, through the slow process of disease and houseless starvation, nearly the half of the Irish [people].[56]

Or, as this same correspondent put it succinctly and with brutal clarity in a later article, 'The system intended to relieve the poor, by making the landlords responsible for their welfare, has at once made it the interest and therefore the duty of the landlords to get rid of them'.[57]

Thus for this writer and for many others in Britain, the Irish landlord, though to some extent the half-willing agent of irresistible forces and pressures, remained devoid of any redeeming features. At the end of his remarkable series of articles the *London News* correspondent characterised Irish landlords, 'speaking of them as a body and admitting many exceptions', as 'extremely selfish, ignorant, negligent, profligate, and reckless. To the serf-like people they have al-

---

54 *I.L.N.*, 20 October 1849.
55 Ibid.
56 *I.L.N.*, 15 December 1849.
57 *I.L.N.*, 22 December 1849.

ways been more oppressors than protectors, and have thought of them only as sponges out of which they were to squeeze the utmost possible amount of rent, to squander on their own pleasures.'[58] That quintessential voice of the English middle classes, the Lancashire cotton manufacturer and Quaker John Bright, was equally disparaging of Irish landlords. Speaking at the Corn Exchange in Manchester in January 1850 on the need to remedy Irish popular grievances, he declared that Irish landed proprietors, with 'some brilliant exceptions', were 'for the most part ... beggared', 'almost universally despised, and to a large extent detested' – calculated remarks which, no doubt as he had expected, elicited loud cheers from his audience. The landlords, insisted Bright in phrases that by now were almost formulaic, 'very grossly neglected all the duties of their office and of their position'. Bright's severe strictures on landlords, of course, were not limited to those of Ireland, for in closing this address, he roundly asserted that 'the aristocracy of the United Kingdom has heaped evils unnumbered upon Ireland'.[59] (Bright's denunciation of the British and Irish 'aristocracy' at Manchester was part of the wider movement for what was called 'free trade in land' – a movement seeking changes in the law relating to landownership that would have eliminated certain legal privileges currently enjoyed by the landed elite of both countries.)

But did not the English middle classes have any complicity in the imposition of an amended poor law on Ireland in mid-1847? Surely they did. This had been reflected above all in middle-class determination to shift the financial burden of relieving Irish destitution onto the shoulders of Irish landed proprietors. The terms in which Irish landlords were discussed in parliament and in the British press clearly display the tell-tale features of scapegoating, and perhaps it is not fanciful to see in all this the displacement of British middle-class guilt. The shifting of the financial burden was accomplished under the Poor Law Amendment Act of June 1847 in the face of many protests and much evidence that Irish property could not bear this huge burden without bankrupting many landlords and causing the collapse or near-collapse of the poor-law system. Even after the dire consequences of the amended poor law became plain in Britain, there was no widespread disposition to reassume any substantial share of the costs of relieving the mass destitution associated with the famine. In March 1849, some eighteen months after any significant expenditure by the British government had ended, the *London News* proclaimed, 'Great Britain cannot continue to throw her hard-won millions into the bottomless pit of Celtic pauperism'.[60] This may safely be taken as the authentic or at least the dominant voice of the British middle classes. What has been called 'donor fatigue' manifested itself in Britain at a very early stage of the Great Famine.

58 *I.L.N.*, 19 January 1850.
59 *I.L.N.*, 12 January 1850.
60 *I.L.N.*, 10 March 1849.

Admittedly, this was very far from the way in which the educated British public assessed the overall British contribution to the relief of an Ireland prostrated by famine. The common British view, well expressed by the *London News* in November 1848, was that 'in a time of commercial pressure and distress we have consented to enormous pecuniary sacrifices for the sake of Ireland and are ready to do so again if we can be assured that our bounty will not do harm rather than good to its recipients'. Coupling a grossly inflated claim with a threadbare excuse, the paper declared:

> if Ireland has offered to the world the spectacle of a gigantic misery, England has also offered to the world the spectacle of an unparalleled effort to relieve and to remove it. If the splendour of our benevolence has not kept pace with the hideousness of her misery, it has not been from any want of inclination on the part of the living race of Englishmen, but from the sheer impossibility of remedying in one year the accumulated evils of ages, and of elevating the character of a people too poor and sorrow-stricken to attempt to elevate themselves.[61]

Here, in the slighting reference to 'the character' of the Irish people, we have a highly significant pointer to one of the principal explanations for the fact that donor fatigue displayed itself in Britain at such an early stage of the famine. If Britons were well along toward spending £10 million to relieve Irish starvation by the spring of 1847, without being able to see any signs of permanent improvement, the question arose as to whether the root of the problem was financial or – as seemed much more likely to most educated Britons – moral and 'racial' or cultural.[62] What Britons confronted in Ireland, proclaimed the *Times* in March 1847, was 'a nation of beggars', and thus the challenge was enormous: 'We have to change the very nature of a people born and bred, from time immemorial, in inveterate indolence, improvidence, disorder, and consequent destitution'.[63] England, claimed the paper, had been trying for years to eradicate or correct the worst features of the Celtic character – 'its inertness, its dependence on others, its repulsion of whatever is clean, comfortable, and civilized'.[64] Irish Catholic priests, representatives of a religion despised by the *Times*, were

---

61 *I.L.N.*, 25 November 1848.
62 This issue of perceived racial differences requires careful handling. In the pages of *Punch*, as Professor Roy Foster has remarked, hostility to the British working classes or to the French could lead to the same kind of 'racialist' caricatures as hostility to Irish peasants and Irish nationalists. In addition, as Foster notes, 'Irish comic papers of a nationalist bent represented the English as grasping, prognathous, subhuman bogeymen'. See R.F. Foster, 'Paddy and Mr Punch' in *Paddy and Mr Punch: Connections in Irish and English History* (Harmondsworth, Middlesex, 1993), p. 192.
63 *Times*, 23 March 1847.
64 *Times*, 6 April 1847.

roundly chastised as a body because allegedly they never preached against 'that which is notoriously the crying evil of Ireland – its universal sloth'.[65] It was not exactly all their own fault that the Irish people were in this lamentable condition. If Englishmen had been 'goaded by oppression and stupefied by neglect', declared the *Times*,

> they would sit, like the Irish, with folded arms on the edge of subterranean or untried wealth, or in the face of anticipated but unrepelled famine; they would lounge, like the Irish, on the shore of a sea whose produce they never sought, and cumber the surface of a soil whose fertility they never cared to augment.[66]

In this situation, what was England's duty, its mission? 'We must educate and elevate Ireland', insisted the *Times*, 'by teaching her people to educate and elevate themselves.'[67] The paper pointed in self-satisfied fashion to all that the English people and government had already done for famine-stricken Ireland – as much as 'the most exacting foe or the most jealous rival could have imposed on our submission or our conscience'. Even greater feats could be achieved by English charity 'were it absolutely needful that England should take the work upon herself'. But such extreme generosity was neither necessary nor advisable while Ireland and the Irish, though not deficient in resources, displayed only 'a crafty, a calculating, a covetous idleness' and 'a thorough repudiation of all self-exertion'.[68] In the face of such deep-seated Irish moral incapacity, what could large additional amounts of British money really accomplish? This was the thrust of what to us must seem perhaps the most callous lines to appear in the pages of the *Times* in all of the famine years: 'But what art, what policy, what wealth is cunning enough, wise enough, rich enough to assuage the moral evils and stay the moral disease of a vast population steeped in the congenial mire of voluntary indigence and speculating on the gains of a perpetual famine'.[69] Even though this 'voluntary indigence' was considered extremely difficult to eradicate, the *Times* had urged the adoption of an amended poor law partly in the belief that it would 'give to the peasant a right and a title which may at once insure his industry and his independence'.[70] Since the diagnosis was horribly wrong, it is scarcely surprising that the prescribed course of treatment failed to yield the desired cure.

65 *Times*, 8 April 1847.
66 *Times*, 31 March 1847.
67 *Times*, 14 April 1847.
68 *Times*, 26 March 1847.
69 Ibid.
70 *Times*, 2 April 1847.

But if the amended Irish poor law disappointed British expectations in several critical respects, on balance its consequences probably satisfied most educated Britons. In April 1849 the *Times* distilled its results in a quite positive manner:

> The rigorous administration of the poor law is destroying small holdings, reducing needy proprietors to utter insolvency, compelling them to surrender their estates into better hands, instigating an emigration far beyond any which a government could undertake, and so leaving the soil of Ireland open to industrial enterprise and the introduction of new capital.

Like many other Britons, this editorial writer was not at all blind to the huge accompanying social dislocation, but what mattered in the end was that the ground had apparently been cleared for a new agrarian era: 'We see Ireland depopulated, her villages razed to the ground, her landlords bankrupt – in a word, we see the hideous chasm prepared for the foundation of a future prosperity ... '.[71] For some people in Britain a 'hideous chasm' was, however regrettably, the price which had to be paid for 'a future prosperity'.

71 *Times*, 2 April 1849.

Can there be an Archaeology of the Great Famine?

CHARLES E. ORSER JR.

When most people think about archaeology, they typically imagine either pith-helmeted scientists poking around crumbling ruins or rugged explorers slashing through dense jungles in search of ancient statues. In both cases, the object of the archaeologist's search is the far-distant, mysterious past. Archaeologists are well known for their interest in antiquity. Ancient history will always fascinate them, because like everyone else, they are intrigued by the humanity of men and women now long dead. But rummaging around in the ancient past is not the only place to find modern archaeologists. Today, many archaeologists investigate subjects that only a few years ago would have seemed decidedly unarchaeological. A growing number of archaeologists examine recent history. One basis for this research into modern history is that 'We know more about some aspects of daily life in the ancient Babylon of 3000 BC. than we do about daily life in parts of Europe and America a hundred years ago.'[1]

One area of research for these 'historical' archaeologists is particularly exciting because it sheds light on men and women who seldom wrote about themselves and who were seldom written about by their contemporaries. This large mass of people includes the men and women who experienced the Great Famine. Recent advances made in studying another group of largely undocumented people, New World African-American slaves, demonstrate historical archaeology's power. Unfortunately, the archaeology of the Great Famine is only in its infancy, and extensive work has yet to be accomplished. Nonetheless, I can provide preliminary comments about an archaeological project beginning in County Roscommon that points the direction for future research.

Historical Archaeology and the World's Forgotten Men and Women

Since the late 1960s, American historical archaeologists have defined their field as a way to study the spread of Europeans into the non-European world after AD 1500.[2] They began by excavating military forts, trading posts, mining and lum-

---

1 D.J. Boorstin, *Hidden History* (New York, 1987), p. 14.
2 C.E. Orser, Jr. and B.M. Fagan, *Historical Archaeology: A Brief Introduction* (New York, 1995); James Deetz, *In Small Things Forgotten: The Archaeology of Early American Life* (Garden City, N.Y., 1977)

ber camps, plantation mansions, and religious missions. Their work usually served to provide architectural details for building reconstruction projects.

During the course of these architectural projects, many historical archaeologists realized that they faced a unique opportunity. The broken and discarded artifacts they found around ruined foundations and in yards often held the keys to illuminating the living conditions of the men and women who once lived inside the buildings. When reassembled, the once-broken bowls and shattered bottles presented a tangible reality of past life. In many cases, the artifacts had been used and discarded by people who were not the elite men and women whose life histories fill most of today's history books. Instead, they were slaves, servants, farmers, laborers, and others who had little lasting voice in the official records of the past. Cultural anthropologist Margaret Mead referred to these underrepresented men and women as 'the inarticulate'. These were people 'who did not write or who were not written about'.[3]

Understanding the exciting sociological potential of their excavations, many historical archaeologists shifted their attention from the architecture of the elite to the societies of the poor, the disenfranchised, and the illiterate. These forgotten men and women, though largely absent in the writings of most historical chroniclers, could be given voice in the objects they left behind. These often subtle items, broken dishes, discarded bottles, lost buttons and coins, could serve as the monuments and documents of the heretofore 'inarticulate'. Today, historical archaeologists have examined diet, health and welfare, housing conditions, sanitation, and personal ownership using the 'non-traditional' sources of history they know best: artifacts, building remains, fences, wells, and other features strewn across relict landscapes.

The ability of historical archaeology to provide new information about the world's inarticulate is well represented by its studies of New World slavery. Through a growing number of excavations, historical archaeologists have shed light into the darkened corners of the slave experience. For example, while excavating antebellum slave cabins at Kingsley Plantation, Florida, Charles Fairbanks discovered gunflints, parts of flintlock muskets, and fragments of lead waste from the moulding of bullets. He also found the bones of several species of nocturnal animals mixed among the cabin refuse. Putting the two finds together, Fairbanks surmised that the slaves, after working all day in the humid fields of coastal Florida, supplemented their meager diets with the animals they could snare at night. The plantation owner did not mention this foraging activity in his records and Fairbanks had not suspected it prior to excavation. The gun parts and the animal bones, however, provide mute testimony to the plant-

---

3 Margaret Mead, 'Anthropologist and Historian: Their Common Problems' in *American Quarterly*, iii (1951), pp. 6-7; Robert Ascher, 'Tin-Can Archaeology' in *Historical Archaeology*, viii (1974), p. 11.

er's economic need to keep his slave property alive even in the face of possible armed insurrection.

Other studies of American slavery demonstrate equally well the power of historical archaeology. For instance, Diana Crader studied excavated animal bones from the slave quarters at Thomas Jefferson's Monticello Plantation and, like Fairbanks, made remarkable discoveries. She learned, for instance, that beef played a large part in the diet of Jefferson's slaves and that some slaves ate better than others.[4] Thus, it seems that not all slaves were fed the historically recorded staples of corn and pork alone. Also, in feeding some slaves better than others, Jefferson may have sought to create a hierarchy in his slave force based on health and nutrition. Crader's work is especially meaningful since the historical documentation for Monticello is so vast. Although numerous volumes have been written about the plantation's famous owner, we must develop our understanding of the majority of the plantation's population with evidence collected from beneath the ground. Other archaeologists have demonstrated that some slaves retained elements of their African heritage in the New World. On plantations along the eastern seaboard and in the Caribbean, archaeologists have unearthed reminders of Africa in housing, pottery, clay smoking pipes, and even in religious objects.[5] These artifacts help to portray the richness and vitality of slave life as it existed beyond the tragic reality of enslavement.

Most of the historical archaeologist's information is not available in the historical record. Professional journalists, literate travelers, plantation owners, politicians, and census enumerators all wrote about slaves in some fashion. Sometimes they visited several estates and penned detailed accounts of their experiences. The vast majority of these writers, however, never addressed the most mundane aspects of slave life that would interest archaeologists. Observers generally did write about slave dishes or the manufacture of pottery by slaves and they almost never mentioned slave diet. Most writers described slave housing, but they never mentioned whether and to what degree slaves could affect the design and construction of their cabins. Many of the issues may have been simply too private or delicate to write about. How could these historical journalists ever imagine that archaeologists would wish to know whether plantation slaves used privies or where they threw their trash? Also, many aspects of slave life were not revealed in written accounts because slaves undoubtedly hid them from the prying eyes of outsiders. Secret religious services and special medical treatments would be prime examples.

4 C.H. Fairbanks and S.A. Mullins-Moore, 'How Did Slaves Live' in *Early Man*, summer (1980), p. 3; D.C. Crader, 'Slave Diet at Monticello' in *American Antiquity*, lv (1990), pp. 690-717.
5 T.R. Wheaton and P.H. Garrow, 'Acculturation and the Archaeological Record in the Carolina Lowcountry' in T.A. Singleton (ed.), *The Archaeology of Slavery* (Orlando, 1985), pp. 243-8; Leland Ferguson, *Uncommon Ground: Archaelogy and Early African America, 1650-1800* (Washington, 1992); M.C. Emerson, 'Decorated Clay Pipes from the

Historical archaeology has the ability to lift the curtain of silence and to peek behind history, revealing what might otherwise never be known. Archaeologists can probe the depths of privies and wells, and look under floor boards and between bricks. They can recover rosaries and drilled cowrie shells that contain clues about slave religion, and show with tangible evidence that slaves made pottery and sometimes influenced the design of their houses. Each excavation reveals new information about the slave experience.

American historical archaeologists have studied several other underreported groups including Chinese immigrants, Italian railroad workers, Sicilian sugar plantation laborers, and Irish canal builders.[6] Historical archaeologists have broad interests, but they have generally restricted themselves to the colonized world. They have studied English colonists in America and Australia, Dutch fur traders in New York, Native American horticulturalists, Portuguese slavers in West Africa, and slaves in the American South and the Caribbean. Oddly, though, historical archaeologists have made no major inroads in Europe. The reason is directly relevant to the archaeology of the Great Famine.

The Roots of Modern Historical Archaeology

Today's historical archaeology is resolutely 'historical' in subject matter, but much of its intellectual tradition springs from the anthropological roots of American archaeology. The perspective is best summarized by the famous dictum that 'American archaeology is anthropology or it is nothing.'[7] In line with this thinking, most American historical archaeologists view their research as anthropological, though their subject matter is irrefutably historical.

When announcing the creation of the Society for Historical Archaeology in 1967, *Current Anthropology* reported that the focus of the new society 'will be the era since the beginning of the exploration of the non-European world by

Chesapeake: An African Connection' in P.A. Shackel and B.J. Little (eds), *Historical Archaeology of the Chesapeake* (Washington, 1994), pp. 35-49; C.E. Orser, Jr., 'The Archaeology of African-American Slave Religion in the Antebellum South' in *Cambridge Archaeological Journal*, iv (1994), pp. 33-45.

6 R.L. Schuyler (ed.), *Archaeological Perspectives on Ethnicity in America: Afro-American and Asian American Culture History* (Farmington, N.Y., 1980), pp. 89-130; Priscilla Wegars (ed.), *Hidden Heritage: Historical Archaeology of the Overseas Chinese* (Amityville, N.Y., 1993); Priscilla Wegars, 'Who's Been Working on the Railroad? An Examination of the Construction, Distribution, and Ethnic Origin of Domed Rock Ovens on Railroad-Related Sites' in *Historical Archaeology*, xxiii, no. 1 (1991), pp. 37-65; D.W. Babson, *Pillars on the Levee: Archaeological Investigations at Ashland-Belle Helene Plantation, Ascension Parish, Louisiana* (Normal, Il., 1989); C.E. Orser, Jr., 'The Illinois and Michigan Canal: Historical Archaeology and the Irish Experience in America' in *Eire-Ireland*, xxvii (1992), pp. 122-34.

7 G.R. Willey and Philip Phillips, *Method and Theory in American Archaeology* (Chicago, 1958), p. 2.

Europeans.' The Western Hemisphere was the main focus of research, but Oceania, Africa, and Asia could also be included. European subjects were considered largely outside the purview of historical archaeology.[8] By definition, historical archaeologists studied the same colonized regions of the globe typically studied by cultural anthropologists.

Historical archaeology's European cousin is post-medieval archaeology. Post-medieval archaeology began with the Post-Medieval Ceramic Research Group, an association of individuals interested in English ceramics from the 1450-1750 period. Within a few short years, the group's focus expanded beyond ceramics, and they renamed their organization the Society for Post-Medieval Archaeology. The society's stated interest was the period from 1450 to 1800, because 'there is something distinctive about the years between the impact of the Renaissance and Reformation at one end and the onset of the Industrial Revolution at the other.'[9] European post-medieval archaeology seems like the logical extension of medieval archaeology. Historians generally perceive the historical and cultural trends of the Middle Ages to blend into the post-medieval period, and post-medieval archaeologists are generally interested in the same sorts of questions as their medievally focused colleagues.[10]

The easy gradation from the 'Middle Ages' to the 'post-medieval period' is not so easily imagined outside Europe. When Europeans took their cultural institutions around the world, they and the indigenous peoples they met created a new world. The new ways of life were unlike anything that had existed before, and represented nothing less than a 'decisive break in world history.'[11] The New World was not just a remade version of the Old World; it was something new and unique, created from diverse strands of culture and tradition.

Historical archaeologists working in the colonised regions of the globe immediately recognized the break between the Old World and the New World. In North America, for example, the remains of the historic period do not resemble prehistoric artifacts. Shiny brass kettles replaced baked clay pots, steel knives took the place of chipped stone tools, and multicolored glass beads appeared where once there were only drilled shells.

8 'Institutions' in *Current Anthropology*, viii (1967), p. 509.
9 'Editorial' in *Post-Medieval Archaeology*, i (1968), pp. 1-2; K.J. Barton, 'Origins of the Society for Post-Medieval Archaeology' in *Post-Medieval Archaeology*, i (1968), pp. 102-3; Society for Post-Medieval Archaeology, 'Prioridades de Investiçáo em Arqueologia Pós-medieval' in *Arqueologia Industrial*, i (1993), p. 93.
10 See, for example, C.O. Cederlund, 'The Regal Ships and Divine Kingdom' in *Current Swedish Archaeology*, ii (1994), pp. 47-85; Miguel Martins, 'A Arqueologia pós-medieval' in *História*, xiv (1992), pp. 84-9; Paul Stømstad, 'Um Exemplo de Arqueologia Industrial na Dinmarca' in *Arqueologia Industrial*, i (1993), pp. 145-8; Francisca Represa, 'La Arqueología Postmedieval en España: Una panorámica de Urgencia' in *World Archaeological Bulletin*, viii (forthcoming).
11 Samir Amin, *Eurocentrism*, trans. Russell Moore (New York, 1989), p. 1.

In Europe, the start of the early modern period was not as abrupt as in the colonies, though it clearly had several unique characteristics.[12] In archaeological terms, only minor changes may signal the beginning of the post-medieval age. In any case, Irish archaeologists, faced with an embarrassment of prehistoric riches, have yet to focus major attention on the post-medieval period. When they do think about this time, they generally terminate the period at about 1750.[13] Excavation of the post-1750 period usually occurs as part of a larger project focused on a much earlier period.[14]

Irish archaeologists cannot be blamed for their overwhelming interest in the island's rich and tantalising prehistoric past. Prehistoric ringforts, standing stones, and aligned networks of field stones excite wonder in almost everyone. Lost civilizations and forgotten peoples have always charged the human imagination and they will do so forever. Given this reality, we may well expect that Irish archaeologists, even when they begin in earnest to study their island's post-medieval and early modern history, will begin with the earliest sites.[15] Still, the archaeology of New World slave sites shows that much can be learned by investigating post-1750 sites.

Irish Cottiers and American Slaves

Though they were contemporaries, impoverished Irish agricultural laborers, or cottiers, and African-American slaves represented two completely different historical and cultural traditions. Nevertheless, visitors among both Irish cottiers and American slaves drew several intriguing parallels between them. For example, in 1749, Anglican bishop and philosopher, George Berkeley, wrote 'The negroes in our Plantations have a saying – 'If negro was not negro, Irishman

---

12 Fernand Braudel, *Capitalism and Material Life, 1400-1800*, trans. Miriam Kochan (New York, 1973). Some English archaeologists, in fact, are beginning to examine the transition from feudalism to modern life. Two interesting studies are N.W. Alcock, *People at Home: Living in a Warickshire Village, 1500-1800* (Chichester, 1993) and Matthew Johnson, *Housing Culture: Traditional Architecture in an English Landscape* (Washington, 1993).

13 Michael Ryan (ed.), *The Illustrated Archaeology of Ireland* (Dublin, 1991).

14 Tadhg O'Keefe, 'Omey and the Sands of Time' in *Archeology Ireland*, viii, 2 (1994), pp. 14-17.

15 B.S. Blades, 'English Villages in the Londonderry Plantation' in *Post-Medieval Archaeology*, xx (1986), pp. 257-69; N.F. Bannon, 'Excavation at a Farm in the Bonn Townland, County Tyrone' in *Ulster Journal of Archaeology*, xliv (1984), pp. 177-81; N.F. Bannon, 'Excavations at Brackfield Bawn, County Londonderry' in *Ulster Journal of Archaeology*, liii (1990), pp. 8-14; Eric Klingelhofer, 'The Renaissance Fortifications at Dunboy Castle, 1602: A Report of the 1989 Excavations' in *Journal of the Cork Historical and Archaeological Society*, xcvii (1992), pp. 85-96; Brian Lacy, 'The Achaeology of British Colonisation in Ulster and America: A Comparative Approach' in *The Irish-American Review*, i (1979), pp. 1-5.

would be negro".[16] Over one hundred years later, English author and staunch anti-Catholic clergyman, Charles Kingsley, wrote during a visit to Sligo in 1860, that he was 'haunted by the human chimpanzees' he saw in that 'horrible country'. He continued, 'to see white chimpanzees is dreadful; if they were black, one would not feel it so much, but their skins, except where tanned by exposure, are as white as ours.'[17] Two years later, the English satirical magazine *Punch* referred to the Irish as 'A creature manifestly between the Gorilla and the Negro.'[18]

Such observations were apparently common, because in the 1840s Frederick Douglass, the great African-American orator, repeatedly reminded his Irish audiences that their island's cottiers, though disenfranchised and impoverished, were not slaves.[19] Still, many commentators continued to draw parallels between them. For example, many said that the 'coffin ships' had conditions 'as bad as the slave trade,' and that many Irish landlords were 'very much like slave holders with white slaves.'[20] It seems that the urge to compare Irish tenant farmers and African-American slaves was too powerful to ignore.

What is perhaps more remarkable is that many writers described cottier and slave living conditions in the same terms. These similarities appear in two famous eyewitness accounts, one by Englishman Arthur Young, and the other by English actress Fanny Kemble. Young toured Ireland in the late 1770s, and Kemble lived for a time on a cotton plantation in Georgia in the late 1830s. Both described the houses of the poor agriculturalists using words so similar that they could have been cribbed from one another. Young described the cabins of the Irish as 'the most miserable looking hovels', while Kemble called the slave quarters 'miserable hovels'. Young said that the Irish houses 'generally consist of only one room,' and Kemble said 'These cabins consist of one room.' Both Young and Kemble remarked on the rudeness of the cabins' furniture. Young mentioned the ubiquitous 'pot for boiling potatoes', and Kemble noted 'capacious caldrons' in the slave quarters.[21]

16 George Berkeley, 'A Word to the Wise: Or, An Exhortation to the Roman Catholic Clergy of Ireland' in A.C. Fraser (ed.), *The Works of George Berkeley, D.D.* (Oxford, 1871), p. 439.
17 Quoted in Luke Gibbons, 'Race Against Time: Racial Discourse and Irish History' in *Oxford Literary Review*, xiii (1991), p. 96.
18 Quoted in R.F. Foster, *Paddy and Mr Punch: Connections in Irish and English History* (London, 1993), p. 184.
19 J.W. Blassingame (ed.), *The Frederick Douglass Papers, Series One: Speeches, Debates, and Interviews, Volume 1, 1841-46* (New Haven, 1979), pp. 77-8.
20 Cecil Woodham-Smith, *The Great Hunger: Ireland, 1845-1849* (London, 1991), pp. 228, 297.
21 Arthur Young, *A Tour of Ireland with General Observations on the Present State of that Kingdom Made in the Years 1776, 1777, and 1778* (London, 1780), p. 25; F.A. Kemble, *Journal of a Residence on a Georgian Plantation in 1838-1829* (New York, 1863), pp. 30-1.

Despite these similarities, the cottiers who tilled the rocky townlands of Ireland were not the European equivalent of the enslaved Africans who labored in the fields of the New World. Each population was distinct in history, culture, and circumstance. But what is significant is that the outsiders who went among both groups drew startlingly similar conclusions about them. In many cases, they saw similar things and even used the same descriptive words. It may well be that extreme poverty and dispossession looks the same everywhere, but the material similarities between Irish cottiers and African-American slaves are interesting nonetheless.

In the light of the perceived similarities between Irish cottiers and American slaves, we can expect historical archaeology to have success examining nineteenth-century cottier life. With this idea in mind, and with over twelve years experience studying African-American slavery, I began an archaeological project with the expressed purpose of discovering evidence about peasant living conditions before, during, and after the Great Famine. The subject of my study is the townland of Gorttoose in County Roscommon, just east of Strokestown.

The Men and Women of Gorttoose

Cottiers settled on Gorttoose in the late eighteenth century, probably around 1780. When Griffith made his survey in the mid-nineteenth century, Gorttoose measured 102.4 hectares (253 acres) in area, and about 200 tenants lived there.[22] The O'Conor Roe family originally owned the Gorttoose land, but lost it when Cromwell granted it to Nicholas Mahon, one of his officers. The Mahons moved into O'Conor Roe's bawn, or fortified enclosure, at Strokestown and eventually built a large Palladian mansion around the ancient structure. This large mansion, Strokestown Park House, today incorporates the Famine Museum.[23]

The Great Famine was a defining moment for the people of Gorttoose, and this terrible event gave them a permanent place in history. The ravages of the famine impelled their landlord, Major Dennis Mahon — a descendant of Nicholas Mahon — to evict them along with almost 3000 others from the twenty-seven townlands on the Mahon estate. Thirty-five of the evicted families, or 185 individuals, were from Gorttoose.[24]

22 Richard Griffith, *Valuation of the Several Tenements Comprised in the Union of Strokestown, in the County of Roscommon* (Dublin, 1857), p. 52.
23 R.F. Foster, *Modern Ireland, 1600-1972* (London, 1989), p. 599; Nicholas Canny, *The Elizabethan Conquest of Ireland: A Pattern Established, 1575-76* (Sussex, 1976), p. 112; S.J. Campbell, *The Great Irish Famine: Words and Images from the Famine Museum, Strokestown Park, County Roscommon* (Strokestown, 1994), p. 10; Niall Ó Ciosáin, 'Hungry Grass' in *Circa*, lxviii (1994), pp. 24-7.
24 Browne, 'The Mahon Evictions'.

Like all landlords, Mahon expected his tenants to pay their rents. Those that did not pay were merely an economic burden. In the 1840s, John Ross Mahon, the major's cousin and principal agent during the Great Famine, conducted a survey of eight townlands and discovered that 479 families had paid no rent for two years. The rent-in-arrears totalled over £603.[25] By Mahon's reckoning, tenants who could not pay had to be removed from the estate. Those who could not be removed would go to the workhouses or be kept alive by public works projects. Under the advice of John Ross Mahon, Mahon believed that he could do little to relieve the suffering of his non-rent paying, starving tenants. Perhaps thinking they would be better off in North America, or maybe simply to spare himself further economic drain, he began shipping them out of Ireland on 27 May 1847. Notes on file at Strokestown Park House, often scrawled by unpracticed hands, beseeched Mahon to help the cottiers through the famine. The petition of James Smyth in 1846 is typical: 'The Application of James Symth of Ballyhabberd begs your honour will cause him to get work at Cutting down Curraghroe hills. The Applicant is a poor Starving Man and has six in family.' Smyth is not on the published list of Mahon evictees. On the other hand, on 11 January 1848, John Ross Mahon received the following appeal from a literate agent: 'A poor man named Edwd. Homes has Begged of me to write to you to Say he is prepared to pay a year's Rent for the quarter of land on which he now lives on in Gurthoose. If you can do anything for him I will be Most thankful.' The Edward Holmes family, containing five members, was on the list of evictees.

When the story began to circulate that Mahon chartered 'coffin ships' for the evictees, the remaining tenants vilified him. Their hatred grew when they heard rumors that one of the ships sank during the Atlantic crossing. On 2 November 1847, their anger erupted into violence when the lover of an evicted girl, who was reported drowned but was actually alive, shot and killed Mahon on the road to Roscommon.[26] The verdict is still out on whether Mahon was an evil landlord or just someone caught in the grip of terrible circumstances. Pat Browne, a farmer in Strokestown and the brother of the local bishop, said that Mahon was lenient with his tenants. Conversely, Father Michael McDermott, the local parish priest, was reported to have said from the pulpit that 'Major Mahon is worse than Cromwell.'[27]

In any case, Major Mahon has become infamous in the history of the Great Famine. The terror of the forced evictions, the horrendous condition of the passengers on board ship, and the drama of his murder tell the tale of the Great Famine in lurid, disturbing detail. Historical archaeologists cannot be expected to unearth new evidence to explain the way in which Mahon was actually shot,

25 Campbell, *The Great Irish Famine*, p. 42.
26 Woodham-Smith, *The Great Hunger*, pp. 324-5.
27 Campbell, 'The Strokestown Famine Papers'; Woodham-Smith, *The Great Hunger*, p. 325.

and they can say nothing about the Atlantic crossing. What archaeologists can do, however, is to provide physical evidence that sheds new light on the social conditions of cottier life just before, during, and after the Famine. Broken ceramic dishes, discarded smoking pipes, fragmented bottles, and lost buttons help to tell the personal side of the Great Famine. Though the evidence is filtered through the archaeologist's analytical lens, the findings are a way for the poor men and women to find a voice in the present.

In Search of the Men and Women of Gorttoose

Archaeologists must find sites before they can excavate them. Poor men and women did not live in large houses or build great monuments to themselves. Their former homes are usually not readily obvious above ground for they were not meant to last. In fact, it is the impermanence of their settlements that helps to make the dispossessed men and women of the past all the more silent and ignored. Archaeologists working in Ireland receive tremendous assistance from the Ordnance Survey. The surveyors did not locate or even recognize every human feature across the landscape, but archaeologists find their maps to be invaluable nonetheless.[28]

The Ordnance Survey map for Gorttoose, drafted in 1837, shows six clusters of one or two buildings each in the townland. A nineteenth-century estate map with handwritten annotations on file at Strokestown Park House identifies the head tenants of these clusters. The houses shown on the map undoubtedly belonged to them. Though the system of rural land tenure was as complex in Ireland as anywhere in the world, the agricultural relationships of the nineteenth century can be distilled to just three classes: landlords, head tenants, and sub-tenants. Sub-tenants, or cottiers, were the laboring poor who felt the fullest effect of the periodic famines that swept through Ireland. Head tenants rented land from landlords and then re-rented it to sub-tenants, thereby becoming landlords themselves.[29] Because tenants made their farming arrangements directly with their landlords, estate owners usually knew little about the sub-tenants. As a result, the sub-tenant cottiers of Gorttoose and of a thousand other townlands are largely overlooked in historical records. The names of sub-tenants can sometimes be gleaned from documents, but the accounts generally pass a judgement of historical silence on them. For Gorttose, the names of the sub-tenant heads of households are recorded in the list of evictees published in 1848.

28 Brendan Connor, 'A Current Tale of Interest' in *Archaeology Ireland*, viii, 3 (1994), pp. 33-5; J.H. Andrews, *A Paper Landscape: The Ordnance Survey in Nineteenth-Century Ireland* (Oxford, 1975).
29 J.S. Donnelly, Jr., *The Land and the People of Nineteenth-Century Cork: The Rural Economy and the Land Question* (London, 1975), pp. 9-10.

Knowing the names of sub-tenant families does not allow archaeologists to find their former homesites. As a result, archaeologists must adopt surveying methods that will aid in site discovery. I decided to use a combination of surface survey, a chemical soil test, and oral interviewing to locate abandoned sites at Gorttoose. My survey crew, composed of Illinois State University students, discovered two previously unknown archaeological sites using these techniques.

The first site, associated with head tenant Roger McGuire, consisted of a scatter of 1309 artifacts lying on the ground surface. These artifacts alone indicated the former presence of a home on this spot. The artifact collection included broken dinner dishes of many styles, pieces of thick, utilitarian stoneware crocks, fragments of blue and green bottles, white clay smoking pipes, and metal buttons. All the items date from the late eighteenth century to the early twentieth century, and are the kinds of things one could expect to find at any domestic site. Records show that the McGuires were at Gorttoose by at least 1795, and our main informant, a farmer whose head-tenant family was present during the 1847 evictions, said that the McGuires continued to live on this spot until 1927. Their house was demolished in 1931.

We discovered a second site using soil phosphate analysis, a non-destructive method of locating past settlements based on the chemical composition of the soil. The method rests on the concept that humans and animals leave phosphates in the soil through their normal activities. A house built on piers would be easy to locate with phosphate analysis, if dogs, chickens, and other animals had regularly gone underneath it, disturbing the soil in the process. Because phosphates do not move in the soil once they are deposited, areas showing high phosphate content generally contain former settlements.[30]

We constructed a grid of 5-meter (16-foot) squares over a portion of an empty field that was the approximate center of Gorttoose, and collected seventy-four soil samples. The tests revealed three areas of high phosphates. No artifacts or building rubble appeared on the ground surface, though a nineteenth-century estate map indicated that Mary Murray had once been the head tenant in this part of Gorttoose. The areas of high phosphate content may represent her former home.

Unfortunately, neither site has yet been the subject of archaeological excavation. When excavation is possible, however, the research will focus on what can be learned from the artifacts and the housing remains. We also hope to use these homes of head tenants to guide us to the homes of cottiers, and eventually to use the remains from head-tenant and sub-tenant houses in a comparative

30 R.C. Eidt, 'A Rapid Chemical Field Test for Archaeological Site Surveying' in *American Antiquity*, xxxviii (1973), pp. 206-10; R.C. Eidt and W.I. Woods, *Abandoned Settlement Analysis: Theory and Practice* (Shorewood, Wis., 1974); W.I. Woods, 'The Analysis of Abandoned Settlements by a New Phosphate Field Test Method' in *The Chesopiean*, xiii (1975), pp. 1-45.

manner. Paralleling the work on American slave sites, historical archaeologists should be able to reconstruct the material culture of peasant families. The issue of what peasants actually possessed is not as straightforward as it may seem. As noted above, Young generally presented a picture of peasant life devoid of material amenities. Evans, on the other hand, portrayed rural Ireland as a place alive with a rich material culture. Many of the most vivid and lasting pictures of the peasants' homes come from fiction. For example, in *The Kellys and the O'Kellys*, regarded by some as Trollope's best Irish novel, Trollope writes of the Irish cabin: 'It isn't that the chairs and tables look filthy, for there are none. It isn't that the pots, and plates, and pans don't shine, for you see none to shine.'[31] Trollope's vision of the typical Irish cabin is compelling and evocative, but does it represent reality? With this literary image in mind, it was probably not a coincidence that an Irish historian told me in 1993 that the archaeology of cottier society was not reasonable because the people had nothing for archaeologists to excavate.

The perception that Irish peasants were completely without material culture is pervasive, but undoubtedly unrealistic. All peoples around the globe approach the world around them with the aid of material things. Also, material things do more than simply help people to survive. Artifacts are actively engaged in society; they carry and help to create meaning, they establish relations between people, and they have the power to expand and to restrict action and thought. In other words, the world of artifacts is alive and powerful, not dead and inert.[32] One kind of meaning that holds particular promise relates to the ability of artifacts to symbolize the resistance to oppression and the struggle for cultural survival.

In his study of contemporary Malaysia, James Scott outlined how tenant farmers daily struggled with their landlords. The conflicts reached far beyond property rights, the possession of the crop, and the flow of cash. In fact, landlords and their tenants clashed over such subtle areas as the appropriation of symbols and the right of the tenants to tell their own history. Scott argued that the daily resistance of tenants contained numerous 'hidden transcripts'. Again using American slavery as a guide, we may image that cottier artifacts may help to reveal what Scott terms the 'arts of resistance.'[33]

---

31 Young, *A Tour of Ireland*; E. Estyn Evans, *Irish Folk Ways* (London, 1967); Anthony Trollope, *The Kellys and the O'Kellys, Or Landlords and Tenants* (London, 1993), p. 54; Foster, *Paddy and Mr Punch*, p. 144.

32 Mihaly Csikszentmihalyi and Eugene Rochberg-Halton, *The Meaning of Things: Domestic Symbols and the Self* (Cambridge, 1981); Mary Douglas and Baron Isherwood, *The World of Goods* (New York, 1979); Grant McCracken, *Culture and Consumption: New Approaches to the Symbolic Character of Consumer Goods and Activities* (Bloomington, 1988); C.H. Orser, Jr., 'Consumption, Consumerism, and Things from the Earth' in *Historical Methods*, xxvii (1994), pp. 61-70.

33 J.C. Scott, *Weapons of the Weak: Everyday Forms of Peasant Resistance* (New Haven,

Daily tensions and strains occur wherever landlords and tenants co-exist, and Ireland was no exception. Occasionally, the stresses were acted out in dramatic fashion. Landlords seized property, evicted tenants, and shipped families off their land. Tenants hid livestock, threatened their landlords, and sometimes even killed them. Records reveal that all was not quiet at on Mahon's estate, as tenants stole his wool and timber and eventually murdered him.[34] Though no armed rebellion ever arose at Strokestown, the tenant-landlord relations there were obviously in a state of constant flux and negotiation. The common, everyday artifacts found at Gorttoose may reflect some of the tensions that had tragic reality during the evictions of 1847. Can we assume, that if the cottiers really did prefer wooden, metal, and leather vessels over continental ceramics, as Evans maintained, that they did so to resist landlord domination and assimilation?[35]

Archaeology also will provide specific information about the size, design, and orientation of cottier cabins at specific townlands regardless of above-ground preservation. Many American slave masters demanded better slave housing near their mansions, and it is intriguing to wonder whether the houses in sight of Mahon's mansion were larger and better made that those out of his immediate line of vision. In addition, archaeology will be able to shed light on the nature and characteristics of clachans, or rundale villages.[36] These small settlement clusters appeared at Gorttoose in association with the more linear settlements required by Mahon.

Conclusion

The archaeology of cottier society at the time of the Great Famine is only just beginning. Comparable research at contemporary African-American sites suggests that archaeologists will eventually have much to say about the material aspects of cottier life. Archaeologists will provide significant new information about material culture, housing, and landlord-tenant relations. Before long, we hope to begin removing the soil from the sites at Gorttoose, searching for clues to the realities of cottier life. Once the sod is stripped and the artifacts are washed, sorted, and inventoried, the real process of discovery will begin. At present, the historical archaeology of the Great Famine is only a promise. But, it is a promise with thrilling potential and unbounded opportunity.

1985); J.C. Scott, *Domination and the Arts of Resistance: Hidden Transcripts* (New Haven, 1990).
34 Pakenham-Mahon Papers, Strokestown House.
35 Evans, *Irish Folk Ways*, pp. 73-4.
36 E.E. Evans, *The Personality of Ireland: Habitat, Heritage, and History* (Dublin, 1992), pp. 60-1; Kevin Whelan, 'Settlement Patterns in the West of Ireland in the Pre-Famine Period' in Timothy Collins (ed.), *Decoding the Landscape* (Galway, 1994), p. 63.

II Representations

A Stone on the Cairn: The Great Famine in Later Gaelic Manuscripts

NEIL BUTTIMER

Most accounts and studies of the Famine are in English or other languages, even though Irish was the spoken tongue of many if not the majority of those who perished in the catastrophe. Recent research has demonstrated the existence of a challenging body of evidence about the event in twentieth-century folklore sources where Ireland's ancestral voice is prominent.[1] This essay reviews another largely Gaelic archive for the insight it affords on the issue. The vernacular manuscript tradition which evolved in early Christian times remained vigorous down to the nineteenth century.[2] Scribes who lived during or survived the calamity noted different aspects of their experience of it. Their witness is valuable both with regard to specific detail but also in a wider sense. The manuscripts belong to a civilisation acquainted with misfortune. They thus furnish a perspective on distress in general as well as this manifestation of it in particular. These matters are sketched below, following the chronological sequence customary in Famine explorations. It must be stressed from the outset that discussion of certain topics raised (disease, for instance) is necessarily perfunctory because of their technical nature. Nonetheless, the paper will have succeeded if it draws attention to a corpus of information hitherto overlooked in Famine scholarship.

Background

Descriptions of the 'Great Hunger' in Gaelic documentation reflect a well-established pattern of recording various instances of natural or social disorder occurring in Ireland from the early medieval era onwards, together with strategies for coping with them.[3] Data from the seventeenth century show the conti-

---

1 C. Ó Gráda, *An Drochshaol: Béaloideas agus Amhráin* (Dublin, 1994). For related material in English see Cathal Póirtéir, 'Folk memory and the Famine' in idem (ed.), *The Great Irish Famine* (Cork, 1995), pp. 219-31, a volume which also mentions (p. 5) its editor's forthcoming extended treatment of the Irish- and English-language folklore evidence.
2 For an excellent description of the culture see P. de Brún, 'Gan Teannta Buird ná Bínse' in *Comhar* xxxi (1972), xi.
3 The medieval portion of William Wilde's well-known table of Irish famines 900-1850 is principally based on information drawn from the chiefly Gaelic contemporary annals; see E.M. Crawford (ed.), *Famine: The Irish Experience 900-1900* (Edinburgh, 1989), pp. 1-30; similar sources also furnish a considerable amount of the data for the next paper in

nuity of this practice into modernity. The harsh winter of 1683-4, when the ground was frozen to a depth of several feet by a cold spell that lasted until summer 1684, is the subject of contemporary commentary in Irish and English, in both verse and prose. The following quatrain is an example of the former medium:

> Duisín caogad míle becht. ochtmoghad a trí i néinfecht;
> ó thecht in ríg dhíol ár gcáin. gusin sioc chlaoi na cnapáin.

> A dozen fifties, a thousand exactly, eighty and three both together, there were from the Advent of the Great King that paid our fine for us down to the frost that ruined the buds.[4]

Much more was written or composed on the harshness of the years 1739-41 during which sustained bad weather and a series of poor harvests resulted in mortality rates unsurpassed in Ireland until over a century later, if even then.[5] Other forms of adversity were remarked on down to the outbreak of the Famine itself. Cholera spread throughout the country in 1832. Scribes observed its arrival in their localities, and copied prayers to be said to overcome its effects together with other reflections on its implications.[6]

Given the diverse ways the tradition registers such phenomena, it seems appropriate to treat with greater care statements couched in imaginative terms which may nonetheless accurately reflect the affairs of the nation on the eve of the Famine. This applies to the poem commencing 'Céad míle fáilte romhat, a bhanríon na scéimhe!' ('A hundred thousand welcomes to you, o beauteous queen!'). The piece, attributed to the Gaelic enthusiast and versifier Brian Ó

the same volume, M.C. Lyons, 'Weather, Famine, Pestilence and Plague in Ireland, 900-1500' (pp. 31-74).

4 The quatrain occurs in British Library MS Egerton 161: f. 35 *b*, and has been edited and translated by S.H. O'Grady, *Catalogue of Irish Manuscripts in the British Museum* (London, 1926), i, p. 609. For a note in English on the frost in a Gaelic source see RIA MS 23 L 34: p. 249 *i*. H.H. Lamb, *Climate, History and the Modern World* (London and New York, 1982), pp. 221-3 describes the nature and impact of contemporary weather conditions; I thank Kenneth Nicholls, Department of History, UCC, for the latter reference.

5 Some of the relevant material has been published by C.G. Buttimer, 'An Irish text on the 'War of Jenkins' Ear''in *Celtica* xxi (1990), pp. 75-98, and P.A. Breatnach, 'Togha na héigse 1700-1800' in *Éigse* xxvii (1993), pp. 120-1. For the context see D. Dickson, 'The Other Great Irish Famine' in Póirtéir (ed.), *The Great Irish Famine*, pp. 50-9; cf. also idem, 'The Gap in Famines: A Useful Myth?' in Crawford (ed.), *Famine: The Irish Experience*, pp. 96-111.

6 The presence of cholera in Cork is noted in RIA MS 23 C 19: p. 346 *i*, for example. For a prayer to be said against it see Maynooth MS R 66: p. 394. UCC Torna MS T.xxiv: pp. 129 ff. contains a sermon which appears to deal with the disease.

Tumultaigh (Bernard Tumulty) from Drogheda, was apparently composed in 1845 when a visit by Queen Victoria to Ireland was thought imminent.[7] The text is an address in the latter's honour, praising her appearance and character as she arrives to consolidate her friendship with the Irish public. The work underlines the extent to which the people of Ireland are in need of whatever assistance and good-will the monarch can provide:

> Uch! a bhanríon mhín! 's gan aon nduine leár n-éagaoin!
> 'Gus inn creachta, 'gus gointe, 'gus scaipthe chum gach réigiúin,
> Gan éadach, gan oideas 'nár seachránaithe sclábhaithe,
> Is dream an uabhair ár ndiaidh sa mbaile go cumhachtach![8]
>
> ...
>
> 'S na mílte fáil bháis tré anródh 's na críochaibh!
> A Dhé uilechumhachtaigh! cá bhfuil creideamh an Bhíobla?

> Alas! gentle queen!, there is no one to lament us! We are destroyed and injured and scattered to every region, unclad, unlettered, like wandering slaves, and a haughty crew pursue us powerfully at home!
>
> ...
>
> There are thousands dying of distress in the land! Omnipotent God! where is the faith of the Bible?

If the Famine was not in progress by the time these lines were completed, the poem may nevertheless already foreshadow the circumstances in which the tragedy would shortly unfold.

Letters from the late 1840s reveal that Ó Tumultaigh's optimism respecting the British sovereign was not universally shared. William Hackett from Midleton, county Cork, member of a prosperous local distilling family and an amateur of Irish antiquities, corresponded regularly with the county Louth Gaelic scholar Nioclás Ó Cearnaigh (Nicholas O'Kearney), by then resident in Dublin.[9] In

---

7 The item occurs in RIA MS 23 E 12: pp. 258-9. Spelling in the following excerpts from this and other contemporary verse is standardized to reflect late twentieth-century editorial practices, and changes in punctuation have also been introduced. (Prose excerpts in which metrical guidance is absent will not be standardised, and will be subjected to minimal alterations in punctuation.) My English translations of both verse and prose citations are intended to be literal but not such as to impede readability. B. Ó Buachalla, *I mBéal Feirste cois Cuain* (Dublin, 1968), Treoir, s.n. Tumalty, Bernard, provides information on the poet.

8 The MS reads *cómhaach*.

9 See S. Duffy, *Nicholas O'Kearney: The Last of the Bards of Louth* (Coalisland, 1989) and S. Ó Dufaigh and D. Ó Doibhlin, *Nioclás Ó Cearnaigh: Beatha Agus Saothar* (Dublin, 1989) for O'Kearney. I thank Professor Seán Ó Coileáin for making these items available to me, and for helpful comments on an earlier draft of the article. Hackett's interest in Irish culture has been explored by B. Ó Conchúir, *Scríobhaithe Chorcaí 1700-1850* (Dub-

1849 Hackett wrote to his colleague that 'The country people here have a tradition that the reign of a queen is portentous of evil to Ireland', citing popular recollections of dispossession in the time of Mary Tudor, or the 'fire sword famine' of her sister, Elizabeth I's age.[10] Another Gaelic document suggests the excommunication imposed on Martin Luther at the Council of Trent was due to expire in 1845.[11] However improbable the latter consideration, at least it demonstrates that differing degrees of sentiment and veracity inform pre-Famine Gaelic discourse. Equivalent levels of perception and understanding surface again in representations of the disaster itself.

The Great Famine in Gaelic manuscript evidence

The causes, development, duration and effects of the Famine are currently receiving renewed notice.[12] The following summary of these points is intended merely to highlight the event's more significant moments for the purpose of structuring presentation of the various kinds of Irish-language testimony subsequently considered. A hitherto unfamiliar disease (*phytophthora infestans*) struck the potato crop – the staple food of considerable sections of the population – in the autumn of 1845. Matters worsened when the crop's 1846 harvest failed drastically, leading to the serious deterioration of early 1847. Illnesses coinciding with mass starvation proved as devastating as food shortages proper in many cases. Privately-sponsored or publicly-supported relief measures were augmented or developed, including the work-house system or construction schemes, while substitute foodstuffs like meal were also imported in response to current exigencies. The fact that hundreds of thousands of people had lost their lives before it abated confirms the magnitude of the crisis.

Manuscript sources shed light on each of these stages, as the following outline reveals. Contemporaries were obviously aware of the difficulties affecting the primary source of sustenance. In a composition entitled 'Laoi cascartha na

lin, 1982), Innéacs, s.n., idem, 'Thomas Swanton, Réamhchonraitheoir in Iar-Chairbre' in *Journal of the Cork Historical and Archaeological Society*, xcviii (1993), pp. 50-60, especially note 62, and in the aforementioned volumes on O'Kearney.

10 The correspondence occurs in RIA MS 24 E 20: p. 286.

11 See NLI MS G 306: p. 129.

12 C. Kinealy, *This Great Calamity: The Irish Famine 1845-52* (Dublin, 1994) offers a comprehensive account of the period. References in Ó Gráda, *An Drochshaol*'s bibliography to articles and books not mentioned by Kinealy should be noted, together with C. Ó Gráda, *Ireland: A New Economic History 1780-1939* (Oxford, 1994), pp. 173-209 and the papers in Póirtéir (ed.), *The Great Irish Famine*. Two earlier titles now enjoy a classic status, R. Dudley-Edwards and T. Desmond Williams (eds), *The Great Famine: Studies in Irish History, 1845-52* (Dublin, 1956), re-issued in 1994, and C. Woodham-Smith, *The Great Hunger* (London, 1962), though these works contain little if any discussion of Irish-language sources.

bpotátaí' ('A poem on the potatoes' destruction') the midlands versifier and
scribe Peadar Ó Gealacáin (Peter Gallegan) speaks of 'ár saorbharr breá séanmhar'
('our noble, auspicious crop') being 'i lámha an éaga' ('in death's hand's').[13] In
its absence, other forms of nourishment were of little consequence, he claims:

> Níl rófhlaith gan eolchaire[14] is éagnach
> 's ní sómasach a dhéantar a bhféasta,
> fíon Spáinneach, beoir ársa no *tea* glan
> ní áirím gur sású sin d'aon neach.

> There is not a great leader without sorrow or lamentation, and their
> feasting is not relaxed. Spanish wine, mature beer or pure tea, I do not
> believe these satisfy any one.

O Gealacáin suggests the following measures to safeguard the potato harvest are
ineffective:

> Ní díon dóibh balla daingean dá thréine,
> scioból nó lafta nó *cagework*,
> nó beannacht na sagart nó éigse,
> i n-uaimh thalmhan dá gcasadh 'na sréathaibh.

> A firm wall, however strong, does not protect them, neither does a barn,
> a loft or cagework, or the priests' or poets' benediction when they are in
> a pit in the ground being turned in rows.

The last-mentioned quatrain demonstrates the rootedness of contemporary ver-
sification in the world around it. A further composition survives in which measures reminiscent of certain of the foregoing are recommended to preserve the
potato crop. This bilingual prose work in the form of a printed page is now
located among a set of mainly handwritten records.[15] It bears the title 'Extract
from the Letter of a "Western Rector"', with an Irish-language version 'Pairt
don' litir fhir Seagailse [sic] 'san Iarthar' facing. The text and its accompanying
diagram describe how to select and arrange a pit to keep potatoes free of disease:

> Togh ionad tirim spearuimhil don bpoll. Ann sin dean poll-gaoithe leathan
> go leor, air barra na talmhan, a bhfoirm thrinse osguilte no abhfoirm
> linteire, le gearadh thrinse naoi norluighe no troig ar leathad 7 ar

13 This text is found in NLI MS G 199: pp. 330-4. Ó Buachalla, *I mBéal Feirste cois Cuain*,
passim, deals with its author.
14 *ulcaire* is the MS reading.
15 See RIA MS 3 C 7: p. 364.

doimhneachd, 7 le cuir mion cloch air a dtreasna air. Tarraig an trinse no an linteirese air fhad an phoill 7 fag osguilte 'na dha cheann e, ionnus go ngeabhach an ghaoth thrid go thaosga. Chum na gaoithe a ghabhail nios fear (an nidh is nios [*sic*] riochdanaiche), dean poill-gaoithe a dtaobhaibh an phoill a m-ballaibh go reasanta a bh-fad o cheile. Air urlar an t-rinse se deantar an poll, ag tabhairt aire air poill-gaoithe d'fagailt ag an bharra, chum an gal a leigint amach. Is uraisd e so a dheanamh le fóid a chasadh tiomchuil feac ráine.

Let a dry and airy site be chosen for the pit; then let an air-pipe or funnel be made, of tolerable width, either on the surface of the ground, in form of a French drain, or in that of a lintern, by cutting a trench nine inches or a foot in depth and breadth, and laying stones loosely across it; and let this funnel be carried the whole intended length of the pit, and left open at both ends, freely to admit the air. To render the ventilation – and ventilation is the great desideratum – still more complete, let air-holes be made in the sides of the pit, at moderate distances.

The English version of the succeeding set of instructions (the copy of which is slightly damaged in parts) is as follows:

Over this frame-work let [...] pit be constructed, care being taken to leave valves or air-holes at the top, which may be done by the simple process of a sod turned round the handle of a spade, to permit the escape of the heated air. In a word, *let the air pass freely underneath the pit, and allow it an easy escape above.* Thus will the pit be kept cool – the progress of fermentation effectually checked – and the Potato, even though diseased, preserved. I found it so with my own pits. The Potato, which was put in diseased and soft, came out dry and hard, and the affected part came off by a touch of the nail like a dry scab, leaving the Potato dry and healed beneath it.

The Irish excerpt shows the influence of conventional, literary spelling but also traces of dialect and speech patterns. It probably echoes real-life debate about how to counter the potato blight. If it is indeed the work of a Protestant minister, the item may further illustrate the assistance members of the established church rendered their fellow-citizens (regardless of denominational interest), examples of which are known for many areas of the country.

These counsels were largely ineffective in the absence of a proper scientific comprehension of both the nature of and the cure for the disease. Irish-language evidence is at one with its counterpart in English in revealing the fate in store for many. Mícheál Ó Raghallaigh (Michael O'Riely) from west county Clare (one of the worst-affected regions) has left this description of the situation in his district during one of the Famine's most notorious phases. The scribe had a deep regard for traditional Irish historiography; the entry, which reads like a medieval annal, is typical of his annotation of contemporary early nineteenth-century incidents:

> AD 1847 Bliadhain na gortan .7 an riachtanais. Oir do sgrios an ghaothruadh blath .7 gasa na bpotátuídhe. ionnus gur loibh siad uile. Ni raibh potátá le buaint as talamh ag aon duine san bfomhar mur badh gnáth. bliadhanta eile. Ni raibh an corcaidh go maith mur badh gnáth. na an mhin ann. Dá bhrigh sin bhí gorta .7 riachtannais air gach aon duine san ríoghacht acht tanaig iliomad minne .7 earbhuir go hEirinn as *America* .7 as rioghachtuibh eile. D'eug mórán do na daoine an gach áit san rioghacht. Fiabhrus .7 tinnios cuirp do thanaig orra do bhár an oicrais .7 is leis a déug na daoine san tír seo. Do thuit breis .7 míle duine san bporóiste so. ar feadh tri mhídh .i. Cill Mhainnithinn a cCorcamruadh.

> AD 1847 The year of famine and need, because the strong wind destroyed the potatoes' flowers and stems, so that they all rotted. Nobody had a potato to pick from the earth in autumn as was usual in other years. Oats were not as good as usual, nor was there meal. Therefore everyone in the kingdom was famished and in want, but much meal and corn came to Ireland from America and other realms. Many people died everywhere in the kingdom. Fever and sickness overcame them as a result of hunger, and that is how people in this country died. More than a thousand fell in this parish in three months, i.e. Kilmanaheen in Corcamroe.[16]

The months are not specified, but they probably encompass the start of the year when conditions were likely to have been particularly adverse. A further Gaelic document sheds additional light on the timing and character of the crisis Ó Raghallaigh mentions. The scribe Séamus Ó Caoindealbháin (James Quinlivan), when residing in the neighbourhood of Askeaton, county Limerick, copied a text entitled 'Oráid a naímsir plágha et doghruingeádha eile' ('An oration in time of plague and other difficulties'), beginning 'A Dhia na Trócaire, A Dhia na truaighmhéile' ('O God of mercy, O God of pity').[17] He dated it 'an tochtmadh lá iar fidhche d'óigmhí 1847' (perhaps 28 January). An English-language pre-

---

16 Maynooth MS R 70: p. 490. This Gaelic composition should be further explored in the context of the type of extant local evidence for county Clare listed in D. Lindsay and D. Fitzpatrick (eds), *Records of the Irish Famine: A Guide to Local Archives, 1840-1855* (Dublin, 1993), passim.

17 NLI MS G 326: p. 391. B. Ó Madagáin, *An Ghaeilge i Luimneach 1700-1900* (Dublin, 1974), pp. 81-4 offers a short account of Quinlivan.

scription occurs shortly after the oration in the same source and may hint at the 'plague' Ó Caoindealbháin had in mind: 'One drop of Hydrocyanic acid, and one drop of creasote, with an ounce of cinnamon water immediately arrests the spasmodic action of cholera.'[18] The shortage of food, the prevalence of disease and the accompanying psychological trauma had a negative impact on such other features of normal life as fertility and reproduction.[19] Impediments to these functions may be at issue in a composition beginning 'O Iesus Crist, son of the dibhine bounty of God be my aid'; the copyist Riocard Paor (Richard Power) transcribed the work and dated it 30 September 1850.[20] The item's preface (in which Gaelic spelling conventions are readily detectible) alludes specifically to child-birth:

> The follóing prayer hath ma[n]y remarcable properties, so as to obtain a good death to any person who says it debhoutly once aday [*sic*], with a good intention to the glorí of God, and debhótion of the Blessed Bhirgin. And saying it debhoutly for any woman in labour, it forwards with God's blessing, a speedy and safe delibherí, with many other benefits.[21]

Riocard Paor was then employed in the 'Districth [*sic*] Lunatic Asylum Waterford.'

Ó Raghallaigh's account mentioned schemes established to assist the needy. These figure in our manuscript sources also. A record of payments made to road workers in the neighbourhood of Fieries, north of Killarney, county Kerry, is found in a document compiled by the scribe Gearóid Mac Gearailt (Garrett FitzGerald) from the same county.[22] The period of payment seems to be from November 1846-January 1847, comprising some of the Famine's more critical moments. The decline in their customary sources of support meant that exponents of native culture would have required this and other types of assistance as a matter of urgency. Edmund Bennet from Croom, county Limerick, corresponded on 5 October 1847 with Waterford-born Seán Ó Dálaigh (John O Daly), a Gaelic enthusiast and bookseller then living in Dublin, stating he had recently earned little 'as school teaching has in a great degree failed in my neigh-

18 NLI MS G 326: p. 410.
19 For a discussion of this matter see P. Hickey, 'Famine, Mortality and Emigration: A Profile of Six Parishes in the Poor Law Union of Skibbereen, 1846-7' in P. O'Flanagan and C.G. Buttimer (eds), *Cork: History and Society* (Dublin, 1993), pp. 873-918 (especially 897-9).
20 NLI MS G 506: p. 302. E. Ó Súilleabháin, 'Scríobhaithe Phort Láirge 1700-1900' in W. Nolan and T. Power (eds), *Waterford: History and Society* (Dublin, 1992), pp. 293-5 discusses the scribe.
21 P. Ó Macháin, *Catalogue of Irish manuscripts in the National Library of Ireland* (Dublin, 1990), xi, pp. 14-15 has published this English entry.
22 NLI MS G 400: pp. 253-74.

bourhood.'[23] Within a year, Corkman John Windele (1801-65), a court official and patron of Irish scholars, wrote to Ó Dálaigh as follows: 'people have no money for literature. Scarcely any even for food which promises to run up to a high figure.'[24] The plight of the learned conveyed in this remark is borne out in the following instance. On completing a version of the poet Eoghan Rua Ó Súilleabháin's song 'Cois abhann inné 's mé ag taisteal i gcéin' in 1847, a copyist from the east-Cork parish of Ballynoe earnestly implores an unidentified person to continue providing patronage in this troubled address:

> Gaibh leathsgeal na locht do cidhfir annso am dhíaig da bhrigh gur tré bhuaireamh aígne, 7 ríachtanas an tsaoghuilsi mé féin 7 mo mhuirrear air easba bídh 7 eadaig, do sgríobhas an beagán so, 7 aithcim air tonóir feachuinn le suil na truadhmheile orruinn 7 comhair éigin do thabhart orruinn. do bhrigh nach fuil dfalltas agam acht corroin annsa tseachtmhuin a faire lae 7 oídhche. Guídhim fad saoghail fa meanamna 7 fa luthghair an sláinte mhaith, 7 a crich mhaith do bheith air dhéire do beatha. Is mise do seirbhiseach dileas go bás; Seádhan Ó Moihill Gleantán.

> Please excuse the errors you see in what follows, because it is on account of mental distress and the necessities of life − I and my family being in want of food and clothing − that I have written this little amount. I beseech your honour to look mercifully upon us and to assist us in some way, because my only income is a crown a week for guarding day and night. I wish you a long, high-spirited, happy and healthy life, and a good conclusion at the end of your days. I remain your faithful servant until death, Seán Ó Moithill, Glaunthane.[25]

Help was not always forthcoming when requested. The Famine fostered evasiveness in human relations, whether through greed, a hoarding mentality or to avoid contact with the sick and the infected. This hesitancy appears to surface in the Gaelic evidence as well. Could the presence of a short discourse on 'our national weights and measures', discussing the demerits of the metric system, now found in a Cork manuscript of 1846, indirectly reflect anxiety about such topics as the proper estimation and equitable distribution of relief supplies?[26] A

---

23 NLI MS G 389: pp. 179-81; see also N. Ní Shéaghdha, *Catalogue of Irish manuscripts in the National Library of Ireland* (Dublin, 1986), ix, p. 23.

24 NLI MS G 389: pp. 335-7, Ní Shéaghdha, *Catalogue ... National Library of Ireland*, ix, p. 27. Ó Conchúir, *Scríobhaithe Chorcaí*, pp. 188-90 discusses Windele.

25 NLI MS G 691: p. 22, published by Ní Shéaghdha, *Catalogue ... National Library of Ireland*, xii, pp. 94-5 (incorporating slight modifications to her punctuation and other readings, following a comparison with the MS). For the scribe see Ó Conchúir, *Scríobhaithe Chorcaí*, p. 163.

26 NLI MS G 659: pp. 121-3.

further Cork document from 1851 contains an account of the identification of a person's character from his complexion.[27] Even though the tract seems to focus on moral traits, might there have been a preoccupation with tokens of physical well-being (or its opposite) also? Finally one may note the survival of 'A sermon preached by the Revd John Meany, Parish Priest of Kilrossenty, Co. of Waterford' transcribed in 1850. Its theme is 'Air Charthanacht nó Grádh na cComharsan' ('On Charity or Love of Neighbour').[28] Was the latter as scarce as other commodities in Gaelic society in mid-century?

Meany's sermon was composed in Irish, but the Famine brought the language's very survival as a widespread vernacular seriously into question. This fact became apparent to various persons interested in both it and its culture. The aforementioned Seán Ó Dálaigh spoke of the marginalisation of Gaelic in a lecture to a Dublin Confederate Club in November 1847.[29] The events of the day are uppermost in the speaker's mind: 'Alas poor Ireland! and that you are poor and hungry and starved every thing about you plainly indicates.' Ó Dálaigh traces the language's persecution since the arrival of the Normans. He argues it would be inappropriate to jettison it now, as it is capable of developing a sense of identity and self-worth in Irish people of a kind he deems particularly desirable in present circumstances. When considered as a medium of communication, the lecturer claims Gaelic phonology is 'more peculiarly adapted to the descriptions of the soft, tender, plaintive and elegiac kind'! Others promoted the cause of Irish differently. John Windele appears to have petitioned the Registrar General to include a question on its status as a spoken language in the 1851 census, the first occasion on which such information was elicited.[30] Data in this and succeeding censuses have greatly assisted the study of the complex decline of Gaelic in the nineteenth century and after.[31] The erosion of other aspects of indigenous civilisation attracted notice also. William Wilde began to collect remnants of Irish folk belief before the informants themselves would be swept away. He corresponded with certain of the scholars previously mentioned in this account, William Hackett from Midleton and Dublin-based Nioclás Ó Cearnaigh, asking for assistance with his undertaking.[32] Even though contact

27 NLI MS G 662: pp. 84–5.
28 RIA MS 23 O 71: pp. 206 ff. Ó Súilleabháin, 'Scríobhaithe Phort Láirge', p. 291 discusses the priest. D.A. Kerr, '*A Nation of Beggars'?: Priests, People, and Politics in Famine Ireland 1846–1852* (Oxford, 1994), particularly pp. 30–68, has explored the role of the Catholic clergy in the Famine. S. Connolly, *Religion and Society in Nineteenth-Century Ireland* (Dundalk, 1985) summarises the wider background.
29 NLI MS G 416, a manuscript devoted entirely to the lecture.
30 For a draft of the letter see RIA MS 12 C 2: p. 583. Windele's summary of the results of the 1851 Census may be found in RIA MS 12 M 12: ff. 830–1.
31 M. Nic Craith, *Malartú teanga: an Ghaeilge i gCorcaigh sa Naoú hAois Déag* (Bremen, 1993) details scholarship on this issue.
32 Wilde sought information on popular customs from William Hackett in early 1849, as Hackett's letter to O'Kearney dated 31 March of the same year indicates; see RIA MS

between them later broke down, publications like the pioneering *Irish Popular Superstitions* (1852) demonstrate that Wilde's work bore fruit. His account of the manner whereby rural depopulation diminished the vitality of the native tradition is one of the more haunting evocations of the Famine's immediate consequences.

Large-scale emigration followed hard on the heels of other losses and added to the sense of devastation.[33] This subject would require extended treatment in its own right, but one may highlight the presence of information on it in the Gaelic record, where it features in both Irish- and English-language compositions. Take, for instance, the didactic verse on the proper behaviour of an exile beginning 'Ar farraige má thaistilir le cúrsa an tsaoil' ('If you travel overseas on life's journey'), copied by the scribe Mícheál Ó hÉalaithe (Michael Healy) from Kilcorney, county Cork, in a manuscript written during 1846-52.[34] Brian Ó Luanaigh (Brian O'Looney) from county Clare transcribed sentimental pieces like 'The Emigrant's Farewell by Patrick Higgins ...', a poem which begins 'I'm leaving you at last Mary', in a document he completed in the years 1850-60.[35] A fuller picture of Gaelic speakers' experience of departure might emerge from considering this material jointly with other similar forms of testimony, particularly entries in folklore sources.[36]

Explanations

It is therefore clear that the Famine did not pass by unobserved in contemporary Gaelic manuscripts. The scribes also considered the event's origins and import. Their attitude towards these issues is more complex than might be imagined could emerge in the Irish-speaking world. We may return to those musings of Peadar Ó Gealacáin which provided an initial impression of the potato blight, the disaster's proximate cause.[37] Ó Gealacáin felt that more profound forces underlay the catastrophe:

24 E 20: p. 227. See also Duffy, *Nicholas O'Kearney*, pp. 76-82, Ó Dufaigh and Ó Doibhlin, *Nioclás Ó Cearnaigh*, pp. 66-70.
33 David Fitzpatrick, *Irish Emigration 1801-1924* (Dundalk, 1985) sketches the phenomenon.
34 NLI MS G 422: p. 343.
35 NLI MS G 634 (a): p. 54.
36 The text given in Ó Gráda, *An Drochshaol*, pp. 70-1 deserves to be contrasted with NLI MS G 250.186 [3]. See also G. Neville, ' 'She Never Then After That Forgot Him'': Irishwomen and Emigration to the United States in Irish Folklore' in *Mid-America: an Historical Review* lxxiv, 3 (October, 1992), pp. 271-89 for a treatment of associated material.
37 See above, note 13.

'Sé shílim, 's ní scríobhaimse bréaga,
's bíodh a fhianaise ag saoithibh atá aosta,
gurb é dhíbir ar saorbharr breá séanmhar
ceart Chríosta ar dhaoithibh gan chéadfa.

It is my opinion, and I write no lie – may venerable learned people be
my witness – that what banished our noble, auspicious crop was Christ's
vengeance on senseless fools.

The people incurred the Creator's displeasure because of their immoderate interest in the affairs of this world, in dancing, dressing and disputation:

Tráth chonaic Dia gach olc 's gach mí-rún,
goid is fuadach, feall is daorbhreith,
's gach peaca eile dárbh fhéidir smaoineadh,
d'fhéach sé anuas le fuath is le míoscais.

Is iomdha fógra fuair na daoine
le heaspaí, tinte is fóirneart gaoithe,
pláigh is gorta, ocras is íota,
is píonóstaí eile nach féidir dom míneadh.

As siocair gach olc dár tharla i nÉirinn
d'éag na potátaí, mo chrá 's mo ghéar-ghoin,
ach a Rí na ngrása a bhásaíos na céadta
go sábhála tú feasta iad trí do dhaonnacht.

When God saw each evil and each ignoble ambition, theft and ravishing,
treachery and ill-judgement, and all other sins imaginable, he looked
down with hatred and anger.

People received many warnings, want, fire and storms, plagues and famines, hunger and thirst and other inestimable punishments.

As a result of all of Ireland's evils the potatoes died, my grief and tor-
ment! But, graceful King who dispatches hundreds, save them hence-
forth through your humanity.

Would other members of the Gaelic community agree with Ó Gealacáin's
contention that the Famine arose from divine retribution? One might initially
be disposed to think so on learning of the existence of an Irish-language tract
entitled *Craobhsgaoile No Mininiughadh Leabhar An Taisbeanach (An Exploration*

or an Explanation of the Book of Revelations). Aindrias Ó Súilleabháin (Andrew O'Sullivan), a scribe from Cahirciveen, county Kerry, copied the compilation in 1854.[38] The celebrated New Testament book in question describes the painful destruction to be visited on the earth's inhabitants in general and on sinners in particular at the end of the world. Could certain sections of the Irish population have thought that apocalyptic predictions were being verified in their case in Famine times as a result of their own innate defects? Other moralising texts were replicated in significant numbers immediately before and after 1850. These include the poem frequently designated 'Comhrá an Bháis agus an Duine Thinn' ('The Conversation between Death and the Patient'). Might the Gaelic-speaking public have largely concurred with the latter's viewpoint that human beings are by nature inherently imperfect and incapable of escaping decay? Death boasts of his achievements in the following vein during his colloquy with the Patient:

> Beirim an t-óg ó dheól na gcíoch liom,
> Beirim an leanbh 's a bhanaltra i n-aoineacht,
> Beirim an fear óna mhnaoi liom,
> Beirim an té phós araoir liom,
> Beirim na boicht liom bhíos ag díolaim.

> I take with me the sucking infant,
> I take the child and nurse together,
> I take the husband from his partner,
> I take the one who wed last evening,
> I take with me the poor a-begging.[39]

One can only wonder at the chords these lines struck in readers or listeners during the Great Hunger. The advice which accompanies them is that Man should seek solace from the spiritual comfort provided by prayer and holy persons like saints rather than in worthless worldly wealth.[40]

The Book of Revelations' complex message has been interpreted in various ways. One of its meanings appears to be that God's faithful followers will be spared while their enemies are destroyed in the final cataclysm. The aforementioned excursus on the Apocalypse Aindrias Ó Súilleabháin wrote out in 1854 is

38 NLI MS G 368: pp. 329-47.
39 The lines are cited from RIA MS 23 L 24: p. 80 (not written during the Great Famine). Analogues to the work's bleak atmosphere may be found in J. Huizinga, *The Waning of the Middle Ages* (Anchor Books edition, New York, 1954).
40 A comparison between the use made of literature as an aid to recovery from disaster and traditional communities' employment of folklore for the same purpose may be worthwhile; for the latter strategy see L. Minc, 'Scarcity and survival: the role of oral tradition in mediating subsistence crises' in *Journal of Archaeological Anthropology* v, 1 (March, 1986), pp. 39-113 and also the Conclusion of this essay.

in fact a model of Catholic apologetics, anathematising Protestantism as the ultimate object of divine anger. Others in the Gaelic world seem to have drawn a correspondingly firm distinction between the just and wrongdoers in the Famine context. Certain copyists suggest the event was perpetrated treacherously on the Irish who did not deserve their fate. This sentiment may be implicit in the writings of the Clareman Mícheál Ó Raghallaigh, one of whose texts was explored above. On completing a version of a devotional tract he states he stopped 'a dtarradh lá fithchiod do Lúmhnas AD 1848 .i. bliadhainn an áir 7 an ocrais ionnar éag na millte duine le huireasbadh bígh' ('the 22 August AD 1848 i.e. the year of slaughter and hunger during which thousands died for want of food').[41] Even if the connotations of the term *ár* ('slaughter') are not absolutely incontrovertible, it would be difficult to doubt the opinion of another copyist from the same county regarding events similar to those Ó Raghallaigh relates. Brian Ó Luanaigh who transcribed the emigration poem 'I'm leaving you at last Mary' noted earlier stated it was 'Written after the odious extermination of 47.'[42]

Statements of a more comprehensive kind than these brief comments are also extant. Nioclás Ó Cearnaigh's verse composition 'Éire án gan cháim ba lachtmhar' ('Illustrious unblemished Ireland was bountiful'), which he himself entitles 'Cruadh-ghorta na h-Éirionn noch chrádh a clannain go díochrach feadh 1846.7.8' ('Ireland's harsh famine, which grievously tormented its children during 1846.7.8'), consists of one hundred and twenty-five quatrains.[43] The poet examines the calamity against the backdrop of this country's historic relations with Britain. Ireland prospered until such time as contact between the two islands was established. The relationship appears never to have favoured the Irish, when one recollects matters like the suffering inflicted on them during Cromwell's presence here or the iniquitous Penal Laws. Ó Cearnaigh blames the English government unequivocally for this latest instance of criminal neglect on its part, indicting such figures as the Prime Minister, Lord John Russell, and the Lord Lieutenant, George William Frederick Villiers, fourth earl of Clarendon:

> Seán beag Ruiséal pocán gan éifeacht
> Bhí an tan ina cheannphort ós na réigiúin;
> Fear ionaid an Rí i nÁth Cliath níorbh fhearr é
> Clarendon ciapach, cíorlach, scléipeach.

41 Maynooth MS R 69: p. 427 *m*, published by P. Ó Fiannachta, *Lámhscríbhinní Gaeilge Choláiste Phádraig, Má Nuad: Clár* (Maynooth, 1967), iv, p. 67.
42 NLI MS G 634 (a): p. 54.
43 NLI MS G 545, described by Ó Macháin, *Catalogue ... National Library of Ireland*, xi, pp. 79-80. The text is not given in Ó Dufaigh and Ó Doibhlin, *Nioclás Ó Cearnaigh*.

Little John Russell, a bloated, ineffectual fellow
Was at that time commander of the regions;
The King's deputy [*sic*] in Dublin was no better,
 The tormenting, upsetting braggart Clarendon.

Irish landlords such as William Gregory (afterwards husband of William Butler Yeats's colleague Lady Augusta Gregory) merit censure as well for their merciless conduct towards their tenants:

Bhí stócach bríobach i gcríochaibh Chonnacht,
Greagoire íocas, fíor a ainm,
Do rinn' sé dlighe do dhíchuir céadta
I ngach crích de chríochaibh Éireann.

There was a bribing youth in the province of Connacht, paying Gregory – his name is accurate – he made a law which banished hundreds in each of the territories of Ireland.

Ó Cearnaigh was associated with the Young Ireland nationalist movement, and his contact with this organisation might have given an edge to the foregoing work's partisanship.[44] The movement's anti-Britishness increased as a consequence of the Famine. The organisation supported the 1848 rebellion against a state system which could allow a tragedy of such proportions to take place, in its opinion.[45] The survival in contemporary Gaelic sources of verse compositions supporting certain of the rebellion's leaders may strengthen the impression that Irish speakers viewed the Famine as an injustice.[46] There is a final oblique hint of scribes' attitudes towards the tragedy. In 'Éire án gan cháim ba lachtmhar' Nioclás Ó Cearnaigh employed the type of metre and form characteristic of seventeenth-century Gaelic political poetry lamenting Ireland's fate in Cromwellian and later times.[47] This verse was copied abundantly during the late 1840s and 1850s,[48] a sign, perhaps, of the manner in which contemporary hardships were envisioned.

44 For this contact see Duffy, *O'Kearney*, pp. 31-8, Ó Dufaigh and Ó Doibhlin, *Nioclás Ó Cearnaigh*, pp. 28-34.
45 See K. T. Hoppen, *Ireland since 1800: Conflict & Conformity* (London and New York, 1989), pp. 28-31.
46 See the poem entitled 'Lament of Wm. Smith O Brien and the State convicts of 1849' in NLI MS G 634 (a): pp. 32-3 and the papers relating to the 'State trials at Clonmel in 1848' in RIA MS 12 O 17 (3).
47 C. O'Rahilly (ed.), *Five Seventeenth-Century Political Poems* (Dublin, 1952).
48 See, for example, NLI MS G 422: pp. 212 ff. ('Aiste Dháibhí Cúndún', dated August 1846), ibid.: pp. 282 ff. ('Aiste Sheáin Uí Chonaill', dated February 1852), Maynooth MS DR 4: p. 315 ('Aiste Sheáin Uí Chonaill', MS dated 1854).

Conclusion

This paper does not aim to apportion responsibility for the Great Famine, but seeks instead to focus attention on a distinctive body of evidence about to it. A comparison of the event with similar occurrences elsewhere will probably reveal whether circumstances other than an unavoidable natural disaster contributed to the débâcle. In this connection, when Gaelic speakers contrasted their conditions with those of other communities, particularly from the seventeenth century onwards, the history of the people of Israel was frequently invoked.[49] Coincidentally, the fiftieth anniversary of the liberation of the death camps is being remembered in Europe as the commencement of the Famine one hundred and fifty years ago is recalled in Ireland. One could scarcely claim that the planned and casual brutality of the former was on the same scale as the latter. Nonetheless, there are striking parallels between the nineteenth-century Irish case and that of Jewish and other groups in the twentieth century. The following reminiscences of an English army officer relating to his service in Germany in 1945 echo the situation in Ireland approximately a hundred years previously in some uncanny respects. Captain Robert Daniell was in pursuit of German troops fleeing eastwards when he came across train carriages full of rotting corpses. He suspected a concentration camp was nearby, and sought his superior's permission to investigate. The journalist who has recently published the story[50] reports the captain's memories of entering the compound thus:

> Behind the first door he broke open he found the camp hospital, a hangar full of bunk beds eight tiers high. Every bed was occupied, but 90 per cent of the patients were dead, many of them drowned in excreta from the beds above ... He visited three more buildings. In the first two were hundreds of people, as thin as skeletons, in the last stages of starvation ... In the third hangar Daniell found the swollen, naked body of a woman, five or six days dead, and sitting on it, playing at drawing lots with straw, a group of young children.

Daniell's own final words are as follows:

49 This understanding persists into the twentieth century. For a well-known instance see 'What points of contact existed between these languages ['ancient Hebrew' and 'ancient Irish'] and between the peoples who spoke them? ... their dispersal, persecution, survival and revival', James Joyce, *Ulysses* ([1922] Penguin Modern Classics edition, Harmondsworth, 1969), pp. 608-9. In this and other respects the proposition that Joyce's 'dislike of the Irish language and everything associated with it was pathological' by David Greene, 'Michael Cusack' in C.C. O'Brien (ed.), *The Shaping of Modern Ireland* (London, 1960), p. 77 is wide of the mark.
50 *Independent on Sunday*, 15 January 1995.

There were at least 3000 inmates still just alive. They were all starving, and skeletons to look at. The irony of the whole thing was that outside the wire lay the most fertile parts of the German Rhineland, with fields of potatoes and green vegetables of every kind. Inside the wire the only thing there was to eat was a pile of rotting potatoes.

My two hours were up and I had to go and rejoin the 29th armoured brigade. That was the last I saw of Belsen.

Many writers who survived locations like the foregoing have left accounts of their experiences from within, Primo Levi, Simone Weil, Elie Wiesel. There is a measure of overlap between their descriptions and the Gaelic records considered here, however fragmentary the latter may seem.[51] Discussion of the Irish language and its civilisation from the second half of the nineteenth century usually emphasises their demise. The time-honoured comparison with Jewish tradition may again be *à propos*. Neither culture departed in unbroken silence.

---

51 It should be noted that a third type of evidence also exists in the Irish language concerning the Great Famine, namely Revival literature which uses the event as a source of inspiration in the same way as Patrick Kavanagh did in English with reference to the intellectual and spiritual impoverishment of his own time. See for instance the short story entitled 'Gorta' ['Famine'] in Máirtín Ó Cadhain, *An tSraith ar Lár* (Second impression, Dublin, 1970), pp. 27-31. This great twentieth-century Gaelic prose stylist's work is replete with explorations of distress and decline (material, social and psychological) which may perhaps be described as post-Famine in their resonances.

Literature, Memory, Atrocity

CHRIS MORASH

[Scene: Pub interior]

Bull McCabe: Who would insult me by bidding for my field here in Carraig-thomond?

Mick Flanagan: There might be outsiders, Bull.

Bull: Outsiders? Outsiders? Are these the same 'outsiders' who took the corn from our mouths when the potatoes went rotten in the ditches?

Flanagan: Ah, now Bull ...

Bull: Are these the same 'outsiders' who took the meat from the tables when we lay in the ditches with the grass juice running green from our mouths?

Flanagan: Take it easy ...

Bull: Are these the same 'outsiders' who drove us to the coffin ships and scattered us to the four corners of the earth? Are these the same 'outsiders' who watched whilst our valley went silent except for the sound of the last starving child?

Flanagan: The English are gone, Bull.

Bull: Gone. Because I drove 'em out. Me. And my kind. Gone. But not forgotten, Flanagan. No 'outsider' will bid for my field.[1]

This scene from Jim Sheridan's 1990 film, *The Field*, is among the more recent (and, given the film's success, among the most widely distributed) representations of the Great Irish Famine of the 1840s. However, like many such representations, it can only invoke the Famine because of an almost invisible form of anachronism which becomes apparent when we focus on the language used by Richard Harris's character, the Bull McCabe: 'took the corn from *our* mouths'; '*we* lay in the ditches with the grass juice running green from *our* mouths'; 'drove *us* to the coffin ships and scattered *us* to the four corners of the earth'. When McCabe speaks of the Famine, it is as if it were something that had happened to him, something he remembered. And yet, as the pub owner, Mick Flanagan, reminds us, 'the English are gone' – that is to say, at the very least, the film is set after 1922; indeed, the car and clothes owned by Tom Berenger's

---

1 Jim Sheridan (dir.), *The Field* (Granada Films, 1990).

character, 'the Yank', suggest that it may be set more than a decade later.[2] This means that in order to have an actual memory of the Famine, the Bull McCabe would have to be at least in his nineties – which he obviously is not unless he is an exceptionally spry ninety.

How do we explain this apparent anachronism? Has Sheridan slipped up in his chronology? Or is it naive to expect such verisimilitude in a film which tries so earnestly in its final moments to mythologise the past? Neither answer is fully satisfactory. Instead, we must think of 'memory' as it is used in this scene as the middle term in an equation connecting literature and atrocity.

Literature

When I first saw this scene in *The Field*, I was reminded of a passage dealing with the Famine in Canon Sheehan's 1905 novel, *Glenanaar*:

> It is an appalling picture, that which springs up to memory. Gaunt spectres move here and there, looking at one another out of hollow eyes of despair and gloom.[3]

Although Sheehan claims that this image of the Famine 'springs to memory', 'memory' is here playing the same trick that we saw in *The Field*. Neither Canon Sheehan, nor the narrator-priest who is his fictional replacement, could, in fact, 'remember' the Famine. Sheehan was not born until 1852, when the Famine was, for all intents and purposes, over. So, as in the case of Bull McCabe, we have to ask: what is he 'remembering'?

We can begin to find an answer to this question by looking at the rest of the passage:

> It is an appalling picture, that which springs up to memory. Gaunt spectres move here and there, looking at one another out of hollow eyes of despair and gloom. Ghosts walk the land. Great giant figures, reduced to skeletons by hunger, shake in their clothes, which hang loose around their attenuated frames ... Here and there by the wayside a corpse stares at the passers-by, as it lies against the hedge where it had sought shelter. The pallor of its face is darkened by lines of green around the mouth, the dry juice of grass and nettles.[4]

2 Sheridan deliberately strips *The Field* of the references to television and aeroplanes which occur in the John B. Keane play on which the film is based, thereby locating it earlier than the 1965 setting of the play.

3 Patrick Sheehan, *Glenanaar* (London, 1905; Rpt. Dublin, 1989), pp. 198-9.

4 Ibid., pp. 198-9.

All of the images which appear in this passage can be found in earlier attempts to write the Famine. This suggests that what Sheehan is actually 'remembering' are other Famine texts. Indeed, in many cases, his memory extends to the vocabulary of those earlier texts, particularly in his use of the word 'spectre'. For instance, if we turn back to the Famine literature of the late 1840s, we will find poems such as 'The Spectre':

> Far west a grim shadow was seen, as 'tis said,
> Like a spectre from Famine and Pestilence bred:
> His gaunt giant-form, with pale Poverty wed ...[5]

Employing a variation on this motif, the *Mayo Constitution* reported in 1848 that 'the streets of every town in the county are overrun by stalking skeletons'.[6] Moreover, this image of the Famine as a 'stalking skeleton' or 'spectre' was still in use as Sheehan was writing in 1905. For instance, a Catholic Truth Society pamphlet from the turn of the century, entitled *The Famine Years*, contains the following passage:

> The dread *spectre* of famine had already set foot on the shores of Ireland, and was making ready to *stalk* through the fruitful land, from north to south, from east to west [emphasis added].[7]

Later in the same Catholic Truth Society pamphlet, we find the image of the corpse with a green mouth, mentioned by both Sheehan and the Bull McCabe:

> In Mayo a man, who had been observed searching for shell-fish on the seashore, was afterwards found dead, after vainly endeavouring to satisfy the cravings of devouring hunger with grass and turf.[8]

Once again, this image has a genealogy as an image of the Famine going back to the 1840s, and can be found in Famine-era texts such as 'The Boreen Side', by James Tighe, which first appeared in 1849:

> A stripling, the last of his race, lies dead
> In a nook by the Boreen side;
> The rivulet runs by his board and his bed,
> Where he ate the green cresses and died.[9]

5 H.D., 'The Spectre: Stanzas With Illustrations' in Chris Morash (ed.), *The Hungry Voice: The Poetry of the Irish Famine* (Dublin, 1989), p. 261.
6 'Death by Starvation' in *United Irishman* i, 5 (11 March 1848), p. 46.
7 Joseph Guinan, *The Famine Years* (Dublin, 1908), p. 15.
8 Ibid., p. 15.
9 James Tighe, 'The Boreen Side', in Morash, *The Hungry Voice*, p. 73.

In tracing the use of these images as representations of the Famine of the 1840s, I am not disputing that they correspond to a concrete reality, albeit an absent one. Their appearance in numerous newspaper reports, travellers' journals, and government documents of the period suggests that such horrific images were originally intended to be mimetic representations of things that actually existed. For instance, in a newspaper account of an inquest held in 1848, we find the image of the corpse with the green mouth:

> A poor man, whose name we could not learn ... lay down on the road-side, where shortly after he was found dead, his face turned to the earth, and a portion of the grass and turf on which he lay masticated in his mouth.[10]

What interests me about such representations is not whether or not they were once empirically true; we can never fully answer that question. Instead, I want to focus on the way in which they were transformed in the process of textual transmission, which happens in and through language.

We must begin by recognising that even before the Famine was acknowledged as a complete event, it was in the process of being textually encoded in a limited number of clearly defined images. Indeed, for an event which we customarily think of as being vast, the archive of images in which it is represented is relatively small and circumscribed. As the nineteenth century progressed, these images became more and more rigidly defined, taking on the characteristics of Lyotard's 'rigid designators'. By the 1870s the Famine had become an increasingly potent element in the propaganda war which accompanied the struggle for land ownership, and as a consequence Famine images such as the 'stalking spectre' and the green-mouthed corpse were repeated in magazines like the *Irish Monthly Magazine* until they had the boldly defined outlines of religious icons. By the turn of the century, such images were so widely known that they could be said to constitute a form of collectively maintained 'memory'.

Memory

When I call these images from the archive of Famine literature 'memories', I am not thinking of memory here as passive recollection; instead, I am thinking of what memory theorists call 'constructive memory', which integrates past, present and future in such as way as to create the impression of a 'unified personal history'.[11] When constructive memories are shared by a group of people – as

10 'Inquests' in *United Irishman* i, 14 (13 May 1848), p. 211.
11 Gillian Cohen, *Memory in the Real World* (East Sussex, 1989), p. 219. See also Maurice Halbwachs, *The Collective Memory* (New York, 1980).

indeed they must be if they originate in a printed text – they create the impression of a unified collective history, in which the memories of the individual and memories shared by the literate members of society as a whole are the same. If we think of textually generated memories in this manner, it becomes apparent that they have an ideological function – indeed, they are almost pure ideology, insofar as they create an illusion of complete identity between the individual and society.

In order to understand the ideological function of these textually generated memories, it is necessary to understand something of their form. Like the Bull McCabe's account of the Famine, or the passage from Canon Sheehan's *Glenanaar*, most representations of the Famine tend to be made up of static, iconic tableaux, each existing in a single timeless moment. Even attempts at longer Famine narratives, stretching from William Carleton's 1847 novel, *The Black Prophet*, to John Banville's 1973 novel, *Birchwood*, incorporate these iconic representations of the Famine, but rarely use them as causal elements in the plot. In *The Black Prophet*, for instance, when the conventional blackmail story which gives the novel its form has been resolved, the Famine disappears. In the case of *Birchwood*, with its postmodern refiguration of cause and effect in narrative structure, the Famine is brought in as yet one more element in a shifting collage of public and family history. In these two very different Famine novels, and in others written in the decades which separate them, we find that there is no single metanarrative of the Famine in literature. Instead, we find that the Famine as a textual event is composed of a group of images whose meaning does not derive from their strategic location within a narrative, but rather from the strangeness and horror of the images themselves, as dislocated, isolated emblems of suffering.

The disconnected form of these images means that they are available for appropriation by other narratives, other forms of discourse. Reading through the literature of the Famine, one finds that such appropriation is rife. For instance, in John Mitchel's *Last Conquest of Ireland (Perhaps)* of 1864 there is an often quoted passage describing the condition of the countryside after the failure of the potato crop. It appears, however, in the midst of his account of the nationalist attempt to win an election in Galway in 1847:

> In the depth of winter we travelled to Galway, through the very centre of that fertile island, and saw sights that will never wholly leave the eyes that beheld them:– cowering wretches, almost naked in the savage weather, prowling in turnip-fields, and endeavouring to grub up roots which had been left, but running to hide as the mail-coach rolled by; ... groups and families, sitting or wandering on the high-road, with failing steps and

dim, patient eyes, gazing hopelessly into infinite darkness; before them, around them, above them, nothing but darkness and despair.[12]

With the Miltonic echoes of the final phrases, this is a powerful representation of human suffering; however, it appears in Mitchel's narrative only as an aside in a chapter that is primarily concerned with the campaign for the Galway election. Mitchel later makes a half-hearted attempt to suggest that in such extreme conditions, he was 'justified in urging so desperate a measure' as revolution.[13] The passage, however, is not fully integrated in the text, and it is the failure of the nationalists to win the Galway election rather than the suffering of the 'cowering wretches' which becomes the rationale for taking up arms.

Moreover, this passage in *The Last Conquest* shares with a number of other Famine texts a detached perspective, as the narrator views the starving peasantry through the windows of a moving coach. For instance, there is an often re-printed account of the Famine by Father Theobald Matthew in which he describes travelling from Dublin to Cork by coach, and seeing 'the wretched people seated on the fences of their decaying gardens, wringing their hands and wailing bitterly the destruction that had left them foodless'.[14] Later, in a 1937 Famine novel by Louis J. Walsh, entitled *The Next Time*, the hero, travelling by coach from Dublin to his home in Gortnanaan, sees 'cowering wretches, almost naked in the savage weather, endeavouring to grub up roots that had been left behind in the ground'[15] in a passage which, like many others in the novel, shamelessly echoes Mitchel's *Last Conquest*.

Hence, the fragmentary way in which the Famine is represented makes it liable to appropriation by larger narratives, such as those of Mitchel, Fr Matthew, and Louis J. Walsh. Having no narrative of their own, put possessing a hard-edged clarity that has been refined through decades of repetition, these Famine icons are transmitted to us like something flashing by the windows of a moving coach – unforgettable glimpses of a narrative whose full development is always just beyond our line of vision.

Atrocity

We can begin to understand the resistance of these Famine icons to longer, sequential narratives by turning to two Famine texts. The first, a poem called

---

12 John Mitchel, *The Last Conquest of Ireland (Perhaps)* (Glasgow, n.d [1861]), p. 147.
13 Ibid., p. 150.
14 Theobald Matthew in John O'Rourke, *History of the Great Irish Famine* (Dublin, 1875), p. 149.
15 L.J. Walsh, *The Next Time: A Story of 'Forty Eight* (Dublin, 1919), p. 155.

'The Three Angels', was written in 1848 by a working class nationalist, John De Jean Frazer:

> Some gathered their kith to a fugitive band
> And sought the stars of a happier land; —
> Themselves and their kindred, thro' sheer despair,
> Some slew, in belief that *to slay* was *to spare*! —
> A cannibal fierceness but ill-suppressed
> In many — made some — we must veil the rest![16]

Frazer's poem can be read in the context of a passage from William Carleton's 1851 novel, *The Squanders of Castle Squander*, in which he describes a cemetery being desecrated by wild dogs:

> Round about the awful cemetery, were numbers of gaunt and starving dogs, whose skeleton bodies and fearful howlings indicated the ravenous fury with which they awaited an opportunity to drag the unfortunate dead from their shallow graves and glut themselves upon their bodies. Here and there an arm; in another place a head (half-eaten by some famished mongrel, who had been frightened from his prey), or a leg, dragged partially from the earth, and half-mangled, might be seen; altogether, presenting such a combination of horrible imagery as can scarcely be conceived by our readers.[17]

These images of cannibalism and desecration of the dead constitute another of the memories which make up the archive of Famine literature. In the texts of both Frazer and Carleton, however, there is an inability to complete the image. 'We must veil the rest', writes Frazer; 'such horrible imagery', writes Carleton, 'can scarcely be conceived by our readers'. Commenting on representations of the Irish Famine, Steven Marcus notes: 'The constant refrain of those who observed the famine is, "It cannot be described". "The scenes which presented themselves were such as no tongue or pen can convey the slightest idea of ". "It is impossible to go through the detail". "Believe me, my dear Sir, the reality in most cases far exceeded description. Indeed none can conceive what it was but those who were in it." ' As Marcus points out, these are very modern voices, telling us that 'however mad, wild, or grotesque art may seem to be, it can never touch or approach the madness of reality'.[18] They also help to explain

---

16 John 'de Jean' Frazer, in Morash, *The Hungry Voice*, p. 187.
17 William Carleton, *The Squanders of Castle Squander* (2 vols., London, 1852), ii, p. 138.
18 Steven Marcus, 'Hunger and Ideology' in *Representations: Essays on Literature and Society* (New York, 1990), pp. 10-11.

why the literature of the Famine contains so many iconic fragments. The un-willingness of these commentators to describe the scenes of Famine suffering is more than simply mid-Victorian prudishness or a conventional nod in the di-rection of an unspeakable sublime. After all, it was in the interest of Irish nation-alist writers and those campaigning for greater government intervention to emphasise the suffering caused by the Famine; and yet a militant nationalist such as John De Jean Frazer is as inclined to 'veil the rest' as his imperialist, free market counterparts. Instead, we must consider structural incompletion as a feature of the representation of atrocity.

'Atrocity' is a word to be used with the greatest of care in relation to the Famine, for it suggests elements of intentionality which simplify matters to an unacceptable degree. Nonetheless, Lawrence Langer's 1975 study, *The Holo-caust and the Literary Imagination*, provides a useful definition of the term when considering the writing of the Famine when he writes of a similar inability to construct sequential narratives among writers dealing with the Holocaust. 'The kind of atrocity at issue here', he writes, 'assaulted the very coherence of time and led to the breakdown of "chronology" as a meaningful conception'.[19] When we are talking about atrocity – at least in Langer's sense – we are talking about suffering that is disproportionate to its causes: hugely, grossly disproportionate. Because atrocity upsets our sense of cause and effect, it hampers our ability to construct sequential narratives which follow the conventions of mimetic liter-ary representation. It may well be as a consequence of this breakdown of literary convention that the literature of the Famine is constructed as an archive of free-floating signs, capable of incorporation in any number of sequential semiotic systems, including the constructive personal memory which seeks to unite past, present and future in the creation of an individual identity.

In an early essay, 'A Kind of Survivor', George Steiner attests to the ability of such textually generated shards of memory to become a part of an individu-al's sense of identity. Steiner begins the essay by describing himself as a 'kind of survivor' of the Holocaust:

> Not literally. Due to my father's foresight ... I came to America in Janu-ary 1940, during the phoney war. We left France, where I was born and brought up, in safety. So I happened not to be there when the names were called out ... But in another sense I am a survivor, and not intact ... If that which haunts me and controls my habits of feeling strikes many of those I should be intimate and working with in my present world as remotely sinister and artificial, it is because the black mystery of what happened in Europe is to me indivisible from my own identity.[20]

19 L.L. Langer, *The Holocaust and the Literary Imagination* (London, 1975), p. 251.
20 George Steiner, 'A Kind of Survivor', in *Language and Silence: Essays 1958-1966* (London, 1985), p. 164.

The literature of the Famine provokes something of the same response; when we read a Famine text, we too feel that we are 'a kind of survivor'. It may be that when we encounter these shattered fragments of the past, we wish to complete them; and the only way in which we can do so is by internalising them, making them part of the narrative of our own memories.

When we do embrace these icons as part of our own past, however, we must undertake a project which Steiner's recent literary criticism has resisted with a stridency which makes his work look increasingly archaic; we must constantly remind ourselves that we are participating in ideology. In accepting these shared memories, we are enlisting ourselves as part of a group – a nation, a tribe, a race. In keeping these memories alive, we may be doing no more than bearing witness, trying to make whole that which the form of these images tells us can never be made whole. But such a longing for wholeness is not without its dangers; and it is here that the final mention of the Famine in *The Field* can act as a warning. As the Bull McCabe beats the 'outsider' to death by slamming his head repeatedly against a rock, he bellows to his son:

> See this fella here? See this Yank? His family lived around here, but when the going got tough they ran away to America. They ran away from the Famine – while we stayed. Do you understand? We stayed! We stayed!! We stayed!!![21]

This should serve to remind us that while memories created by literature and born of atrocity may often seem like a testimony of human decency, they nonetheless have the potential to perpetuate the atrocity which they memorialise by providing the justification for a future which is envisaged in terms of the iconic, clearly-defined narrative structure which the past so often lacks.

21 Sheridan, *The Field.*

The Female Gaze:
Asenath Nicholson's Famine Narrative

MARGARET KELLEHER

Asenath Nicholson's record of 'The Famine of 1847, '48 and '49', first published in 1850 as the third part of her study of Irish history entitled *Lights and
Shades of Ireland*, is one of a large number of eye-witness accounts from the
period. These descriptive and individualised narratives by contemporary observers such as Nicholas Cummins, William Bennett, William Forster and Syd-
ney Osborne constitute a significant but frequently neglected historical source.
The omission or scant reference to these writings in Famine historiography
suggests a fear, on the part of some historians, of their emotive potential along
with a suspicion that they do not constitute a sufficiently objective source. In
those histories where eye-witness accounts are mentioned, they frequently serve
as a type of shorthand for famine's effects, given in isolation from other aspects
of the Famine study and without any detailed analysis of their original context,
audience or reception. Substantial work is yet to be done on the nature and
influence of observers' accounts, in relation both to the original context in
which they appeared and the occasions in which they have been reproduced,
albeit infrequent. The texts of these accounts themselves deserve a close examination, moving beyond questions of putative accuracy to the type of detail
chosen for representation, the existence of recurring motifs, the role of the
observer and the creation of a famine spectacle. Drawing from cinematic theories of 'gaze' and 'spectacle', this article presents a re-reading or re-visioning of
Asenath Nicholson's famine account; re-vision, in the words of Adrienne Rich,
being 'the act of looking back, of seeing with fresh eyes, of entering an old text
from a new critical direction.'[1]

Contemporary film criticism, in particular the work of feminist film theorists, provides a richly suggestive perspective from which to view the writings of
Nicholson and others. In a pioneering article, entitled 'Visual Pleasure and Narrative Cinema' and published in 1975, Laura Mulvey argued that mainstream
cinema invites the spectator to identify with a male gaze which objectifies the
female; woman is thus the object of the gaze, 'to-be-looked-at-ness'.[2] Mulvey's
identification of 'woman as image, man as bearer of the look' is exemplified

1 Adrienne Rich, 'When We Dead Awaken: Writing as Re-Vision' in *On Lies, Secrets
and Silence* (New York, 1979), p. 35.
2 Laura Mulvey, 'Visual Pleasure and Narrative Cinema' in *Screen* xiv, 3 (1975), pp. 6-18.

throughout representations of famine, in which individual victims are characterised most frequently as female, by predominantly male observers. Developing Mulvey's work, some film critics have investigated the nature of a female
gaze and the positioning of a female spectator: what happens when a woman
looks?[3] In exploring these questions, feminist film theory faces many of the
problems and dangers encountered by feminist literary studies: defining the realm
of the female may involve positing a female specificity, woman as nature, as
mother, which reproduces and reinforces the old dualisms of culture and nature. Female perspectives also risk becoming an unchallengeable 'authentic'
expression. With reference to this particular study of Nicholson's famine text,
the danger is of positing a 'pure female gaze'.

The writings of Judith Mayne and Christine Gledhill, two more recent theorists, resonate in interesting ways with Nicholson's narrative. In arguing that
film theory's over-concentration on the psycho-linguistic has neglected social,
economic and political practices, Gledhill's work parallels the move by other
feminist writers from the 'textual' to the 'social' subject.[4] Her work is of particular interest in studying famine texts, both in its emphasis on the importance
of social and economic formations and in its identification of 'textual negotiation'. Gledhill defines the dynamics of a text and of its reception as processes of
'negotiation' in which 'meaning arises out of a struggle or negotiation between
competing frames of reference, motivation and experience'; the critic is thus
one who analyses 'the conditions and possibilities of reading', who 'opens up
the negotiations of the text in order to animate the contradictions in play.'[5]

Drawing from analysis of the novel, Judith Mayne similarly defines narrative
as a 'form of negotiation', in this case between the private and the public spheres,
with female writing in novels and in cinema involving an 'intensification' of
such negotiations.[6] As a summary of women's relationship to the cinema, Mayne
has formulated the expressive phrase, 'the woman at the keyhole':

> On one side of the corridor is a woman who peeks, on the other, the
> woman who is, as it were, on display ... The history of women's rela-

---

3 See Linda Williams, 'When the Woman Looks' in M.A. Doane, P. Mellencamp and L.
   Williams (eds), *Re-Vision: Essays in Feminist Film Criticism* (Maryland/ Los Angeles,
   1984); Lorraine Gamman and Margaret Marshment, *The Female Gaze* (London, 1988)
   and E.A. Kaplan, *Women and Film: Both Sides of the Camera* (London, 1983).
4 Christine Gledhill, 'Recent Developments in Feminist Film Criticism' in *Quarterly
   Review of Film Studies* iii, 4 (1978), republished in Doane et al., *Re-Vision*, pp. 18-48;
   idem, 'Pleasurable Negotiations' in E.D. Pribram (ed.), *Female Spectators* (London, 1988),
   pp. 64-89.
5 Gledhill, 'Pleasurable Negotiations', pp. 68, 74-5.
6 Judith Mayne, 'The Woman at the Keyhole: Women's Cinema and Feminist Criticism' in *New German Critique* xxiii (1981), republished in Doane et al., *Re-Vision*, pp.
   49-66.

tionship to the cinema, from this side of the keyhole, has been a series of
tentative peeks; that threshold ... crossed with difficulty.[7]

The key-hole and threshold mark the boundary between public and private
spheres, between outside and inside; rooms and homes being viewed tradition-
ally as women's space. Drawing on the work of women film-makers, Mayne
contemplates what happens 'if women cast a cinematic gaze inside rooms': the
construction of narrative space from a female perspective.[8] Nicholson's famine
writing, read in light of these studies, demonstrates the operations of a female
gaze, its specific negotiations and thresholds 'crossed with difficulty'.

Asenath Hatch Nicholson was born in Vermont in the late eighteenth century, where she worked as a teacher, before moving to New York in the 1830s.
A strict teetotaller and vegetarian, and follower of Sylvester Graham, a Presby-
terian minister, she opened the Graham Temperance Boarding-house in New
York, later described as 'the resort of hundreds of choice spirits from all parts of
the country, including most of the names of those who were engaged in measures of social reform.'[9] Nicholson first arrived in Ireland in June 1844; her book,
*Ireland's Welcome to the Stranger; or, Excursions through Ireland in 1844, and 1845, for
the purpose of personally investigating the condition of the poor*, first published in 1847,
records her travels around Ireland, staying in lodging-houses and in cabins, including the homes of servant-girls whom Nicholson had employed in New
York.[10] As well as 'personally investigating the condition of the poor' Nicholson
sought to distribute and read the Bible among the Irish, having obtained a stock
of Bibles, some in English and some in Irish, from the Hibernian Bible Society.
Nicholson's independence of spirit and her ability to disturb and perplex her
contemporaries are clear from the memorable editorial published in the *Achill
Herald* of June 1845:

> She lodges with the peasantry, and alleges that her object is to become
> acquainted with Irish character. This stranger is evidently a person of
> some talent, and although the singular course which she pursues is ut-
> terly at variance with the modesty and retiredness to which the Bible
> gives a prominent place in its delineation of a virtuous female, she pro-
> fesses to have no ordinary regard for that Holy Book ... It appears to us
> that the principal object of this woman's mission is to create a spirit of
> discontent among the lower orders and to dispose them to regard their

7 Ibid., pp. 54-5.
8 Ibid., p. 55.
9 J.L., 'Introduction' in Asenath Nicholson, *Annals of the Famine in Ireland, in 1847, 1848,
   and 1849* (New York, 1851).
10 Asenath Nicholson, *Ireland's Welcome to the Stranger; or, Excursions through Ireland in 1844,
   and 1845, for the Purpose of Personally Investigating the Condition of the Poor* (London, 1847).

superiors as so many unfeeling oppressors ... There is nothing either in her conduct or conversation to justify the supposition of insanity, and we strongly suspect that she is the emissary of some democratic or revolutionary society.[11]

Nicholson's particular denominational affiliation remains unclear; Alfred Sheppard, author of the preface to the 1926 reprint of *Ireland's Welcome*, notes that nowhere does Nicholson give a clue to her own denomination, 'if indeed it had any other member than herself'.[12] Similarly, in *Lights and Shades of Ireland*, Nicholson gives a detailed account of the various denominations existing in Ireland such as Presbyterians, the Society of Friends, Methodists and others, and describes herself as 'a listener who belongs to no one of them'.[13]

Returning to Ireland in late 1846, Nicholson spent the next two years travelling around famine-stricken areas: based in Dublin for six months, she moved in July 1847 to the north of Ireland, visiting Belfast, Donegal, Derry, Arranmore; the autumn of 1847 and winter 1847-8 she spent in the west, including Tuam, Ballina, Achill Island; in summer and autumn 1848 she visited Munster, before leaving Ireland in late 1848 or early 1849. Nicholson's account of what she had seen, entitled 'The Famine of 1847, '48 and '49', was first published in London in 1850, along with her accounts of early Irish history and of 'saints, kings, and poets, of the early ages'. In April 1851, the famine account was published in New York as a separate volume; a 'tale of woe' which, according to its editor 'J.L.', 'should be read by the whole American people; it will have a salutary effect upon their minds, to appreciate more fully the depth of oppression and wretchedness from which the Irish poor escape in coming to this land of plenty.'[14]

Both Nicholson's commentaries and the author herself emphasise the breadth and depth of her investigation, entering people's homes, in city and countryside: 'walking and riding, with money and without, in castle and cabin, in bog and in glen, by land and by water, in church and in chapel, with rector, curate and priest.'[15] In the preface to *Lights and Shades* the author warns the reader of the horrors, the 'fearful realities' which she has witnessed, and stresses the uniqueness of her perspective:

> The reader of these pages should be told that, if strange things are recorded, it was because strange things were seen; and if strange things

---

11 *Achill Missionary Herald and Western Witness*, 25 June 1845, p. 65.
12 A.T. Sheppard, 'Introduction' in Asenath Nicholson, *The Bible in Ireland* (abridged version of *Ireland's Welcome*; London, 1926).
13 Asenath Nicholson, *Lights and Shades of Ireland* (London, 1850) p. 419.
14 J. L., 'Introduction' in Asenath Nicholson, *Annals of the Famine in Ireland, in 1847, 1848, and 1849* (New York, 1851).
15 Nicholson, *Lights and Shades of Ireland*, p. 438.

were seen which no other writer has written, it was because no other writer has visited the same places, under the same circumstances. No other writer ever explored mountain and glen for four years, with the same object in view; ... And now, while looking at them calmly at a distance, they appear, even to myself, more like a dream than reality, because they appear out of *common course*, and out of the order of even nature itself. But they *are* realities, and many of them fearful ones – *realities* which none but eye-witnesses can understand, and none but those who passed through them can *feel*.

The distinctive nature of her position is attributed both to her identity as woman: 'My task was a different one – operating individually. I took my own time and way – as woman is wont to do, when at her own option'[16], and as 'foreigner':

I was attached to England as the race from which I descended, and pitied Ireland for her sufferings, rather than I admired her for any virtues which she might possess; consequently my mind was so balanced between the two, that on which side the scale might have preponderated, the danger of blind partiality would not have been so great.[17]

Later Nicholson identifies a bias to which she, as female outsider, is distinctively vulnerable: 'the danger of that excessive pity or blind fondness, which a kind mother feels for a deformed or half-idiot child, which all the world, if not the *father* himself, sets aside as a thing of nought.'[18]

Nicholson's famine narrative includes a number of striking individualised accounts, offered almost reluctantly and quite apologetically, as 'specimens, not wishing to be tedious with such narrations, only to show the character of the famine, and its effects in general on the sufferers, with whom I was conversant.'[19] Two of the most memorable descriptions of famine victims occur quite early in the narrative, while Nicholson is still in Dublin, and provide interesting examples of Nicholson's singular 'negotiations', with regard to her own position and her encounters with others.

Nicholson's first sight of 'a starving person' occurs in Kingstown/Dun Laoghaire:

A servant in the house where I was stopping, at Kingstown, said that the milk woman wished me to see a man near by, that was in a state of actual starvation; and he was going out to attempt to work on the Queen's highway; a little labour was beginning outside the house, and fifteen-

16 Ibid., p. 229.
17 Ibid., pp. 8-9.

18 Ibid., p. 10.
19 Ibid., p. 233.

pence-a-day stimulated this poor man, who had seven to support, his rent to pay, and fuel to buy.[20]

The description of her encounter with the starving man is prefaced by an apostrophe to the reader:

> and reader, if you never have seen a starving being, *may you never!* In my childhood I had been frighted with the stories of ghosts, and had seen actual skeletons; but imagination had come short of the sight of this man ... [he] was emaciated to the last degree; he was tall, his eyes prominent, his skin shrivelled, his manner cringing and childlike; and the impression *then* and *there* made never *has* nor ever *can* be effaced.[21]

Nicholson's observations contain motifs common to other eye-witness accounts: the physical description of the man, the sense of a reality exceeding the possibilities of imagination. Much less frequent is her explicit inclusion of political and economic analysis, in this case a ringing condemnation of official methods of payment: 'Workmen are not paid at night on the public works, they must wait a week; and if they commence labour in a state of hunger, they often die before the week expires.' In contrast to many other eye-witness accounts in which encountering and distributing famine relief requires male authorization and mediation, frequently from local ministers, priests or doctors, Nicholson's distribution of food occurs during the family's absence, with help provided by the servant. References to entrances and gates, which carry crucial material consequences, permeate Nicholson's narrative: the labourers are 'called in' to the kitchen for food while others are fed at the door; the eventual locking of the gate, the barring of access, painfully signifies the exhaustion of supplies; while an unexpected donation from New York allows the unlocking of the gate, once the 'man of the house' has left for his business in Dublin.

Soon after this episode, Nicholson details another encounter, on this occasion with a widow who she meets 'creeping upon the street, one cold night', carrying 'a few boxes of matches, to see if she could sell them, for she told me she could not yet bring herself to beg; she could work, and was willing to, could she get knitting or sewing.'[22] The woman is reluctant to give Nicholson the number of her home; having given an indirect promise to call some future day and meaning to take the woman 'by surprise', Nicholson recounts that 'at ten the next morning my way was made into that fearful street, and still more

20 Ibid., p. 224. This episode and other extracts from Nicholson's famine narrative have been anthologised in Seamus Deane (ed.), *The Field Day Anthology of Irish Writing*, (3 vols., Derry, 1991), ii, pp. 133–45.
21 Nicholson, *Lights and Shades of Ireland*, pp. 224–5.
22 Ibid., p. 230.

fearful alley, which led to the cheerless abode I entered.' Her journey through the city's 'retired streets and dark alleys' involves 'finding my way through darkness and filth' until 'a sight opened upon me, which, speaking moderately was startling.' The description of this sight, as Nicholson's gaze travels around the room, from the dark corner at her right to the other side of the empty grate, includes features common to other famine accounts: the empty fire, the woman without a dress, pawned to pay rent, the man without a coat 'likewise pawned', and Nicholson's initial muteness at the sight. Less frequent is the breaking of the pause by the widow Nicholson had encountered earlier; very rarely in such accounts do the suffering victims speak. In this case, a conversation takes place, one of the women is named, and, even rarer, the encounter emerges as the first of many such visits: 'daily did I go and cook their food, or see it cooked.'[23]

Nicholson's repeated crossing of the threshold of this 'forbidding', 'uncom-fortable' and 'wretched' abode occurs in marked contrast to many other eye-witness accounts in which the beholder remains standing at the threshold or outside. The following extract from the Earl of Dufferin's account of his one-day visit to Skibbereen in 1847 is typical in its positioning of the male spectator:

> Conversing on these subjects, we reached a most miserable portion of the town; the houses were mere hovels, dark and dismal in the inside, damp and filthy to the most offensive degree. So universal and virulent was the fever, that we were forced to choose among several houses to discover one or more which it would be safe to enter. At length, Mr Townsend singled out one. We stood on the threshold and looked in; the darkness of the interior was such, that we were scarcely able to distin-guish objects; the walls were bare, the floor of mud, and not a vestige of furniture.[24]

The perspectives offered by Dufferin and other contemporary observers further exemplify Laura Mulvey's comments on the gendered split between spectacle and narrative: women, or famine victims, represent 'icon' or 'spectacle' while the male protagonist 'articulates the look and creates the action.'[25] In Nicholson's narrative, however, both the female protagonist/ narrator and the women she observes possess an active role. Most rarely, Nicholson's entrance into the peo-ple's home and her giving of food are reciprocated: 'Often late in the evening would I hear a soft footstep on the stairs, followed by a gentle tap, and the unassuming Mary would enter with her bountiful supply of fire kindling.'[26] In

23 Ibid., pp. 231-2.
24 Earl of Dufferin and Hon. G.F. Boyle, *Narrative of a Journey from Oxford to Skibbereen during the Year of the Irish Famine* (Oxford, 1847), pp. 12-13.
25 Mulvey, 'Visual Pleasure', pp. 12-13.
26 Nicholson, *Lights and Shades of Ireland*, p. 232.

addition, as part of a continued emphasis throughout her narrative on women's desire and duty to work, Mary and her friend are presented as 'good expert knitters and good sempstresses' who repair Nicholson's clothing.

The account of the 1840s famine provided in *Lights and Shades of Ireland* is also distinguished by its interweaving of detailed analysis of famine's causation with representation of famine's effects. Nicholson engages directly and vehemently with contemporary views such as the attribution of famine to God's providence: 'God is slandered, where it is called an unavoidable dispensation of His wise providence, to which we should all humbly bow, as a chastisement which could not be avoided'.[27] Her comments on the availability of food provide an early treatment of what has become one of the most controversial issues in famine history: the question of the existence of 'sufficient' food in Ireland; while they also anticipate late twentieth-century debates as to the relation between famine and entitlement to food:

> and never was a famine on earth, in *any* part, when there was not an abundance in *some* part, to make up all the deficiency; ... Yes, unhesitatingly may it be said, that there was not a week during that famine, but there was sufficient food for the wants of that week, and *more* than sufficient.[28]

Nicholson also castigates the government systems charged with transportation and distribution of grain, her strong individual grievance being the wasting of grain on the making of alcohol, while she deems many government officials or 'hirelings' guilty of crimes ranging from unnecessary delay in distribution of relief to direct embezzlement of government funds. Arguing that if the 'immediate breaking forth' of famine 'could not have been foreseen or prevented, its sad effects might have been met without the loss of life', she concludes, in a bitter satire of political economy, that 'the principle of throwing away life today, lest means to protect it to-morrow might be lessened, was fully and practically carried on and carried out.'[29]

On a number of occasions in her narrative, Nicholson draws analogies between the position of American slaves and the Irish lower-classes: 'never had I seen slaves so degraded ... These poor creatures are in as virtual bondage to their landlords and superiors as is possible for mind and body to be.'[30] In a passage strikingly prophetic of studies on the origins and ambivalences of colonial discourse,[31] she declares that existing laws

27 Ibid., p. 237.
28 Ibid., pp. 237-9.
29 Ibid., p. 239.
30 Ibid., p. 301.
31 See, for example, Homi Bhabha, 'The Other Question: The Stereotype and Colonial Discourse' in *Screen* xxiv, 6 (1983), pp. 18-36.

possess the unvarying principle of fixing deeply and firmly in the heart of the oppressor a hatred towards the very being that he has unjustly coerced, and the very degradation to which he has reduced him becomes the very cause of his aversion towards him.[32]

Along with her detailing of encounters with individual famine victims and her forceful political analysis of 'oppression', Nicholson stresses that her 'greatest object in writing this sketch of the famine' was 'to show its effects on all classes, rather than to detail scenes of death by starvation.'[33] Yet the distinctive quality both of Nicholson and of her writings arises from her extensive visits among the lower classes of Irish society. This 'looking into' the lives of the poor, ironically, at first facilitated Nicholson's entrance into upper-class society:

> The people of Dublin, among the comfortable classes, whatever hospitality they might manifest towards guests and visitors, had never troubled themselves by looking into the real *home* wants of the suffering poor. Enough they thought that societies of all kinds abounded, and a poorhouse besides, were claims upon their purses to a full equivalent for all their consciences required, and to visit them was quite *un-lady-like*, if not dangerous. To many of those I had access as a matter of curiosity, to hear from me the tales of starvation, which they were now to have dealt out unsparingly; and so kind were the most of them that the interview generally ended by an invitation to eat, which was never refused when needed, and the meal thus saved was always given to the hungry.[34]

Nicholson's account affords to the 'comfortable classes' a certain voyeuristic pleasure, 'the impression of looking in on a private world unaware of the spectator's own existence',[35] a curiosity, even voyeurism, shared by future audiences.

These visits, however, were to render the American 'foreigner' increasingly suspicious to her contemporaries. Nicholson herself mimics the voices of her critics, such as the 'nominal professor': ' "We do not understand your object, and do you go into the miserable cabins among the lower order".'[36] Although, in the early part of her famine narrative, Nicholson comments that the events of 1846 onwards allowed easier and more frequent access for outsiders, 'Poverty was divested of every mask; and from the mud cabin to the estated gentleman's abode, all strangers who wished, without the usual circuitous ceremony, could

32 Nicholson, *Lights and Shades of Ireland*, p. 408.
33 Ibid., p. 25.
34 Ibid., p. 234.
35 Williams, 'When the Woman Looks', p. 83.
36 Nicholson, *Lights and Shades of Ireland*, p. 429.

gain access,'[37], the later chapters suggest that her visits into Irish homes, particularly the homes of the poor, were made increasingly difficult by famine. *Ireland's Welcome to the Stranger*, Nicholson's earlier work, includes many accounts of staying overnight in cabins, with detailed descriptions of cabin interiors and bedding arrangements; significantly fewer of these are to be found in her famine work. On a number of occasions, Nicholson admits her reluctance to enter cabins: of her visit to Arranmore, Co. Donegal, she writes: 'We went from cabin to cabin till I begged the curate to show me no more.'[38] On these occasions, Nicholson's famine discourse displays a marked struggle between competing judgements, sometimes bordering on animalistic terms and struggling to retain a humanised discourse:

> they stood up before us in a speechless, vacant, staring, stupid, yet most eloquent posture, mutely *graphically* saying, 'Here we are, your bone and your flesh, made in God's image like you. *Look at us!* What brought us here?' ... when we entered they saluted us by crawling on all fours towards us, and trying to give some token of welcome.[39]

In some of the most moving scenes in Nicholson's 'sketch' of famine, those seeking relief press against windows and doors, the threshold between the woman observer and famine victims now increasingly difficult to cross. In the home of the Hewitson family in Derry, 'the lower window-frame in the kitchen was of board instead of glass, this all having been broken by the pressure of faces continually there';[40] at Newport,

> the door and window of the kind Mrs Arthur wore a spectacle of distress indescribable; naked, cold and dying, standing like petrified statues at the window, or imploring, for God's sake, a little food, till I almost wished that I might flee into the wilderness, far, far from the abode of any living creature.[41]

Soon afterwards, Nicholson is at dinner with a company of ministers during which she criticises their luxurious fare, in particular their taking of alcohol, citing the suffering of the people; the Marriage of Cana is cited in reply,

> when in an hour after dinner the tea was served, as is the custom in Ireland, one of the daughters of the family passing a window, looked down upon the pavement and saw a corpse with a blanket spread over it, lying upon the walk beneath the window. It was a mother and infant,

37 Ibid., p. 246.   40 Ibid., p. 256.
38 Ibid., p. 271.   41 Ibid., p. 284.
39 Ibid.   42 Ibid., p. 294.

dead, and a daughter of 16 had brought and laid her there, hoping to induce the people to put her in a coffin; and as if she had been listening to the conversation at the dinner of the want of coffins, she had placed her mother under the very window and eye, where those wine-bibing ministers might apply the lesson. All was hushed, the blinds were down, and a few sixpences were quite unostentatiously sent out to the poor girl, as a beginning, to procure a coffin. The lesson ended here.[42]

The episode is an interesting one for a number of reasons; clearly displayed, along with Nicholson's strong objections to alcohol, are her alienation from most of the company inside, her imaginative sympathy with the girl outside which extends to some knowledge of the girl's age and purpose, and her recognition of the desperate efforts of the poor to ensure a proper burial for their dead.

By early 1847, during her travels in Connaught, the overwhelming nature of what Nicholson has witnessed becomes clear:

A cabin was seen closed one day a little out of the town, when a man had the curiosity to open it, and in a dark corner he found a family of the father, mother, and two children, lying in close compact. The father was considerably decomposed; the mother, it appeared, had died last, and probably fastened the door, which was always the custom when all hope was extinguished, to get into the darkest corner and die, where passers-by could not see them. Such *family* scenes were quite common, and the cabin was generally pulled down upon them for a grave. The man called, begging me to look in. *I did not*, and *could not* endure, as the famine progressed, such sights, as well as at the first, they were too *real*, and these realities became a dread. In all my former walks over the island, by day or night, no shrinking or fear of danger ever retarded in the least my progress; but now, the horror of meeting living walking ghosts, or stumbling upon the dead in my path at night, inclined me to keep within when necessity did not call.[43]

In what are now familiar terms in Nicholson's writing, the horror of the family's death is expressed in terms of 'inside' and 'outside', of uncrossed thresholds: the mother fastens the door so that others may not enter, Nicholson is, by now, unable to even 'look in' and, in stark contrast to her earlier 'excursions', increasingly stays 'within'.

In August 1848, in a letter published in the *Cork Examiner*, William O'Connor wrote, with regard to Asenath Nicholson:

43 Ibid., p. 330.

It is a singular spectacle to witness – a lady gently nurtured and brought up, giving up, for a time, home and country and kindred – visiting a land stricken with famine – traversing on foot that land from boundary to boundary, making her way over solitary mountains and treading through remote glens, where scarcely the steps of civilisation have reached, sharing the scanty potato of the poor but hospitable people, and lying down after a day of toil, in the miserable but secure cabin of a Kerry or Connaught peasant.[44]

Nicholson's writings present, in many ways, a 'singular spectacle', both in the details of famine conditions and in the character of their observer. Her account illustrates the negotiations which she attempted, both personally – across geographical and class divisions, and in the narration of famine – between analysis of famine's effects and causation; it remains a significant testimony to the 'fearful realities' of the 1840s famine.

---

44 William O'Connor, letter to *Cork Examiner*, 31 August 1848, quoted in Nicholson, *Lights and Shades*, p. 385.

Historicising the Famine: John Mitchel and the Prophetic Voice of Swift

ROBERT MAHONY

In mid-March 1847, while the Great Famine was taking its catastrophic course in Ireland, the newly-formed Irish Confederation issued the first in its series of historical publications, a two-penny pamphlet titled *Irish Political Economy*. Given the date of its appearance and its provenance in a young organization of advanced nationalists, this pamphlet would be expected to concern itself with the ongoing disaster in rural Ireland. Hence it is curious that the work should consist of three discussions of Irish conditions dating from the first half of the eighteenth century: Jonathan Swift's *Proposal for the Universal Use of Irish Manufacture* (1720), his *Short View of the State of Ireland* (1728), and excerpts from *The Querist* by George Berkeley, which dated from 1735. Both Swift and Berkeley, the bishop of Cloyne in Swift's day, had long been regarded as ancestors of Irish patriotism, although Berkeley somewhat less than Swift, whose works were also more easily available.

The three pieces were introduced with a short preface by John Mitchel, a leading light (and often a leader-writer) in *The Nation* newspaper after Thomas Davis's death. Mitchel was a moving spirit in the withdrawal of Young Irelanders from Daniel O'Connell's Repeal Association in 1846 and their forming the rival Confederation in early 1847; but he was also well aware that such political disputes resembled, in Theodore Hoppen's words, 'a hermetic drama in which the participants and the issues remained almost entirely divorced from the realities of starvation and death.'[1] Indeed, in a letter to William Smith O'Brien, of 19 March 1847 – only four days after the *Political Economy* pamphlet appeared with his preface – Mitchel considered the likelihood of an impending general election and bleakly dismissed parliamentary politics, even agitation for repeal of the Union, as delusive. For he contended that in only a matter of months, and certainly in advance of any election, 'it will be manifest to everybody that the material existence of the Irish people is the thing now at stake – and the mere raising of our political position will be able to excite no great enthusiasm, unless it be made irresistibly obvious that the one object includes the other.'[2] That last clause contained no hint of any optimism on Mitchel's part about the efficacy of the Repeal movement either to ameliorate the effects of the Famine or to mobilize the Irish population to renewed agitation on account of it. Rather, the

1 T.K. Hoppen, *Ireland Since 1800: Conflict and Conformity* (London, 1989), p. 29.
2 Quoted by William Dillon, *Life of John Mitchel* (2 vols., London, 1888), i, p. 156.

reference to the 'irresistibly obvious' was a swipe at O'Connell, whose final letter, read to the Repeal Association in mid-February 1847, noted:

> it will not be until after the deaths of hundreds of thousands, that the regret will arise [i.e. within the British parliament] that more was not done to save a sinking nation.
>
> How different would the scene be if we had our own Parliament – taking care of our own people – of our own resources. But alas! alas! it is scarcely permitted to think of these, the only sure preventatives of misery, and the only sure instruments of Irish prosperity.[3]

To Mitchel, O'Connell had failed to make the connection between Repeal and the Famine 'irresistibly obvious' to the suffering Irish poor – whose inevitably short-term interest in survival rendered O'Connell's style of political action irrelevant. If Mitchel could imply such a dismissal of O'Connell, what relevance could he possibly have seen in reprinting works by Swift and Berkeley, written over a century earlier and thus without any immediate connection at all to the contemporary catastrophe?

Mitchel's 'Preface' to *Irish Political Economy*, however, explicitly connects national survival with the necessity of Irish autonomy, providing thereby a theoretical context for the new Irish Confederation's treatment of the Famine, which, however disastrous, had been only tangential to the recent founding of the Confederation. The Young Ireland seceders had broken with the main body of O'Connell's Repeal Association over issues of both substance and style. In terms of substance, they were not willing to accept O'Connell's disavowal of physical force as a means of achieving separation, nor his own willingness occasionally to cooperate with the Liberal government, or, perhaps more precisely, to attempt to persuade that government to take effective measures to ameliorate the effects of the Famine. Stylistically, they were uncomfortable with the overtly Catholic tone of the Association, concerned that it might alienate landowners and middle-class Protestants potentially of good will toward the objective of Repeal. The Irish Confederation they formed was to have a more pluralist tone, and was more sympathetic to Irish landlords' complaints about the extension of the Poor Law to Ireland (since this, in accord with Liberal ideology, would place the financial responsibility for the relief of the Irish poor on the shoulders of the Irish gentry), although on the question of physical force the Confederation was eventually to tack toward the O'Connellite position.[4] In keeping with its more

3 O'Connell to T.M. Ray, 13 February 1847, *The Nation*, 20 February 1847, p.318. Mitchel quoted this passage in *The Last Conquest of Ireland (Perhaps)* [first published 1859; and in the Irish American Library, vol. iv: *The Crusade of the Period and Last Conquest of Ireland (perhaps)*] (New York, 1873), p. 232.

4 See Richard Davis, *The Young Ireland Movement* (Dublin, 1987), esp. chapters 3-5.

pluralist aims, and its roots in Young Ireland and the programme of *The Nation* newspaper, one of the purposes of the Confederation's own educational programme was to show that Repeal was a modern manifestation of the Irish separatist tradition dominated in the past by Irish Protestants and to which their descendants might be drawn. Confederate clubs were often named for historical Protestant patriots, and pamphlets like *Irish Political Economy*, reprinting Swift and Berkeley, illustrated the tradition of Protestant nationalism.

Like *The Nation* itself, then, the Confederation's purpose included historicizing nationalism. But Mitchel's inclusion of Swift's *Short View* in particular had a starker object as well, historicizing the Famine by implicating it in a longstanding strategy of English control of Ireland. As Mitchel had noted in establishing a Confederate Club in Dublin, named for Swift, the Confederation was intended to show 'how we should re-conquer this country from England'.[5] The goal of reconquest obviously went beyond mere repeal of the Union; indeed in the circumstances of the Famine a reconquest seemed necessary if the 'material existence of the Irish people' was to be secured against the designs of the British government. Demonstrating the longevity of those designs, and that, however natural the potato blight, the fact of the Famine was a direct result of British domination, was Mitchel's ultimate purpose in invoking Swift's complaints dating from 1728. For as Mitchel noted in his preface, 'the warnings, advice and remonstrances, which were addressed to our ancestors one hundred and twenty years ago, suit our condition exactly to this day.'[6]

What appealed to Mitchel about Swift's 'warnings, advice and remonstrances' in the *Short View* was that these were prompted in 1727 by the Dean's general despondency about Irish conditions, rather than by such topical (and by 1847, much dated) concerns as the Wood's Halfpence affair which had occasioned the more famous *Drapier's Letters*. In the *Short View* Swift begins with a list of fourteen features of geography, economics and politics that 'are the true Causes of any Countries flourishing and growing rich', and then examines 'what effects arise from these Causes in the Kingdom of *Ireland*'.[7] Such causes include the fertility of the soil and the presence of good natural harbours, which Ireland possesses, but also an industrious population, a habit of agricultural improvement and economic self-reliance, lacking in Ireland 'not altogether owing to our own Fault, but to a Million of Discouragements.'[8] Even more tellingly, what brings about prosperity in any normal country is also self-government, a chief administrator in constant residence, the restriction of political office to natives, and the spending of both public revenues and privately-received rents and profits within the country. All of these necessary conditions of national

5 Quoted by Davis, p. 136.
6 John Mitchel (ed.), *Irish Political Economy* (Dublin, 1847), pp. iii–iv.
7 *Swift's Irish Pamphlets*, ed. Joseph McMinn (Gerrards Cross, 1991), p. 107.
8 Ibid., p. 109

prosperity are denied to Ireland by virtue of English dominion. England meets all Swift's conditions for national prosperity, but actually precludes their operating in Ireland; indeed, English prosperity is increased by its receiving revenues and rents from Ireland while denying Irish products entry to English markets. While Swift criticizes the Irish who prefer to consume or wear foreign-produced goods, his criticism of English economic and political domination, although covert, is nonetheless obvious, and with it the unspoken remedy, Ireland's freedom from such domination.

Mitchel was attracted, then, by Swift's long since having identified England as responsible for Irish misery on account of a determined policy of governing Ireland in English interests. The dovetailing of his own views with Swift's was recognized in the review of the pamphlet including Swift's *Short View* which soon appeared in *The Nation*. For Swift's contentions, the reviewer noted, have an 'extraordinary applicability ... to our present wants and defects, show[ing] how little of political advancement has taken place here for the last one hundred years. What Swift wrote ... is a perfect picture of our present condition.'[9] Indeed, Swift's picture of peasant life in 1727 was astonishingly similar to contemporary facts: 'The miserable Dress and Dyet, and Dwelling of the People. The general Desolation in most parts of the Kingdom ... the Families of Farmers, who pay great Rents, living in Filth and Nastiness upon Buttermilk and Potatoes, without a Shoe or Stocking to their feet; or a House so convenient as an *English* Hog-sty, to receive them', a picture he regards as perhaps 'comfortable sights to an *English* Spectator'.[10]

The *Short View* in fact had acquired for Swift a certain reputation as a prophet, for well before Mitchel or his reviewer it had been cited as a picture that had not changed over the years. It was discounted, to be sure, by the Earl of Orrery, Swift's sometime friend, when in 1752 he produced his captious *Remarks on the Life and Writings of Swift*, frequently adopting a dismissive tone toward Swift's patriotic writings. Of the *Short view*, he maintained, 'I need take little notice, since the present state of *Ireland* is, in general, as flourishing as possible.'[11] Responding to Orrery, Swift's cousin and enthusiastic defender, Deane Swift, waxed indignant: 'I am sorry, that any man whose whole fortune ... is reported to be in *Ireland*, should be so great a stranger to the groans and miseries of that unfortunate kingdom. But what I chiefly wonder at is, that any man ... could possible reside for the greater part of eighteen years in *Ireland* without remarking to his infinite regret that no people in the *Christian* world are so destitute of raiment, food and all the conveniences of life, as are the inhabitants of that wretched kingdom.'[12]

9 *The Nation*, 27 March 1847, p. 394.
10 *Swift's Irish Pamphlets*, pp. 111-12.
11 Earl of Orrery, *Remarks* (London, 1752), p. 199.
12 Deane Swift, *Essay upon ... Swift* (London, 1755), pp. 199-200.

In the century between Swift's death and the appearance of Mitchel's pamphlet, the *Short View* became something of a touchstone for Swift's patriotism among Catholic commentators. There were, in fact, not so many of these; Swift's patriotic legacy was most often invoked over that century by Irish Protestants, who tended to prefer the rhetorically more memorable *Drapier's Letters*. But for Catholics, the *Short View* was more telling: where Swift as the Drapier was speaking to a particular historical incident, aggravating enough at the time but later needing its context explained, as the 'short viewer' he seemed to be describing a state of affairs essentially unchanged. English markets were long since open to Irish goods, but the other deficiencies under which Ireland laboured in 1728 for the most part remained, and the condition of the people, if not so generally abjectly destitute, was often enough as Swift had described it. While the *Drapier's Letters* reflected the urban perspective of the Protestant middle class in Swift's day, furthermore, the perspective of the *Short View* was broader, hence more rural, and, although Swift does not say so, more directly appropriate to the Catholic peasantry. Thus, when the historical controversialist Dennis Taaffe, a now-and-again Catholic, hailed Swift's patriotism in his *Impartial History of Ireland* in 1811, he gave the Drapier one-ninth the space devoted to the *Short View*.[13] And the certainly Catholic Francis Mahony, writing as 'Fr. Prout' in *Fraser's Magazine* in 1834, celebrated Swift in general and the *Short View* in particular, citing it as 'evidence that the wretched peasantry at that time was at just the same stage of civilization and comfort as they are at the present day; for we find the Dean thus describing a state of things which none but an Irish landlord could read without blushing for human nature.'[14] Perhaps with the British Tory readership of *Fraser's* in mind, however, Mahony refrains from quoting the *Short View* at length, so veiling its implication that responsibility for the state of rural Ireland lay more with English policy than with Irish landlords.

Blaming Irish landlords, of course, formed no part of the Irish Confederation's programme in 1847. Mitchel's 'Preface' to the first Confederation propaganda pamphlet indeed notes that Irish exports of grain and cattle were proceeding even as the Famine raged, implying his own preference for prohibiting exports as the means to relieve it. Overtly, however, he places the responsibility for Irish starvation squarely on the denial of Irish self-government, since advocating a different commercial policy in the absence of an Irish parliament would be fruitless. And although his including in the pamphlet Swift's *Proposal for the Universal Use of Irish Manufactures* and selections from Berkeley's *Querist* imputes his own endorsement of both authors' promotion of Irish self-sufficiency, the immediate relevance of either work to the desperate situation of Ireland in 1847

13 Denis Taaffe, *An Impartial History of Ireland from the Period of the English Invasion to the Present Time* (4 vols., Dublin, 1809-11) iv, pp. 20, 21-30.
14 Francis Mahony, 'Dean Swift's Madness: A Tale of a Churn' in *Fraser's magazine*, x (July 1834), pp. 27-28.

was not obvious, but had to be constructed. Hence they were introduced with Swift's *Short View*, which pictured a rural devastation that had hardly changed at all in the century and more since Swift's time, outlining the enduring premises for Ireland's catastrophe and holding intentional English policy to account for them. The acceptance of such political premises, implicitly, must underpin progress toward Irish economic self-sufficiency.

The significance of Mitchel's reprinting Swift's *Short View* in 1847 extends, then, well beyond its fitting the Irish Confederation's programme of appealing to contemporary Protestants by invoking their patriotic ancestors, and avoiding direct criticism of landlords. For re-presenting the *Short View* contextualized the Famine not in the blunders or accidents of then-current British policy, but as the latest manifestation of a long-established policy of privileging English commercial and political interests over Ireland's in every instance, even if this resulted in the utter annihilation of Ireland. In terms of Mitchel's personal rhetorical proclivities, this is a softer version of what he explicated outright in America a decade later in a series of letters to Congressman Alexander Stephens of Georgia (later the Vice president of the Confederate States of America), originally appearing in Mitchel's *Southern Citizen* in 1858 and soon republished in book form as *The Last Conquest of Ireland (Perhaps)*. This is Mitchel's account of the failure of the Repeal movement, culminating in the abortive Rising of 1848, a failure in which the Famine operates, even more directly than it is cast in the Preface to *Irish Political Economy*, as an instrument of British policy, a devastating tactic in its own right. It is the last, as Mitchel's title indicates, of a catalogue of conquests. Like Swift's *Short View*, Mitchel's book explains how a country much favoured by nature could be prostrated by policy; how

> an island which is said to be an integral part of the richest empire on the globe – and the most fertile part of that empire ... should in five years lose two and a half millions of its people (more than one-fourth) by hunger, and fever the consequence of hunger, and flight beyond sea to escape from hunger, – while that empire of which it is said to be a part, was all the while advancing in wealth, prosperity, and comfort, at a faster pace than ever before.[15]

A second significance of Mitchel's reprinting Swift in 1847 is not without an ironic twist. For as the *Short View* evidenced Swift's sympathy for the Catholic peasantry, and thereby became the document Catholics preferred to invoke when celebrating Swift's patriotism, so Mitchel's making use of it can be seen as his aligning himself with that aspect of the Swift tradition. Like the eighteenth-century Dean of St Patrick's, but much more forthrightly and forcefully, he

15 Mitchel, *Last Conquest* (1873), p. 94.

adopted the cause of the native Catholic population of Ireland. And like Swift as well, his motivation was not love of country, but hatred of its condition; whether Mitchel understood this of Swift we do not know, but in a letter of 1857 he recognised of himself:

> whatever it was that made me act and write as I did in Ireland, ... there was perhaps less of love in it than of hate — less of filial affection to my county than of scornful impatience at the thought that I had the misfortune ... to be born in a country which suffered itself to be oppressed and humiliated by another; less devotion to truth and justice than raging wrath against cant and insolence.[16]

Indeed, in Mitchel's time and later he was often compared to Swift, particularly for his talents of invective and irony. It is the *more* ironic, then, that in Mitchel's *History of Ireland* in 1869 he should have attacked Swift bitterly as an insincere patriot. For although Swift had promoted the use of Irish manufactures, he had not made a forthright and sustained argument for national independence; although he was 'well enough aware ... of the growing misery and destitution of the common people',[17] he never spoke out against the Penal Laws against Catholics; and while the Ireland of Swift's day offered a great catalogue of degradations at English hands, what moved him most memorably was a patent for Irish copper coinage that the English government had awarded to the Englishman William Wood. Rarely even in his lifetime, when personal enemies abounded, was Swift so vilified as at the hands of John Mitchel.

The reason for Mitchel's change of heart toward Swift lies, I think, in that self-revelation of his own patriotic motives as so similar to Swift's. In 1847 Mitchel had aligned himself in the Catholic tradition of regarding Swift as a patriotic prophet; ten years later he admitted that what prompted him to serve Ireland was more hatred at its humiliation than any love of country. By 1869 he was blaming Swift, it would seem, for not progressing so far in his patriotism as Mitchel himself had; for not inveighing against England, explicitly and repeatedly, as the source of Ireland's humiliation. To imply as much, as Swift had done in the *Short View*, had been sufficient validation of Swift's patriotism for Mitchel in 1847, but for Mitchel by 1869 it was no longer enough. Whereas Swift had served as a model of Protestant patriotism for over a century after his death, Mitchel could perceive in his own career, only five years before he was to die himself, a model that far outpaced the old Dean of St Patrick's, and to which, however anachronistically, he could blame Swift for not measuring up.

16 Mitchel to Fr. John Kenyon, c. 1858, quoted in Dillon, *Life of John Mitchel*, ii, p. 104.
17 John Mitchel, *The History of Ireland from the Treaty of Limerick to the Present Time* (2 vols., Dublin, 1869), ii, p. 75.

'A Nation Perishing of Political Economy'?

THOMAS A. BOYLAN & TIMOTHY P. FOLEY

It is difficult to deny the centrality of political economy, the master public discourse of nineteenth-century Britain, in the contemporary debates about the Great Famine, its causes, consequences, and especially the question of the efficiency and equity of the market mechanism in the distribution of famine relief. We would argue that the Famine crucially challenged political economy in Ireland and bore a large responsibility, though not immediately, for fundamental discursive changes in the discipline. The Famine was seen to impugn the very scientificity of political economy and the universality of its laws. It called into question its abstractionism, its methodological deductivism, its homogenising cosmopolitanism, its Anglocentrism. By the end of the 1850s even its most orthodox defenders, such as William Neilson Hancock, were submitting it to a searching moral critique. This process of historicising culminated in the work of two notable Irish practitioners, Cliffe Leslie and John Kells Ingram, who became the leading proponents of the historical school of political economy in the English-speaking world. In this article we will concentrate on the official defence of the discipline in the era of the Great Famine in Ireland.

From the early nineteenth century there was a widespread belief that political economy was a 'science ... unknown in Ireland',[1] and if known was not highly thought of. There were moral critiques after the fashion of Carlyle and Ruskin (as in the work of William Dillon[2] and Hutcheson Macaulay Posnett[3]) and a widely-held view that it was inimical to religion, especially Roman Catholicism. John Henry Newman, as rector of the Catholic University of Ireland, had described it as a science 'at once dangerous and leading to occasions of sin'.[4] Significantly, he was attacking Nassau Senior whose version of political economy was influentially disseminated in Ireland by his friend Archbishop Whately of Dublin and by many of the Whately professors at Trinity College Dublin. It was also felt in various quarters that political economy, though allegedly an impartial, unideological science, was unfriendly to the interests of, vari-

---

1 John Bright in a letter to Gladstone 15 October 1869, British Library, Add. MSS 44112 quoted in R.D.C. Black, *Economic Thought and the Irish Question 1817-1870* (Cambridge, 1960), p. 58.
2 William Dillon, *The Dismal Science: A Criticism of Modern English Political Economy* (Dublin, 1882).
3 H.M. Posnett, *The Historical Method in Ethics, Jurisprudence, and Political Economy* (London, 1882); *The Ricardian Theory of Rent* (London, 1884).
4 J.H. Newman, *The Idea of a University* (London, 1901), p. 86.

ously, the working class, tenants, and the very Irish nation itself. A conservative critique emanated from the *Nation* and a sharply radical one from such revolutionary organs as the *United Irishman, Irish Tribune,* and *Irish Felon.* All versions of nationalism attacked free trade, *laissez-faire*, the doctrine of the sanctity of the market mechanism, and the utilitarian philosophy which underpinned political economy. More radical versions challenged the sacredness of contract and of private property, especially in land. This critique reached its climax during the Famine. The hitherto more-or-less orthodox Isaac Butt became the only academic economist in these islands to defend a version of protectionism. There was widespread clamouring that the 'laws of political economy' (meaning, in effect, *laissez-faire*) should be ignored, or modified in the face of the terrible calamity of the Famine. James Lawson, in a lecture which he delivered in May 1848, 'On Commercial Panics', stated that during the 'distress of the two last years, it was very common to say, "Oh, these are extraordinary times; we cannot apply the rules of Political Economy to them."' At a time when guidance from 'settled principles' was most urgently needed, they were cast aside. If, he added: 'we have any faith in the truth or certainty of science, we must feel fully persuaded that the truths are of universal application; that they cannot be true at one moment and false at the next; that they are not to be taken up in smooth seasons, and laid aside in rough ones.'[5]

Others, like John Mitchel, advocated an *Irish* political economy, an absurd oxymoron in the view of the orthodox. There was none more orthodox than Hancock, and such was his view in an important paper which he delivered to the Statistical Society, 'On the Economic Views of Bishop Berkeley and Mr. Butt, With Respect to the Theory that a Nation May Gain by the Compulsory Use of Native Manufactures'. He said that the *Querist*, published by Berkeley almost a century previously, had been 'recently recommended as a valuable manual of *Irish* political economy, quite as well suited to the year 1847 as it was to 1741'. But 'the idea of having a science of exchanges peculiar to Ireland, under the name of Irish Political Economy, is about as reasonable as proposing to have Irish mechanics, Irish mathematics, or Irish astronomy'.[6] Hancock was referring here to the booklet entitled *Irish Political Economy*, edited by John Mitchel, and published by the Irish Confederation in 1847, which had conscripted Berkeley and Swift as early exemplars of national economics. The essence of Hancock's critique of Butt was that his treatise, avowedly dealing only with a specific situation, was *unscientific* in that it refused to generalize its findings or to relate them to the principles of political economy which were of universal

5 J.A. Lawson, 'On Commercial Panics' in *Transactions of the Dublin Statistical Society*, i (1847-9), p. 1.
6 W.N. Hancock, 'On the Economic Views of Bishop Berkeley and Mr. Butt, With Respect to the Theory that a Nation May Gain by the Compulsory Use of Native Manufactures' in *Transactions of the Dublin Statistical Society*, i (1847-9), p. 3.

validity. The *Querist* was quite unfit to be a scientific manual at the present day, claimed Hancock, and Butt had 'himself deprived his lectures of any scientific authority, by giving them an avowedly unscientific character', for he stated in his introduction that in 'endeavouring to deal with a particular case, I have rather avoided than sought to lay down general principles, or form any system of general results'. Butt deprecated 'all general discussion of protective duties', and confined himself to the case of Ireland; and from the facts of this case he attempted 'to deduce conclusions at variance with the best established principles of economic science'.[7]

Central to the defence of political economy, which was at once both spirited and systematic, was Archbishop Richard Whately, who formerly professed the subject at Oxford. He founded a chair of political economy at Trinity College Dublin in 1832, shortly after his arrival in Ireland, and as a commissioner of national education he was responsible for having the subject taught to schoolchildren. The Barrington Lectures were set up in 1834 to teach the working class throughout the country the elements of political economy. At the height of the Great Famine, in 1847, the Dublin Statistical Society was established, with Whately's encouragement, by the current and some of the former Whately professors, including Hancock and Lawson, ostensibly as a humanitarian response to the Famine. But, due obeisance having been paid to Schull and Skibbereen, a more important purpose emerged: the defence of the principles of political economy, then under unrelenting attack. The 'principles' were those promulgated by the British classical school. However, their Irish acolytes were selective in reading their masters' texts. Their was general hostility towards David Ricardo and all the early references to Mill were unflattering. Lawson, for instance, used Senior in condemning Ricardo's theory of wages and profits:

> that wages fell as profits rose, and profits fell as wages rose, and that any rise of wages was a deduction from profits, and *vice versa*, the effect being to represent the interests of the employer and the labourer diametrically opposed to each other. Mr. Senior made inquiry into the facts, and found, that acording to all experience, wages and profits rose and fell together, and that it was quite impossible that every rise of wages could be a deduction from profits.[8]

The young Cliffe Leslie attacked Mill's view of the 'antagonism of the interests of capitalist and labourer,' a view he found 'unscientific as well as mischievous'.[9]

7 Ibid., pp. 6, 7.
8 J.A. Lawson, 'On the Connexion between Statistics and Political Economy' in *Transactions of the Dublin Statistical Society*, i (1847-9), p. 6.
9 T.E.C. Leslie, 'The Self-Dependence of the Working Classes under the Law of Competition', *Transactions of the Dublin Statistical Society*, ii (1849-51), p. 4.

Most Irish political economists adopted the Senior-Whately version of classical doctrine, which was hostile to the Smithean cost-of-production theory of value and the Ricardian labour theory of value. It was bitterly opposed to trade unions and it was absolutely committed to free trade in general and especially to free trade in land, totally rejecting any state intervention in the process of distribution. Edward Lysaght was correct when he wrote that all economists of reputation (with the exception of Mill) were agreed 'in attributing the wretched state of agriculture in Ireland to the absence, rather than to the excess of competition'.[10]

Political economy in Ireland is best seen in the context of the framework of ideas of the classical school and its diagnosis of Ireland as a case of entrenched underdevelopment. In terms of the Ricardian model Ireland was seen as not having reached the stationary state; rather it was one of arrested development, which could be rectified by appropriate policy measures, which had to be taken in the context of the ideology of free trade, which excluded from debate such issues as protectionism, manipulation of exchange-rates, or major fiscal variation. The classical school was virtually unanimous in their views on Ireland until the later writings of John Elliot Cairnes and John Stuart Mill. Their diagnosis centered on some key concepts in the classical theory of distribution. The pivotal concept was the relation between *population* and *capital* which was crucial to the classical analysis of wages and profits. According to Adam Smith, 'The demand for those who live by wages ... cannot increase but in proportion to the increase of funds which are destined for the payment of wages'.[11] In Ireland, the increase of population had far outstripped the growth of capital, so that the average rate of wages fell to a minimum subsistence level, and combined with the absence of employment opportunities outside of agriculture, created intense competition for land, with resultant subdivision and rack-renting. So a fundamental condition for any economic development was an alteration of the population/capital ratio, either through an increase in capital, a reduction in population, or a combination of the two. To achieve long-term development, agriculture, which employed the vast majority of the population, had to be targeted. Most classical economists believed that a more productive and efficient agriculture could be achieved only through the replacement of Ireland's cottier system with the capitalist leasehold tenancy on the English model. This would involve a large injection of capital and the removal of population to facilitate the consolidation of farms. It was envisaged that most of those dis-

10 Edward Lysaght, 'A Consideration of the Theory, That the Backward State of Agriculture in Ireland is a Consequence of the Excessive Competition for Land' in *Transactions of the Dublin Statistical Society*, ii (1849-51), p. 5.
11 Adam Smith, *Wealth of nations*, bk i, ch.viii. For a clear and succinct account of this topic, see R.D. Collison Black, 'The Classical Economists and the Irish Problem' in *Oxford Economic Papers*, v (1953), pp. 26-40.

placed would be re-employed in agriculture as wage-labourers, earning more than they had done as small-holders. The rest would go to non-agricultural employment, in turn generated by either public or private investment, or encouraged to emigrate.

In general, the classical economists were ill-disposed towards state investment in public works, except to the extent necessary to create the basic infrastructure to facilitate private enterprise. To bring about private investment the state would have to provide security of person and of property, at best a long-term objective, at worst a virtual impossibility, given the allegedly disorderly nature of the Irish character. Nassau Senior believed that the insecurity of person and of property in Ireland arose from 'the tendency to violence and resistance to law' which was the 'most prominent, as well as the most mischievous part of the Irish character'.[12] Given pre-Famine rates of population growth, it followed that large-scale emigration became a necessary condition if this model of development were to be effective. Fundamental to this programme was the assumption that English conditions provided the norm towards which Ireland should be moved as rapidly as possible. Mill in England and Cairnes in Ireland were two pivotal figures in the subversion of this conventional wisdom, by advocating peasant proprietorship, which, they argued, could be no less efficient economically than the English model, and would be more socially and politically acceptable given the depth of Irish tenants' belief in their right to the occupation of the soil rather than accepting the status of wage labourers. But all of that was in the future. At the time of the Famine, political economists associated with the Whately chair and the newly-established Dublin Statistical Society, tirelessly propagandized on behalf of free trade in land, free-market solutions, and the unquestioned superiority of the English model.

During and after the Famine, political economy came under unprecedented attack and the official intelligentsia rushed to its defence. Such was Whately's belief in the efficacy of political economy that at a meeting of the Statistical Society on 19 June 1848, his first biographer remarked, 'a moment when all Ireland was drilling, and Dublin seemed like a slumbering volcano, the Archbishop propounded a panacea against the threatened siege'. That panacea was political economy, and Whately urged Young Ireland to study it.[13] At that meeting he spoke of it as the '*only* means which existed of rescuing the country from convulsion'.[14] The Famine crisis made it all the more important that the principles of political economy should be applied to Ireland. Any relaxation,

---

12 N.W. Senior, *Journals, Conversations and Essays Relating to Ireland* (2 vols., London, 1868), i, p. 33.

13 W.J. Fitzpatrick, *Memoirs of Richard Whately, Archbishop of Dublin: With a Glance at his Contemporaries and Times* (2 vols., London, 1864), ii, pp. 63, 67-8.

14 Richard Whately, 'Report of the Address on the Conclusion of the First Session of the Dublin Statistical Society' in *Transactions of the Dublin Statistical Society*, i (1847-9), p. 5.

however nobly motivated, was a 'killing kindness', to use W.E. Hearn's phrase for protectionism.[15] In a pervasive, and conveniently naturalising, metaphor, Ireland was figured as a diseased body, in need of the strong, even harsh medicine of political economy, which was seen as all the more effective for being unpalatable. Emigration, for instance, depending on one's viewpoint, could be either a damaging haemorrhage or a curative phlebotomy of a plethoric body. Lawson saw famines as 'commercial panics', 'diseases to which the body politic is subject – not chronic diseases, but epidemics as regular in their recurrence as influenza itself, though at longer intervals'. He saw the political economist as the 'physician [who] can best meet and cope with disease, who is most intimately acquainted with the structure and functions of the healthy subject'.[16] As John Joseph Murphy wrote much later, in 1866, 'Ireland is, no doubt, a poorer country than Great Britain; but to relax the application of the principles of political economy in the case of a poor country, would be as reasonable as to relax the application of medical science in the case of a patient of weak constitution'.[17] A powerful dose of *laissez-faire* was the universal panacea for Irish ills, in opposition to those who clamoured for more lenient treatment for Ireland either because of her generally perceived 'anamolous' position or because of the exceptional circumstances of the Famine. In 1847, William Neilson Hancock delivered and published his significantly-titled *Three Lectures on the Questions, Should the Principles of Political Economy be Disregarded at the Present Crisis? And If Not, How Can They Be Applied Towards the Discovery of Measures of Relief?* There was an extraordinary proliferation of public lectures on political economy from the late 1840s on. Economic knowledge, theoretical and applied, was produced from the Whately chair at Trinity College Dublin, and from 1849 by the professors of Jurisprudence and Political Economy at the newly-founded Queen's Colleges at Belfast, Cork, and Galway, all of whom (with the exception of Lupton and Donnell at Galway) were graduates of Dublin University. All of these professors were members, usually very active ones, of the newly-founded (1847) Dublin Statistical Society, later to become, and to remain to this day, the Statistical and Social Inquiry Society of Ireland. The Society was dedicated to the application of economic theory to practical questions and generally to promoting an acceptance of the principles of political economy among the people at large. Its mission was greatly facilitated when it took on the administration of the Barrington Trust in 1849. In 1834 John Barrington had bequeathed a large sum of money for the dissemination of economic knowledge throughout the towns and villages of Ireland, especially to those seen as most in need of it, the lower classes. Professsors of the subject, but also of other disciplines, traversed

15 W.E. Hearn, *The Cassell Prize Essay on the Condition of Ireland* (London, 1851), p. 83.
16 Lawson, 'On Commercial Panics', i, pp. 1, 2.
17 J.J. Murphy, 'The Relation of the State to the Railways' in *Journal of the Statistical and Social Inquiry Society of Ireland*, iv (1864-8), p. 307.

the length and breadth of Ireland broadcasting what John Mitchel ironically called the 'saving doctrines' of political economy.[18] These lectures were very extensively reported in the national and local press. The view was repeated *ad nauseam* that a knowledge and appreciation of the laws of political economy was crucially important because of the great calamity of the Famine. And the subject had been introduced into the national schools by Whately himself for the edification of the children of the poor.

One of the central tenets of political economy was that of the harmony of interests, the finding, not of discord, but of concord in the operations of competitive society. It was, declared Hancock:

> a fundamental principle of economic science that the interests of the various classes in the community are bound up together. The capitalist rarely derives profit without employing labour. The landlord cannot get rent unless both the labourer and capitalist have been engaged in the cultivation of his land.[19]

The interests of the various classes in the community were reciprocal:

> The capitalist cannot prosper without increasing the wages of the labourer, and the rent of land. If the labourer is well off, he increases the demand for the various commodities he consumes, and so raises profits and rents. The greater the amount of land rent, the greater the funds out of which those classes can be supported who take care of the highest interests of humanity. Such are the manifest conclusions of economic science, the dissemination of which is calculated to produce happiness, contentment, and peace-teaching, as they do, individuals, classes, and nations that the true interest of each is the true interest of all; that one class can never be sacrificed to another with impunity; that calamities and blessings alike extend their influence, producing, like stones dropped into a lake, the greatest impression where they fall, but extending their influence in circles ever widening, till the effect has reached the entire family of man.[20]

W.E. Hearn, the first Professor of Greek at Queen's College Galway and a political economist of note, claimed in his 'Introductory Lecture' to the Royal

18 John Mitchel, *History of Ireland*, (2 vols., Glasgow & London, n.d.), ii, p. 210. The phrase which we have used for the title of this paper, 'a nation perishing of political economy', is taken from this work, ii, p. 218.

19 W.N. Hancock, 'On the Economic Views of Bishop Berkeley and Mr. Butt ...', i, p. 12.

20 Ibid., p. 13.

Galway Institution, that 'the interests of the individuals, classes, and nations ultimately coincide, [so] that the true interest of each is the true interest of all'.[21] This theme was centrally addressed in his important lecture to the same body, 'On the Coincidence of Individual and General Interests', and, significantly, as his example he chose the role of the corn dealer in the Famine, arguing that, despite the public odium in which that calling was held, the interests of the corn dealer and those of the people at large coincided.[22] Judging by the political economy papers in the examinations for male national teachers in 1848 and the immediate post-Famine years, the activities of the corn dealers were felt to be in need of justification. In 1848, for example, the following question was asked: 'What is the illustration made use of to show the beneficial action of the corn dealer upon the market of provisions, in times of scarcity'?[23] In another examination in the same year, candidates were asked to show 'in what way the business of the *Corn Dealer* ministers to the public services'.[24] The question was again asked the following year: 'How is it shown that the interest of the Corn Dealer coincides with that of the public'?[25] Hancock defended the activities of provision dealers on the basis of what he described as the 'well-established economic principle, that the interest of consumers and that of producers are really the same', which principle 'is but another form of the doctrine, that both parties gain in every free exchange'.[26] The private self-interest of the corn-dealer was seen, paradoxically, as more productive economically, socially, and morally than the sympathy, altruism, and public spiritedness of state intervention. Whately, although an archbishop, was keenly aware that an excess of benevolence promoted by religion and traditional morality could be dangerous to the body politic unless restrained by political economy.

In his *Three Lectures*, Hancock said that religion and morality were not the province of political economy, which was a science, the domain of intellect, not of feeling. So it was inappropriate, if not indeed immoral, to describe economists, as had been happening with increasing frequency, as '*hard-hearted* and *cruel*'. The hard-headed principles of political economy pointed out that 'the providing food *for sale* in *all* districts, and under *all* circumstances, should be left to the foresight and enterprise of private merchants'. Hancock mentioned the 'common taunt against Political Economy', that it recommended 'the interest of the poor to be sacrificed to the interest of the merchants'. But class-conflict was structurally impossible in this version of political economy: the 'sole reason that Political Economists object to any interference with the provision dealers,

21 W.E. Hearn, 'Introductory Lecture' in *Galway Vindicator*, 6 November 1850.

22 W.E. Hearn, 'On the Coincidence of Individual and General Interests' in *Galway Vindicator*, 6 March 1850.

23 *Fifteenth Report of Commissioners of National Education in Ireland* (1848), p. 305.

24 Ibid., p. 314.

25 *Appendix to Sixteenth Report of Commissioners of National Education in Ireland* (1849), p.182.

26 W.N. Hancock, 'On the Economic Views of Bishop Berkeley and Mr. Butt ...', i, p. 9.

is that their interests and that of the community are identical'. But the unreflecting then very numerous in Ireland – did not perceive 'the wisdom of the Almighty, in making the security of the most vital interests of the community depend not on any general benevolence or public spirit, but on the strongest and most enduring of human motives – self interest'.[27]

Hancock examined and found wanting Butt's arguments for protectionism, which had found no evidence of the operation of the 'wisdom of the Almighty', nor of its personal representative on earth, the 'hidden hand' of Adam Smith, in the Ireland of the 1840s. These arguments were, according to Hancock:

> First – That the consumer must sacrifice his own interest in order to benefit the community. Second – That the poor can gain by government interference with the expenditure of the rich. Third – That wealth has a monopolizing tendency which requires to be controlled.

He rebutted this argument by a familiar appeal to the doctrine of the harmony of interests. To distinguish between the expenditure of the rich and that of other classes in the community, was not merely erroneous but 'most dangerous and objectionable':

> To direct the attention of the poor to the wealth of the rich as standing in the way of their comforts, is to make them envious and covetous of that which, if entirely divided amongst them, would produce to each but a trifling sum, insignificant compared with what they would gain in a short time by their own industry from the expenditure of the same wealth by the rich.

Hancock condemned Butt, clearly no believer in economic harmonies, for subversively speaking of the 'monopolizing power of wealth', and for 'freely and unreservedly' advocating 'the right of the artisan to protection against the grinding influence of riches'.[28]

The harmony of self-interest and social interest was held to come about through the operation of competition, unfettered by unnatural state intrusion. In general, political economists agreed that Ireland's distress was due, not to insufficient state activity in the economy, but to too much 'interference' in the market, especially in the market for land, and they argued that the relief effort was hampered by government intrusion in the food market. In a paper on

27 W.N. Hancock, *Three Lectures on the Questions, Should the Principles of Political Economy be Disregarded at the Present Crisis? And if not, How can They be Applied Towards the Discovery of Measures of Relief?* (Dublin, 1847), pp. 12, 19, 51, 61.
28 W.N. Hancock, 'On the Economic Views of Bishop Berkeley and Mr. Butt ...', i, pp. 9, 12.

laissez-faire which he read to the Statistical Society, in December 1847, when the Famine was at its most intense, Hancock stated that the contrast between 'a destitute peasantry and prolific resources' suggested an investigation into the social arrangements of the country where such an 'anomaly' prevailed. But, he added, that natural resources however lavishly bestowed, were 'valueless as instruments for the production of wealth, unless the arrangements respecting their use' were based on 'sound economic principles'. The result of this investigation had been 'to vindicate the character of our common nature from the charge of general indolence', by showing that such anomalies arose from the 'social arrangements transmitted from less enlightened ages, being at variance with the teachings of science'. The problem had been caused, he believed, by 'past neglect of economic science', specifically by 'a want of reliance on private enterprise' as the 'most prolific source of unsound arrangements', and not on the supposed shortcomings of the Celtic race. According to Hancock, there was no country in the world which afforded a stronger proof of the disasterous consequences of neglecting the doctrine of *laissez-faire* than Ireland. Its economic history, he wrote, displayed 'an extent of interference with private enterprise, quite as remarkable as the misery and distress which the potato failure has so painfully disclosed'. The evils, as Hancock believed them to be, of this pervasive interference, were not confined to its direct economic effects – it had 'perverted the minds of the people on economic questions'. This resulted in a proliferation of theories to account for Irish distress, most of them involving remedial action which included a further extension of government interference. The 'principle of *laissez faire* was *not* tried in the West of Ireland, where the deaths from starvation took place', he claimed; 'the people of Ireland died from want of *money*, and not from want of *food*'. The extreme destitution of the people in the absence of an extensive poor-law, exposed the aged and infirm, who:

> could not take advantage of the relief by public works, to the want of the means wherewith to buy food. But the interference with the trade in food undertaken by the commissariat arrangements, instead of benefitting those unfortunate people, since the lowering of the price, supposing it to be effected, is of no benefit to a man who has no money, increased their danger, by turning away the attention of the public from the only mode of saving their lives by supplying them with the means of buying food.[29]

A constant theme with Hancock was the deleterious effects on economic activity, especially in the market for land, of ideas and practices inherited from feudal or other kinds of pre-capitalist social formations. He, and others, argued

29 W.N. Hancock, 'On the Use of the Doctrine of *Laissez Faire*, in Investigating the economic Resources of Ireland' in *Transactions of the Dublin Statistical Society*, i (1847-9), pp. 3, 4, 7-8.

strenuously against what they saw as the feudal encumbrances which made the alienation of land, and agricultural improvement generally, extremely difficult. They argued for the removal of all legal restraints on dealing in land and for treating it as a commodity, just like commercial property. *Laissez-faire* and free-trade in land were their watchwords. In short, they demanded the replacement of feudal with capitalist economic and social relations. The old restrictions on trade in food, forestalling, regrating, and engrossing, were, Hancock pointed out, abolished as misdemeanours only in 1844. For instance, the causes of sub-letting were, in his view:

> the legislative enactments which afford less than the ordinary security to the tenant who holds his land and lays out capital in its cultivation, and give him at the same time all the extraordinary powers of a landlord for recovering rent from his cottier tenant.

The real remedies for subletting were 'to give the tenant security for improving his farm, and to give no more power for recovering his rent when he sublets than an ordinary creditor has for recovering his debt'. The law of distress, which enabled the farmer to take the law into his own hands against his cottier tenant, was 'one of those feudal institutions which have survived the policy on which they were founded'. Subdivision, he argued, was injurious only where 'unwise restrictions' impeded the accumulation of land. The theory that Irish 'ruin' was due to middlemen was but another form of the old-fashioned prejudice against intermediate dealers, such as in the case of forestallers. There was nothing in the nature of the case

> to make middle parties in transactions necessarily injurious to the com-munity; on the contrary, whenever they arise in the ordinary course of trade, without any special interference of government, as certainly as they gain profit themselves so certainly do they benefit the community. The evils traced to middlemen in Ireland arise not from the parties being middlemen, but from the legal restrictions which render it *unprofitable* for them either to transfer or to improve the land, whilst they are in-duced to sublet by the ample means for levying exorbitant rents, in the power of distress, and priority of recovering rent which they exercise as landlords.

He agreed that absenteeism produced some economic evils, but these he attrib-uted to the feudal law of distress, whose operation was even more baneful when in the hands of agents.[30]

30 Ibid., pp. 7, 12, 13, 14-15.

In an important series of articles, 'On the Economic Causes of the Present State of Agriculture in Ireland', Hancock stated that the main causes to which he ascribed the state of agriculture in Ireland were, 'the legal impediments to the free transfer and sale of land, whether waste or improved; and the legal impediments to the application of capital to agricultural operations'. These included encumbrances of various kinds, such as entails, the high cost of transfer, and other restraints on the power of alienation. He quoted Adam Smith approvingly on the 'disorderley times which gave birth to the barbarous institutions of primogeniture and entails'. The chief object of entails, Hancock stated, was 'to maintain a wealthy and hereditary aristocracy', and it was 'upon its wealth much more than its connection with land that the aristocracy must in future rest its power'. Hancock spoke of the 'old feudal principle that the ownership of improvements follows the ownership of land', which constituted a legal impediment to tenants expending capital in improvement. He quoted a report which spoke of early notions concerning property in land and the relation between landlord and tenant, which had an important social as well as a merely economic dimension. This customary social relationship between a landed aristocracy and its tenantry was radically unequal, whereas the bourgeois-capitalist system advocated by Hancock claimed that its regime of contract was posited in equality:

> Above all, the landlord and tenant were not looked on simply as parties to a contract concerning property, in which the rent on the one hand and the usufruct of the land on the other formed the only terms. They had personal relations which placed the landlord in the condition of a superior, the tenant in that of a dependant, and prevented the notion of a contract (which is found on equality) from being fully developed.[31]

During and after the Famine, the scientificity of political economy was frequently appealed to but because of what were seen as its cold and ruthless prescriptions, it was often augmented by having recourse to an officially superannuated but affectively powerful pre-scientific moral discourse. For reasons of expediency this gift-horse was not looked in the mouth and the lesson of Troy went unheeded. The scientific citadel of political economy was breached by the Trojan horse of morality. Ironically, it was Hancock, the most doughty defender of the discipline, who first relented, submitting its 'laws' to a vigorous and sustained *moral* critique. The new historicisation of political economy demonstrated that its laws, far from being universal in their derivation and application, were, usually, based on 'English experience and ideas', to quote the words

---

31 W.N. Hancock, 'On the Economic Causes of the Present State of Agriculture in Ireland', pt i, p.7; pt ii, p.9; pt iii, pp. 3, 4, 5.

of John Elliot Cairnes.[32] It was later argued that a political economy suitable for Irish circumstances and ideas was, for example, more hospitable to state intervention and small-scale agriculture, and tended to be opposed to the commodification of land, to contract, and to the sacrosanctity of the market. This new version of political economy was propagated, in different ways, by Cairnes and the pioneers of the historical school, Cliffe Leslie and John Kells Ingram. The most famous confrontation between the new and the old political economy occurred in the House of Commons in 1868, significantly in a debate about Irish land. Robert Lowe argued that political economy 'belongs to no nation; it is of no country'. John Stuart Mill replied:

> my Right Hon. Friend thinks that a maxim of political economy if good in England must be good in Ireland ... I am sure that no one is at all capable of determining what is the right political economy for any country until he knows the circumstances.[33]

Tom Kettle, a methodological follower of Leslie and Ingram, saw this historicising project as a 'revolt of the small nations against the Czardom, scientific and political, of the great'.[34] But it should not be forgotten that those who fell in the struggle for survival in the Great Irish Famine played a crucial, if unintended, part in demonstrating that political economy, too, had a nation.

---

32 J.E. C[airnes], 'Ireland in Transition' in *The Economist*, 14 October 1865, p. 1238.
33 *Hansard*, 3rd series, vol. cxc, col. 1525 (16 March 1868).
34 T.M. Kettle, *The Day's Burden* (Dublin, 1937), p. 138.

Reading Lessons:
Famine and the *Nation*, 1845-1849

SEAN RYDER

Under the regular column heading of 'State of the Country' in the *Nation* of 1 July 1848, shortly before the suppression of the newspaper for sedition, a subheading appears advising the reader to 'Read, Mark, Learn, and Inwardly Digest' the contents of the following two columns of reports, which are all concerned with 'exterminations' (a term applied to both evictions and to famine deaths). The advice is worth noting because it draws attention to the ultimately pedagogic and utilitarian intentions of the paper. One is not merely to read, but to make *use* of the material presented, to absorb it into the bloodstream, so to speak, make it food for thought or action. The stories of death and suffering and cruelty and despair are more than brute facts. They are facts which have implications and latent power – for the editors of the *Nation*, the provision of news was a means to an end, not an end in itself. One might say that this small but representative item indicates an important difference between the *Nation* and many present-day newspapers; the contemporary media is more inclined to veer away from such open admissions of its polemic and ideological role, and is more likely to privilege the ideas of 'objectivity' and the reservation of judgement. If we think of this in literary terms, we might argue that where the nineteenth-century nationalist press recognises and accepts the affectivity of language – its power to evaluate, move, to activate and provoke – the media of the twentieth-century has tended to devalue affectivity and aspire instead to the supposedly descriptive and informative. To some extent this is also related to the impact of literary modernism on language and narrative in the twentieth-century. The nineteenth-century conventions of narrative copiousness, sentimentality, commitment, and so on, are the very values rejected by the modernist principles of minimalism, detachment, 'hardness', and objectivity.

Any attempt to assess the representation of an event like the Famine in the nineteenth-century press must bear this difference in mind. To comment in a genuinely useful way on these texts, we have to treat means of representation, discourse itself, as an object of investigation. We can't take language, even the language of journalism, at 'face value', since 'obvious meanings' and 'face values' are not immutable. Where the nineteenth-century audience reads a powerful and enabling expression of national feeling, a contemporary reader may read an overblown and hackneyed piece of propaganda. Both readings say more about their respective historical contexts than about the nature of the texts 'in themselves'. The point is that we cannot assess discourse and representation apart from its material contexts – and this includes everything from the meaning of particular tropes and narrative conventions to the material conditions of production and transmission, such as the publishing trade, the function of the press, and the nature of the readership.

Thus we might begin to investigate the representation of the Famine in the *Nation* by briefly looking at the nature and function of the newspaper itself. The original slogan of the *Nation*, 'To create and to foster public opinion in Ireland – to make it racy of the soil', indicates the intention of its founders to use it as an instrument of national consciousness-raising, thus combining an Enlightenment notion of creation or building anew, with an apparently contradictory romantic belief in the authority of the 'soil' – a kind of uneasy juxtaposition of modernity and tradition. The first part of the formula, the 'fostering of public opinion', points clearly to the pedagogical function of the paper. But this is not just education for the sake of it; Ireland needed to be educated in order to free itself. Education and learning are understood as merely a prelude to action. In the paper's first issue of 15 October 1842, Charles Gavan Duffy writes: '[a newspaper's] slow and silent operation acts on the masses as the wind, which we do not see, moves the dust, which we do see.' Duffy sees the paper as a vehicle for the 'ablest writers in the country' to 'turn with us from the study of mankind in books, to the service of mankind in politics' – in other words, the *Nation* will enable the much needed connection of intellect and politics, of theory and praxis. The most important point here is that the *Nation* did not see itself in terms of neutrality or objectivity. It defined itself in terms of its efficacy.

This object of this efficacy was the production of no less than a unified national culture. In that same first issue, Gavan Duffy writes that the paper's first duty is to teach 'Nationality', but an inclusive one in which sect, party and class differences would 'combine for great and permanent change.' In a significant passage, he argues that:

> With all the nicknames that serve to delude and divide us – with all their Orangemen and Ribbonmen, Torymen and Whigmen, Ultras and Moderados, and Heaven knows what rubbish besides, there are in truth, but two parties in Ireland; those who suffer from her National degradation, and those who profit by it.

For a national mind and body which is fragmented, a newspaper offers a means of producing unity, singularity; a voice for the whole nation. Political, religious, and social heterogeneity is here rhetorically transcended by the allegedly 'truer' and less complicated binary opposition of 'degrader' and 'degraded', with the latter group constituting genuine Irish nationality. This ideological move, made possible by a powerful rhetoric of transcendence and exclusion, meant the displacement and obscuring of those very real and historically rooted divisions in the country, and proposed instead to subsume painlessly all under Wolfe Tone's 'common name of Irishman'. The homogenising character of the project was also reflected in a number of the paper's features: the convention, for instance, of reprinting reports from the local and regional press, thus assimilating them into this new, 'national' voice which transcends the local and regional. What is gained by this practice is the construction of a powerful ideal of cultural unity; but what is devalued or lost is the range of alternative identities – identities based on differences of locality, language, sect, or social class. The reader of the *Nation* is supposedly in the position of the idealised national subject: one who exists beyond the 'local' and 'regional', one who 'naturally' speaks English, one who appears on the face of it to belong to no sect or class at all. As David Lloyd has shown, this 'transcendental' identity-thinking is a common feature of nineteenth-century nationalisms, in Ireland and elsewhere. It belongs to the bourgeois ideology of the universalised subject, which is the dominant ideology informing the nationalism of Young Ireland itself.[1]

Deep contradictions underlie bourgeois ideology, of course, and the *Nation*, like any text, inevitably reproduced some of the contradictions of its informing ideology. Limited by its bourgeois liberalism, the paper decried oppression in general, but disclaimed republicanism, Chartism and socialism; it looked forward, Arnold-like, to a combination of classes, but rejected calls for 'combinations' of workers. It sought to speak for the idealised 'People', but spoke a language which was still alien to half the actual population. Most strikingly, perhaps, it called for the production of a national culture, but did so through the machinery of imperialism. A famous example is Thomas Davis's advice to aspiring poets to learn about the topography of their country from the military project of the Ordnance Survey[2] – it can even be argued that the newspaper trade itself was a development of the capitalist industrialisation of communication which was integral to nineteenth-century imperialism. This 'machinery' originating in the imperialist culture might also be taken to include narrative and representational conventions. The discursive features of the news reports and editorials of the *Nation* are no different in many ways to those of the bourgeois British press and literature of the period, though they are of course pressed into the service of what is ostensibly an anti-imperialist project. It is thus not surprising to find that the 'Young Irelanders', Davis and Duffy and Mitchel, were essentially urban-based, middle-class, English-speaking professionals, as were many of their contributors.

We might ask who precisely would have been reading the *Nation*, especially in a country where, on the eve of the Famine, less than half the population was

---

1 See David Lloyd, *Nationalism and Minor Literature: James Clarence Mangan and the Emergence of Irish Cultural Nationalism* (Berkeley, 1987), chapter 2.

2 'Ballad History of Ireland', *The Nation*, 30 November 1844.

literate.[3] The price of the paper was 6*d*. – in 1845, that would nearly buy two two-pound loaves of 'lower quality' bread in Dublin. But a better indication of its relative expense is the fact that in 1847, a labourer on a public works scheme might earn only 8*d*. to 10*d*. per day[4] – an amount which was often insufficient to feed a family. Clearly then the purchasers of the *Nation* were middle class; but of course one of the strengths of the paper was the fact that one need not buy it to read it – until the split with O'Connell, the *Nation* could be read in any Repeal reading room, and there is also a popular image of the *Nation* being read aloud to rapt but illiterate listeners in villages across Ireland. There is undoubtedly some truth to this image – Malcolm Brown estimates a figure of 10 readers for every single paper sold, which makes for a readership of perhaps 250,000 people per week.[5] But it may also be significant that the distribution of newsagents selling the paper was concentrated in Dublin, Leinster and southern Ulster.[6] All of this would suggest that the majority of *Nation* readers (or at least buyers) were middle-class, English-speaking, and inhabitants of the more economically advantaged and urbanised parts of the country. The experiences of those labouring and cottier classes who were to suffer most in the Famine would have been alien to those readers in terms of language and social class, and the provinces of Munster and Connaught, most devastated by the Famine, would have been literally and imaginatively remote. What's more, the representational conventions employed by the paper's writers, and expected by the paper's readers, would have been closer to the representational models of bourgeois English culture than any other models.

So more precisely, what does the *Nation* tell us about the Famine itself? For one thing it provides, through its regular Saturday publication, a weekly chronology of the Famine, from the first reference to potato blight on 13 September 1845 to the despairing editorials of late 1849, penned by a disillusioned and exhausted Charles Gavan Duffy. It also serves as a convenient digest of the provincial press of the period, on whom it relied heavily for its often harrowing reports on the 'State of the Country.' Through these hundred and fifty issues of densely-packed columns of print, the Famine figures as one of the most potent and pervasive signifiers across a range of discourses, from the agricultural-scientific, to the political-economic, to the religious, to the literary, to the nationalist revolutionary. The *Nation*'s representation of the Famine can thus tell us something about the character of these discourses, and in particular the meaning of the Famine for nationalist thought in the period.

3 See J.W. Freeman, *Pre-famine Ireland: a Study in Historical Geography* (Manchester, 1957), pp. 133–9.
4 Cormac Ó Gráda, *Ireland Before and After the Famine* (2nd ed., Manchester, 1993), p. 131.
5 Malcolm Brown, *The Politics of Irish Literature* (London, 1972), p. 67.
6 Each issue of the *Nation* provided a list of newsagents selling the paper in Ireland and abroad.

It is poignant to follow the early reports of the blight itself, and the various proposals by agricultural and scientific experts to counter or alleviate its effects. In the early days of September and October 1845, the *Nation* gives considerable coverage to the scientific controversy over the cause of the potato disease, with speculation ranging from hot, damp weather, to poor cultivation practices, to excessive electricity in the atmosphere. The true explanation – the fungus – was not considered probable, and there are consequently lengthy proposals for remedies which proved to be of no use whatsoever. By November 1845 'The Potato Disease' is a weekly heading over a substantial range of texts, often occupying 10 or 11 columns of print, and including letters, reports of public meetings, advice on the storage and preparation of potatoes, news of the blight in England and abroad, and so on. The deeper ironies and problems in this discourse emerge when one considers it within the wider context of who was communicating to whom. The advice of scientific experts like Sir James Murray, which the *Nation* reported in great detail, looks tragically inappropriate to the majority of victims of the blight, firstly because it was based upon a misunderstanding of the causes of the disease, but also because it seems to misunderstand the resources available to a huge population often living in destitute conditions. One early piece of advice called for the baking of diseased potatoes at 180° F, advice which presumes the ownership of an oven. Another called for the household production of chlorine gas with which to treat the potatoes. In addition, the *Nation*'s admirably exhaustive coverage of these proposals appears to construct a model which sets English scientific expertise against hapless Irish peasant ignorance, just one of the many points at which this bourgeois nationalist paper becomes more bourgeois than nationalist. The discursive surrealism produced by such contradictions is also reflected in the juxtapositions of reports of immanent starvation with weekly columns of 'Gardening Operations for the Week' (reprinted from the English *Gardener's Chronicle*), which on 18 April 1846 reminded readers, alongside reports of food riots in Tipperary, that

> Scarlet runners and an early crop of French beans should now be sown. The first kidney beans will be as well raised in a hothouse or frame, and transplanted. Sow also a little early red beet, scorzoners and salsify. The globe artichokes should now be dressed.

As the months wore on, the reporting of the effects of the Famine on the Irish populace was to become central to the *Nation*'s nationalist political-economic discourse. The language of 'starvation' was not new to either Irish nationalist or British bureaucratic discourse when the 1845 potato crop failed. For example, the *Times* Commissioner visiting Ireland in August 1845, a month before the blight was first noticed in the country, wrote that 'nearly all the crimes that are committed in Ireland are agrarian ... the cause which produces it is almost universal – namely, want of employment and consequent starvation and discontent' (30 August 1845). This is an argument found over and over again in the minutes of Repeal Association meetings so meticulously reported in the *Nation* every week, and represents the standard O'Connellite position at the outset of the Famine. The 'Great Famine' itself, as its ominous scale began to be recognised in the winter and spring of 1846, was, from this perspective, merely an unusually intense example of a recurring evil rooted in the country's defective economic structure. The Famine was easily put to use by the O'Connellite political-economic view of Ireland under the Union – the view, that is, that British governments inevitably mismanaged Irish affairs, particularly in maintaining an economic order which drained the country of resources and pauperised a large section of the populace.

Judging from his speeches as reported in the *Nation*, O'Connell, in the autumn of 1845, recognised almost immediately the impending disaster that the failure of the potato crop would cause among the poor (and indeed the rich, who, he argued, would become victims of the fever consequent upon famine). As early as October 1845, when the exact extent of crop failure was still uncertain, O'Connell was advocating a number of specific practical measures – some of which, like preventing exports of grain, import supplies of Indian corn, suspension of the distilling industry, and taxing landlords, were also part of his larger Repeal argument in favour of an Irish parliament. The establishment of the latter would enable the Irish themselves to deal with crises like potato failure in a more efficient way than heretofore. This discourse featured strongly in the *Nation*, both in the reported speeches of Repealers and in sympathetic editorials, which often took the form of prophetic warnings to the government and landlords – warnings that scarcity of food, should it occur, might provoke social revolution. As early as 25 October 1845, in an editorial entitled 'The People's Food', the *Nation* warns that unless urgent action is taken:

> agrarian outrage ... will ... stalk, in blood and terror, over the land, leading to a general disorganisation of society and reign of terror which it is fearful to think of.

Reading this editorial more closely, we might also note that in this kind of discourse the term 'People' functions more as a signifier of a transcendental national identity than as a signifier of actual inhabitants of Ireland – who are the 'People' exactly? Is the editor himself a potato-eater? In line with the bourgeois character of the discourse, the text produces rhetorically what it hopes to find in actuality – an identity which escapes the heretofore recalcitrant divisiveness and heterogeneity of Irish culture. To the bourgeois nationalist, dedicated to the production of the unified and homogenous national cultural order, the prospect of uncontrolled revolution, of a kind which escapes the control of central authority, is as terrifying as it is to the government and landlords. It is noteworthy that the *Nation*, while condemning landlord injustices, universally condemned assassinations as examples of 'outrage'. In general Young Ireland courted the gentry for support, and was not opposed to landlordism as such.

What is striking and perhaps liable to misinterpretation by the contemporary secular readers, is the apparently easy mingling of religious and political-economic discourse in discussions of the Famine. O'Connell's speeches in particular are exemplary of this – in one breath he will describe the potato failure as a 'visitation of Providence', with 'famine and pestilence now at our door', and in the next breath list seven practical measures for alleviation of the impending scarcity, including closure of the ports, reducing the allocation of oats to the cavalry, and so on (15 November 1845). Prayers that the 'Almighty may avert ... misfortune' are followed up by accusations of government 'culpable conduct' in the 'crime' of allowing the exportation of oats and 'aggravating starvation and famine' (22 November 1845). Divine causation, in other words, did not preclude administrative culpability – Mitchel was by no means original in his allegation that 'The Almighty, indeed, sent the potato blight, but the English created the Famine.'[7] This was more or less an implication that could be logically derived early on from the speeches of O'Connell and in the editorials of the *Nation*. Similarly, the expectation of divine retribution did not preclude nationalist agitation; in an editorial entitled 'The Last Resource' (17 April 1847), the *Nation* argues that:

> children will grow up in the trodden nation, to pray to the Lord that no peace, no rest, no prosperity, may be vouchsafed to England till GOD's justice to suffering Ireland prevail, and be made manifest to all men. One more effort, then, for dear Ireland, *now*, while this generation may still be saved. Let us meet together – all ranks and classes of Irishmen – in some *National* Council, and take measures, once for all, for our redemption; that we, too, may not be thrown into coffinless graves, amid the bitter scorn and contemptuous laughter of mankind.

As a literary illustration of the same interaction of political and devotional, consider the work of the most popular *Nation* poet, Speranza. Her famous poem 'The Stricken Land' (23 January 1847) juxtaposes political accusation ('But the stranger reaps our harvest – the alien owns our soil') with predictions of divine retribution on these alien 'murderers.' But to read this as merely a plea to 'suffer and be still' in the hope of divine retribution is to fail to realise the power of the political rhetoric which also suffuses the poem. It is poor government – a human and therefore changeable reality – which provides the occasion for God's

---

7 John Mitchel, *The Last Conquest of Ireland (Perhaps)* (Glasgow, 1876), p. 219.

intervention. God intervenes only because humans have failed; the human and divine are interactive rather than mutually exclusive. Consider also the last stanza of the poem:

> We are wretches, famished, scorned, human tools to build your pride,
> But God will yet take vengeance for the souls for whom Christ died.
> Now is your hour of pleasure – bask ye in the world's caress,
> But our whitening bones against ye will arise as witnesses,
> From the cabins and the ditches in their charr'd uncoffin'd masses,
> For the Angel of the Trumpet will know them as he passes.
> A ghastly spectre army before the great God we'll stand,
> And arraign ye as our murderers, the spoilers of our land.

The imagery here is not merely symbolic. It bears a close resemblance to the imagery of the populist agrarian blood and terror which will rise up to stalk the land in O'Connell's speeches or Gavan Duffy's editorials – imagery intended to suggest actual historical possibility. The apocalypse is not merely something to be deferred to the 'end of history'; it may arrive in all-too-literal fashion in the near future. Indeed if we look at a poem by Speranza published in the *Nation* several weeks later (27 March) entitled 'France in '93 – A Lesson in Foreign History', we find her describing an almost identical political and moral cataclysm, this time in purely secular terms, warning of the bloody social and moral chaos which accompanies violent revolution.

The other obvious discourse at work here is the Gothic – the notion of the walking dead, the spectre army, the terror produced by violating the natural order. The use of the Gothic in this instance also indicates the mixture of horror and fascination which the prospect of violent revolution inspired for cultural nationalism – on the one hand a romantic excitement at the idea, and on the other a conservative fear of the collapse of political and social order. We can also see the language of the Gothic employed in the factual reports of the human consequences of famine and eviction in the period. Reports frequently tell of dead who 'are so changed by want as not to be recognised by their friends – their looks wolfish, and glaring as madmen' (2 January 1847). The *Nation* of 18 April 1846 carries a report on the eviction of 277 tenants from the estate of the Marquis of Waterford:

> The faces of these people were subdued with hunger; pale, or rather of a ghostly yellow, indicative of the utmost destitution. They are starving ... We hurried with horror from these frightful visitations, which are *permitted* by Providence for his own wise ends, sick at heart, and out of conceit with the system of doing what one likes with one's own ... I have put nothing down in malice, but every thing in the spirit of truth and fair

play ... I need draw no moral from this; but you might call the attention of the Irish members to it, that they might use the FACTS against the coercion bill, and against traducers of the people.

Here the Gothic is pressed into the service of nationalist politics. It is not merely an indulgence in the fantastic, it is not mere sensationalism (though it is partly these) – here it is primarily a discourse designed to challenge *laissez-faire* economic and social policy, and to be useful in nationalist political agitation.

Many of the reports of actual deaths from famine are taken from inquest reports. These inquests are an important element of the discourse on the Famine, since they provide names, details, a sense of place, and personal histories which are lacking in the generalising famine discourses in poetry and politics. The issue of 2 January 1847 includes the following, from the *Mayo Constitution*:

> the same coroner held an inquest on the body of Bridget Joyce, a widow with four children, who died in a small sheep house in a small field at Gleneadagh. It appeared in evidence that the deceased and her family were in the utmost state of destitution, and one of the children had nothing to wet the lips of its dying parent with but a drop of water or a little snow. The body lay for eight days before a few boards could be procured to make a coffin, in such a state of destitution was the locality. Verdict – death from starvation.
>
> On the 23rd, same coroner held an inquest on the body of Edmond MacHale, a boy, at Caracirable, in Attymass, one of a numerous family. The evidence of the mother as to their destitution was truly melancholy. The last words of the dying child to his family were – 'Mother, give me three grains of corn.' A woman who was present at the melancholy scene, searched the pocket of his jacket and found three grains of corn. Verdict – died from starvation.

Here we see a combination of the conventions of the sentimental tale, especially in the evocation of lost innocence, extreme pathos, and the deaths of mothers and children, with elements of myth and folk-tale, complete with tragic irony and magical numbers. All six of the reports in this section are punctuated by the striking refrain of 'Verdict – died from starvation' which adds another level, the language of official, unemotive, statistical discourse. The cumulative effect of the refrain is to transform the named individuals we have just read about into anonymous dehumanised victims of a mass tragedy, a kind of blackly ironic version of nationalism's ideal of common identity. The other irony is that such revelations, which are here being used as part of a nationalist project, are only made possible because of an imperial British bureaucracy which demands the holding of inquests. As a result, the *Nation* reproduces a perspective which in some basic ways reproduces the perspective of the imperial culture it ostensibly opposes.[8] Such scenes as those described are mediated in a similar discourse for the Dublin reader of the *Nation* as they would be for the London reader of the *Times*. The bourgeois nationalist subject and the bourgeois imperialist subject begin to look like mirror images, though of course in other ways the *Nation* is asking the Irish reader to view these victims as fellow national subjects, thus working to overcome the 'distancing' effect of the mediation itself.

Apart from the fact that they are all features of bourgeois discourse, what links these discursive forms I have described – the religious, the Gothic, the sentimental tale – is their *affectivity*. They are narrative forms which are intended to perform things rather than simply reflect reality in some transparent way (as in the classic realist novel, or in modern journalism, or in scientific discourse). Yet at certain points, the writers of the *Nation* draw attention to language's apparent failure to reflect the reality of the Famine. On 19 February 1848, for instance, a report reprinted from the *Sligo Champion* is prefaced with the statement that 'The misery which the people here are now enduring beggars all description.' Gavan Duffy himself, in the first issue of the newly-revived *Nation* of 1 September 1849, writes that 'No words printed in a newspaper or elsewhere, will give any man who has not seen it a conception of the fallen condition of the West and South.'

But we must be careful about how we interpret these comments. Recent assessments of Famine literature which have stressed the importance of such statements appear to read them in the light of modernist reactions to the Holocaust. In the introduction to his useful anthology of poetry about the Irish famine, for example, Chris Morash quotes George Steiner's pronouncement that 'The world of Auschwitz lies outside speech as it lies outside reason.' Morash adds: 'The same could be said of the world of the Famine. But the attempt to contain that world within language, even if doomed to failure, had to be attempted.'[9] Margaret Kelleher also invokes Steiner in the opening paragraph of her essay on Famine literature.[10] While such a comparison is superficially attractive, there seem to me to be two very basic problems with it. Firstly, it assumes that Steiner's attitude towards the Holocaust is itself unproblematic. But to suggest, as Steiner does, that the meaning of human atrocity is outside reason and representation – 'outside the text' – merely mystifies and romanticises such events. To speak of a 'world' of Auschwitz is already to employ metaphor, to be *within* speech and reason – ironically one can only make claims about language's

8 See also Margaret Kelleher's related and very useful discussion of the audience-orientation of nineteenth-century fiction about the Great Famine in her essay 'Irish Famine in Literature' in Cathal Póirtéir (ed.), *The Great Irish Famine* (Cork, 1995).

9 Chris Morash (ed.), *The Hungry Voice: The Poetry of the Irish Famine* (Dublin, 1989), p. 37. The Steiner quotation is from *Language and Silence* (London, 1985), p. 146.

10 Kelleher, 'Irish Famine in Literature', p. 232.

inadequacy through the medium of language itself. The argument is not just sophistic – the point is that there is, as Derrida has famously written, no 'outside the text'. Even irrationality is a signifier whose meaning is rationally comprehended, and every gesture toward some kind of non-linguistic 'truth' or reality is still a gesture, a sign which has real and often very powerful meanings. It is true that language can only give us constructions which are limited by history and material life, never an expression of 'transcendent truth' – but such a failure is only a problem if one believes the function of language to be merely the disinterested conveyance of some pre-existent 'truth' in a more or less accurate way. For the writers of the *Nation*, on the other hand, writing was much more reader-oriented, more dedicated to efficacy than accuracy, more an instrument for communicative action rather than a looking-glass (even a Joycean cracked one). The point was not necessarily to 'contain' the world of the Famine within language – it was primarily to write about the Famine in a way which would produce certain responses. The affective function of such discourse was strong, even if its representational function seems weak.

The second problem relates to the way we interpret the 'indescribability' of atrocity. To admit to the 'indescribability' of certain Famine scenes, as contemporary commentators on the Famine often did, is not simply to register an ultimate failure of all linguistic or representational conventions. The fact is that in certain forms of nineteenth-century bourgeois discourse, 'indescribability' is itself a trope, a convention, which is itself very meaning*ful*. One finds it originally in the romantic discourse on the Sublime, where it functions to suggest emotionally overpowering experience, in which effect exceeds material representation. This trope of the 'indescribable' takes on a particular social and ethical meaning in the Victorian period, where writers like Dickens use it to signify a state of physical or material degradation which corresponds to a state of moral depravity (the conditions of urban poverty or prostitution, for example). It is also a central trope in another Victorian descendent of romanticism, the Gothic novel, whose conventions we have already seen at work in representations of the Famine. The 'indescribable' and 'unspeakable' are *de rigueur* for such narratives – the whole point of them is to evoke that which is suggestive, excessive, hidden, radically Other. For the bourgeois writer of the 1840s, in other words, there was a ready made set of discourses which lay to hand, and which had 'indescribability' as a built-in feature. To use the trope in the 1840s was not to register a Beckettian encounter with the void. Nor was it exactly the same as the modernist 'unspeakable' and 'unrepresentable' of Conrad and Forster. It does look forward to these modernist texts, it is true, but it is not identical to them.

I think it is also very telling that 'indescribability' of this sort does not appear to be a feature of the discourse on the Famine in the oral tradition, an alternative to the bourgeois discourse of the print medium. The gaps and 'failures' in the oral tradition seem to be more the result of willed silence rather than a breakdown of language. Cathal Pórtéir cites the account of one 'native informant', who felt that certain local accounts of the Famine, involving stealing or taking over the holdings of evicted tenants, were better left untold:

> Several people would be glad if the Famine times were altogether for-gotten so the cruel doings of their forebears would not be again renewed and talked about by the neighbours.[11]

The problem in this case is not the inadequacy of language but the very oppo-site – the *power* of language to reveal certain truths about the Famine, and to stimulate the production of more discourse. It is precisely because language can say *too* much that it causes a problem in such contexts. So, it seems to me to be too simplistic to argue for the fundamental unrepresentability of the Famine; this idea too needs contextualisation.

How efficacious were these representations, ultimately? The *Nation* cer-tainly provided a set of images and perspectives on the Famine which would establish themselves in nationalist discourse for generations. Yet obviously, in the end, the tropes, conventions and exhortations did not do enough to assist a political and cultural revolution of the sort Gavan Duffy, John Mitchel and other Young Irelanders had aspired to. In the issue of 1 September 1849, Gavan Duffy admits that he is 'paralysed' in the face of the Famine's devastation. Faced with such shocking scenes as the ones witnessed during his trip to the West, Duffy's language constructs the victimised Irish men and women as a race be-yond nationality, beyond even basic humanity:

> The famine and the landlords have actually created a new race in Ireland. I have seen on the streets of Galway crowds of creatures more debased than the Yahoos of Swift – creatures having only a distant and hideous resemblance to human beings. Grey-headed old men, whose idiot faces had hardened into a settled leer of mendicancy, simeous and semi-hu-man; and women filthier and more frightful than harpies ... *shrieking* for their prey, like some monstrous and unclean animals ... I have seen these accursed sights, and they are burned into my mind forever.

At the waning of the Famine, Duffy and the *Nation* are in despair, yet even under such conditions, Duffy never entirely loses faith in the potential efficacy of language. In the same editorial, he can still plead that '[t]he grounds of hope are various, but sure. Some of them are plain and clear enough. Plain, clear and eternal, for God has written them in symbols which no one can refuse to see,

11 Cathal Pórtéir, 'Folk Memory and the Famine', in Pórtéir (ed.), *The Great Irish Famine*, p. 230.

although many are too blind and confused to interpret them aright.' The paper goes on to welcome the publication of the Larcom Report on Ireland in 1848, and in a brief foray into literary theory notes that the facts of famine and extermination which Larcom presents are all too familiar to Irish people – yet

> facts with which one is too familiar need sometimes to be placed in a new light to attract attention. The very nature of some things seems changed by the varying of lights and shadows upon them ... The effects of famine seen in Captain LARCOM's statistics might cause some similar emotion in the dulled sensibilities of the Irish public.

Even here, still, cultural nationalism can express the hope of finding redemption through the powers of representation.

The Famine Crisis:
Theological Interpretations and Implications

ROBERT DUNLOP

The social, political and religious convulsions of the Great Famine provide a fitting and constructive interpretative framework in which to situate an analysis of mid-nineteenth-century religious interaction in Ireland. The 'hungry times' became the cockpit for much conflict as attempts were made to bring bread from heaven to the starving people. There is nothing eccentric about attempting to look at the Famine crisis through theological lens. Indeed, I shall argue that the whole tragic experience of the potato failure had a profound and permanent effect on the religious consciousness of the Irish people, those who left and those who survived, those who 'took the soup' and those who winced at 'Peel's brimstone' and 'Trevelyan's corn'.

The sociological crisis and human tragedy created by the Famine occasioned the intensification of efforts to Protestantise the Irish peasants. Their sheer vulnerability through the distress they experienced triggered in the facilitators and promoters of the new Reformation an explosion of genuine compassion, organised targeting and aggressive evangelisation. Theology impelled the mission agents, it informed the reactions of their antagonists, and helped create the sort of subversive spiritual memory from which we have not fully recovered. This brief investigation sets out to examine some of the theological interpretations which emerged in the aftermath of the Famine, and in a second layer of enquiry goes on the assess the implications of the collapse of the main source of sustenance for theological and ecclesiastical survival and co-existence.

It is useful to begin this study in the middle of the fifth decade of the century when the climate shifted from the Malthusian analysis of the 1820s to the Free Trade approach of Cobden and Peel. Sir George Graham, the Peelite Home Secretary, wrote to Peel in October 1845 on the deeper significance of the rotten potatoes in Ireland:

> It is awful to observe how the Almighty humbles the pride of nations. The Sword, the Pestilence, and Famine are the instruments of His displeasure; the Cankerworm and the Locust are His armies; he gives the Word; a single crop is blighted, and we see a nation prostrate, and stretching out its hands for Bread. These are solemn warnings, and they fill me with

reverence; they proclaim with a voice not to be mistaken, that 'doubtless there is a God, who judgeth the earth'.[1]

Behind this sobering Old Testament approach to an agrarian economy lay the prevailing nineteenth-century doctrine of a somewhat static order of things. Catastrophes on the scale of the Great Famine naturally excited the imagination and stretched the minds of those searching for an explanation on both sides of the Irish Sea. Providentialism had many faces within the religious and political world of the day. It sometimes flirted with a genocidal understanding of the complex Irish dilemma. At our distance from events we need to avoid too rigid a reading of the comments and statements of those who often struggled to put a tolerable interpretation on what was going on. Boyd Hilton captures the mood of the time when he writes:

> Whether they stressed the evidences of design in the universe, or the fact that life was a time of probation, most early-nineteenth-century Christians saw the world as a stationary state, and lacked any dynamic conception of the economy such as that adumbrated (though perhaps not anticipated) by Adam Smith.[2]

We get a sense of the complexity of this doctrine of providentialism by turning to Thomas Chalmers, the benevolent Scottish divine, who had an acute sense of self-help and who made an important distinction between scarcities which were evenly spread across a nation and famines which virulently attacked one part of a nation. The Great Irish Famine fell into the latter category and in his scheme known as the 'godly commonwealth', the terrible visitation of distress 'left the task of equalization – if there be enough wisdom and mercy below for the accomplishment of the task – to the ordering of man'. Consistent with his support of Free Trade, he saw the disaster as a 'special providence' which justified interventionist political policies. This stood in contrast with a more *laissez-faire* response better suited to more prosperous times. Although an ardent Scotsman, he identified with the English ruling class, but not in an uncritical manner. Famine had also touched the Highlands and this sharpened Chalmers's understanding of what needed to be done. His theology stopped short of attributing the Famine to a recriminatory visitation of chastisement from the Almighty. For him the providential dimension was linked to the responsibility of the Christian nation to look after the victims of a terrible catastrophe. Although supporting Trevelyan, he called on the government to suspend distillation from grain because it was morally unacceptable that 'the Scotch might luxuriate in spirits, and the English in their potations of beer as usual' while Irishmen starved.

1 Peel Papers, 18 October 1845, BL MS 40451 fos 400-1.
2 Boyd Hilton, *The Age of Atonement* (Oxford, 1988) pp. 66-7.

Relief was not the only concern in Chalmers's theological response; he more than hinted that there was redemptive significance in alleviating Ireland's need:

> Now is the time for Britain to move forward ... to acquit herself gener-
> ously, openly, freely, towards Ireland – and by her acts of princely but
> well-directed munificence to repair the accumulated wrongs of many
> generations ... with the guidance and guardianship of the Holy Provi-
> dence above, a harvest of good will ensue from this great temporary evil;
> and Ireland, let us trust and pray, will emerge from her sore trial, on a
> bright and peaceful career to future generations.[3]

This optimistic note was the by-product of Chalmers's redemptive-recovery theory, which stressed that Britain's response by way of generous relief not only had corrective significance but also provided an arena of re-birth for the victims of both political neglect and natural misfortune. Such theological reasoning presents the challenge of corporate atonement as a way of making amends for past wrongs, while at the same time laying the foundation for social regenera-tion. It at least opened up an alternative to paternalism, the *bete noire* of Anglo-Irish relationships, and paved the way for the notion of benevolence as the inductor of self-help.

Adversarial Responses

Sir Charles Trevelyan, a moderate evangelical with a Clapham sect background, also worked assiduously for the relief of the starving people. He understood the calamity in teleological terms and worked to produce a better state of society in Ireland without interfering with property rights. He was an establishment man who held that indirect permanent advantages would accrue to Ireland follow-ing the crisis because there would be a resulting social regeneration. Yet, there are some chilling sentences in his theological interpretation of what he saw as 'the visitation'. He wrote in strident language, seeing the scarcity as:

> ... the judgment of God on an indolent and unself-reliant people, and as
> God had sent the calamity to teach the Irish a lesson, that calamity must
> not be too much mitigated: the selfish and indolent must learn their
> lesson so that a new and improved state of affairs must arise.[4]

---

3 Thomas Chalmers, 'Political Economy of a Famine' in *North British Review*, vii (1847), pp. 282 and 289.
4 Jenifer Hart, 'Sir Charles Trevelyan at the Treasury' in *English Historical Review* lxxv, 294 (1960), p. 99.

As we shall see, however, he was more or less at one with many of his ecclesiastical mentors and contemporaries.

A rounded reading of Famine historiography compels us to enquire into the theological impact of the Great Hunger on the main religious protagonists who inhabited the territory where the starving multitudes lived and died. This in turn compels us to consider what has become known as 'the new Reformation', sometimes called 'the Protestant Crusade', an intricate world of evangelical missionaries. It is necessary to recognize deep rivulets of practical compassion for the starving people coming out of a rigid theology and an exclusivist ecclesiology. Many of the missionaries were convinced that a substantial amount of blame for the crisis could be laid on the priests and the Roman Catholic system. It was certainly seen as a divine visitation on those who needed 'the new sound of truth to frighten away the devices of falsehood and superstition.'

One of the leading evangelical missionaries of the period was the Revd Alexander Dallas, founder of the Irish Church Missions, who set up a Fund for Temporal Relief with a view to 'relieving the temporal needs of the body in such a manner as to extend the influence for relieving the eternal wants of the soul.'[5] His response to the Famine gives us some idea of the complex attitudes of these latter-day crusaders. Writing an anecdotal account of the Protestant colony at Castlekerke, Co. Galway, we find, for instance, an interesting twist in the theology of Famine blame. In the following extract from *The Point of Hope in Ireland's Present Crisis*, he describes a local convert suffering ostracisation:

> He was a good deal persecuted because he read the Bible and taught Irish, and was on one occasion beaten by the priest. He is still taunted and called names by the neighbours, who say 'tis no wonder the crops would fail, and the land be blasted, when they act so.[6]

Dallas used colourful language when describing mission work amongst the Irish peasantry, concluding that the agents of the Irish Church Missions 'must be able to see the jewel of God in the midst of that dunghill and condescend to be a scavenger to get it.'[7]

The devastation of the Famine also had a substantial impact on the majority Irish Catholic Church. The impact was so overwhelming that the full theological implications only developed in the post-Famine era. Undoubtedly, there were distinctly Catholic interpretations of the tragedy and some trenchant comments are on record, but the immediate result was growing solidarity amongst a people who felt battered and repressed long before the potato crop failed. Dur-

5 A.R.C. Dallas, *The Point of Hope in Ireland's present Crisis* (London, 1849), p. 14.
6 Ibid., p. 17.
7 A.R.C. Dallas, *Address to City Mission at Exeter Hall* (13 January 1851), Irish Church Mission Mss.

ing the year after 'Black '47', the Irish hierarchy, in rejecting the offer of a concurrent state endowment with the Established Church, took the submissive line that 'having shared in the prosperity of their faithful flocks, the clergy of Ireland are willing to share in their privations.'[8] Nonetheless, it should be understood that pre-Famine Catholicism was in a state of some disarray in rural Ireland. According to Miller's analysis, in 1840 only 40 per cent of the population attended church: 'by the standards of the Counter-Reformation fewer than half the Irish Catholics were practising their religion, or could be considered well schooled in its disciplines. The Catholic revival before 1840 had made its greater impact on the urban middle classes and better-off tenant farmers.'[9] What has been termed the 'devotional revolution', allied to the Ultramontane thrust, was orchestrated to recover lost ground and to bring post-1850 Catholicism to Roman heel. One statistic which throws light on the high clericalisation of the Catholic devotional renaissance reveals that in 1845 Ireland had one priest to every 3000 people, in 1870 one priest to every 1476 people.

The shape of post-Famine society in Ireland reflected not only a demonstrable strategy of recovery but also an impressive restructuring of the social order with a traditional core – the family, the nation and the church. Such a formidable coalition paved the way for the sort of confessionalism which has been a constant factor in Irish life well into the twentieth century. Theological conformism was on of the strands of this nineteenth-century religious renaissance. Kerby Miller offers a useful analysis:

> In the 'New Ireland' of the post-Famine period there were three dominant social institutions – the strong farmer type of rural family ... the Catholic Church of the 'devotional revolution' and Irish nationalism, especially in its constitutional and quasi-legal form. All three were innovative in structure and purpose and all were associated with the *embourgeoisement* of Catholic society – adopted by or imposed on Catholic smallholder and labourers.
>
> All three upset or challenged traditional 'peasant' practices and outlooks ... all demanded absolute conformity and proscribed deviations as familial ingratitude, religious apostasy, or even national treason.[10]

The prolific Catholic polemical correspondent, Father James Maher of Graigue, Co. Carlow, in a letter to Richard Whately, the Church of Ireland Archbishop of Dublin, appeals to Scriptural images to scold the Established Church for neglect and carelessness:

8 *Freeman's Journal*, 13 October 1848.
9 David Miller, 'Irish Catholicism and the Great Famine' in *Journal of Social History* (1975), pp. 81–98.
10 Kerby A. Miller in *Studies*, cxxv, 300 (Winter 1986), pp. 538–9.

Prostrate Ireland bleeding at every pore – abandoned in the hour of her need – hunted to death by landlord tyranny, cheated and robbed by vicious institutions – neglected and spurned by the Priest and Levite and marked for the grave through the slow, lingering excruciating process of famine. The Scriptural type of your project, my Lord, was the man who fell into the hands of robbers, on his way from Jerusalem to Jericho, who also stripped him and having wounded him, went away leaving him half dead.[11]

This needs to be read, however, in the context of Akenson's assessment, which suggests a populist reading of the tragedy with some folk overlay:

The initial Catholic folk-interpretation of the Famine was in terms of supernatural judgment. Studies of the Irish folk tradition have shown that the commonplace reaction was to interpret the Famine as some form of divine punishment by the Christian God for the people's sins. Alternatively, it was commonplace to explain events by invoking the action of non-Christian spirits, who, in some way, have been vexed and therefore attacked the Irish people. Whether interpreted in a Christian or a non-Christian form of Supernaturalism the Famine to the Irish people was 'beyond indignation' and was perceived as an event of cosmic significance, not as a merely human conspiracy against the Irish people.[12]

Lasting Implications

Turning our attention to the theological implications of the Famine crisis, it is helpful to investigate the theological and ecclesiological postures which arose in the middle of the nineteenth century. It is as totally unhistorical to attribute Ireland's lasting spiritual malaise to the Great Famine as it is to blame the English nation for the Famine itself. What is not in doubt, however, is the fact that the sociological upheaval experienced in the hungry times had wide theological ramifications. I am prepared to argue that Christianity in Ireland is still recovering from the trauma of the Protestant Crusade, the Catholic Revival and the social dissonance produced by the Famine.

In the first instance, there emerged following the Famine a theology with pietistic strands and sentimental tendencies. This should not surprise us given both the Irish liking for folklore and the need for a release of emotional energy during the hard times. Although it ran in tandem with a defensive, exclusive

11 James Maher, *Letters* (Dublin, 1877), p. 2.
12 D.H. Akenson, *Small Differences – Irish Catholics and Irish Protestants 1815-1922* (Dublin, 1991), pp. 144-5.

theology, this more benign form of religious experience should be recognised. Sheridan Gilley sees the period as the 'golden-age of religious self-help' characterised by a renewal of faith in the laity. He judges that 'this devotionalism was tender, romantic, sentimental; it was the outcome of the soft-centred religion pioneered by Rousseau.'[13] It would seem that the Irish theological palate had a liking for both the hard-shelled bitter mints of severe dogma and the soft-centred creamy mints of popular devotion.

A somewhat strange bed-fellow came in the form of Victorian evangelicalism with its romantic ideas of the happy isles beyond the miseries of the present valley of the shadow of death. While the two opposing theologies have a common provenance and emphasis, they failed to cohere in the ecclesiastical atmosphere of post-Famine Ireland. This shared pious overlay operated within a Manichean framework of black and white, right and wrong, truth and error, Christ and Antichrist, perverts and converts, jumpers and faithful. In the words of George Boyce:

> Catholics and Anglicans, Presbyterians and Methodists, were caught up in a new sense of religiosity, one notable for its central belief that Catholicism and Protestantism were deadly enemies, sworn foes, defenders of the right against the wrong, of truth against error. This religious fervour was not, of course, a constant factor in Irish life; other more material and secular preoccupations intervened. But the churches began to sink their roots deeply into Irish social as well as religious life.[14]

A second form of theological action prompted the emergence of a reactionary, defensive Catholic power bloc. S.J. Connolly has described this phenomenon:

> In the period after the Famine, then, two main developments combined to give the Catholic church and its clergy the dominant position within Irish society ... the first was the growing effectiveness of Catholicism itself – Catholicism considered not just part of the structures of local power and influence, or as an auxiliary to nationalist politics, but as a religion, a system of beliefs, values and rules of behaviour supported by an appeal to supernatural realities. The second was social change, decimating those sections of the population whose behaviour had been the source of greatest concern to pre-Famine churchmen and bringing into being a new and more respectable society in which the church's discipline was from the start more readily accepted ... The triumph of the

13 Sheridan Gilley,'The Church and the Irish Diaspora' in *Journal of Ecclesiastical History*, xxxv, 2 (April 1984), p. 193.
14 George Boyce, *Nineteenth Century Ireland – the Search for Stability* (Dublin, 1990), pp. 124-5.

post-Famine Church was also the victory of one culture over another and when modern Irish Catholicism came into its inheritance it did so only by means of the destruction of a 'rival world'.[15]

The question must be asked – what sort of theological underpinning was used for this social and religious rejuvenation? Dipping into the language of the Cullen era, the Synod of Thurles and the whole Ultramontane crusade, we sense a theology which was dogmatic, defensive, assertive and reactionary. In the words of one commentator, it 'pinned its faith to the patterns thought up long ago at Trent, more personal, more Italian, genuinely more human, but not without some danger of sentimentality.' This brought to the foreground talk of 'godless colleges', 'perverts' and 'converts', depending on which side you were on. Strategy on the ground was organized by theological sharp-shooters of the stature of Cullen and McHale, which resulted in a conservative, combative style of reasoning. The remnants of Neo-Gallicanism went to the shredder, class conflict among Irish Catholics was muted, educational and philanthropic services previously sponsored by the Protestant establishment were assiduously duplicated and, where possible, replaced.

Of special note is the growing, and in some ways, perilous link between religious belief and nationalist politics, despite the anti-clericalism of the Fenians and Land Leaguers. Nationalism and religion fused together the Irish loyalties to Faith and Fatherland and this created Ireland's unique mode of confessionalism which in the end decimated, succeeded and replaced the religious Establishment of the Anglican church. As Gilley notes, 'the essential battle was one external to the Catholic population between natives and aliens, Catholics and heretics, the state of the oppressor and the church of the oppressed.'[16]

Thirdly, the waning of establishment Ireland threw down a deep theological challenge to the Church of Ireland and the smaller bodies known as Protestant Dissenters. Less than twenty five years after the Famine, disestablishment coincided with Vatican I and the declaration of papal infallibility. The smaller Dissenting bodies adopted a theology of survival, buoyed at times with revivalist renewal and Victorian pulpiteering. Nonetheless, a Baptist report speaks mournfully:

Our work is now for the most part confined to the North of Ireland, where the Protestant population is numerous and influential. But this has been the result of circumstances over which the Committee have had no control. The question is often asked, 'What has become of your operations in the South and West?' The answer is a mournful one: 'the awful

15 S.J. Connolly, *Priests and People in Pre-Famine Ireland, 1780-1845* (Dublin, 1982), p. 113.
16 Sheridan Gilley, 'The Church and the Irish Diaspora', p. 195.

famine of 1845-1847 swept them all away – some 3000 members of our churches and congregations were lost to us; and thus Limerick, Birr, Clonmel, Abbeyleix, Youghal and Cork have been abandoned. We have never recovered from that fatal blow. Waterford alone remains to us and it was almost extinct when Mr Douglas took up his abode there'.[17]

The minority Reformed churches continued to smart from the devastation of the Famine era in terms of lost ground through death and emigration, the rapid rise of Catholic power and the lingering memory of the proselytising allegations.

The triumphalism of Nicholas Wiseman's words in the *Dublin Review* reveals the mood of the post-Famine decade among many in the Catholic Church:

> Away go proselytism and souperism, and the nests of pestilence which they have built amidst the neighbourhoods that they have infected and the educational strife, and the stalking missionary, and the sneaking Bible-reader and the lying apostate, and perhaps at length the unbelieving prelate, who scorns revelation and patronises bigotry.[18]

It is an understatement to label this a theology of confrontation. As the nineteenth century wore on, and the Roman ascendancy became more visible, the best we can expect from the minority churches is a theology tailored for survival which, on the ground, turned out to be a continuation of the polemical, confrontational, defensive theology of the famine era. It is particularly sad that the Bible, the primary source of all Christian theology, was used as a polemical blunt instrument to defend a position rather than to unfold spiritual light. It is asking too much to expect balanced theology from the poisoned atmosphere of nineteenth-century religious exchange.

Behind this denominational polarisation lay the emergence in the middle of the century of diverse cosmologies which became self-enclosed and self-referential. Energy was expended on boundary maintenance and this created the limbic regions where those outside the circle of truth were consigned in rejection. Out of this dividing of the people flowed the sort of polemical posturing which is inimical to a more wholesome apologetic. The rehabilitation of the Scriptures in the Irish Catholic community and the more rounded hermeneutic of many twentieth-century Protestant divines serves as a corrective to the bleak, negative theology which was almost as burdensome as the Famine itself.

---

17 *Irish Baptist Magazine* (1885), p. 119.
18 Nicholas Wiseman, *Dublin Review*, xlii (1857), pp. 225-6.

Better Ways – Brighter Times

To conclude, it may be helpful to draw out some theological lessons from the turbulent times of the Great Famine.

Firstly, it is patently obvious that gallant efforts were made by sociologists, commentators, politicians, historians and some of the plain people of Ireland to develop a theological understanding of an immense human tragedy. What is important for us is the fact that they were putting theological questions to human distress, and while perhaps coming up with wrong or incomplete answers, they deserve praise for wrestling with the issues. In the end, some of their theology was deficient, but we must never forget that professional theologians frequently serve up bad theology. From an Irish standpoint, it is appropriate to invoke and revise Metz's famous dictum: 'we cannot do theology with our backs to the Great Famine.'

Secondly, the undercurrents of ecclesiastical incivility of Victorian Ireland stultified theological reflection. Part of the contemporary task is to redeem the rich imagination, so essential for theological work, which surfaced during the Famine crisis and employ it to create what has been called a 'wayfarers theology'. The main themes for a buoyant, enlightening theology are all in place; there is a crying need to engage them productively for the benefit of current spiritual growth.

Thirdly, it is evident that a working theology with an Irish flavour must interface with the painful realities of a turbulent past and struggle to come to terms with the ancient angers of Ireland. Social, political and demographic happenings should feed into the thematic melting pot where popular theology is created. All the stories are there waiting to be tapped: agrarian agitation, the clearings, the coffin ships, the Irish diaspora, 'the fields of Athenry'. If we fail in our modern world to search for light from dark days and find bread in the hungry times we cannot escape Kavanagh's censure: 'We cannot live on memory – not all the remembered beauty of last year can compensate for the stupidity and vulgarity that is this year's harvest.'[19]

Fourthly, it is necessary to struggle with the tension between the two major theories surrounding the Great Hunger: tragedy and conspiracy. John Mitchel's writing of the Famine in the 1860s tells a story of a British conspiracy which 'tries to seduce the Irish from the True Faith with soup and damnable heresies.' From within the interpretation which is weighted on the side of tragedy, the note of chastisement is evident, with purgatorial resonances. Such a doleful understanding of providentialism is echoed in *The Plague* by Albert Camus. The central actor in the drama, Father Paneloux, at first rationalises the tragedy:

19 Patrick Kavanagh, 'Twenty-Three Tons of Accumulated Folk-Lore' in *Irish Times*, 18 April 1939.

'The sufferings of children were our bread of affliction, but without this bread our souls would die of spiritual hunger.'[20] Such a reading of tragic events fits well into much popular recounting of Famine devastation and in the end produces both a doleful theology and a dour spirituality. Paneloux later abandons his faith after a small child dies of the plague. Things are not so in the folk memory of the Irish. In theological terms, natural calamity has been seen as a necessity, a spiritual cleansing agent administered by the Deity for the benefit of His devotees. As long as this way of looking at life's exigencies consorts with the improvement theory of the human journey, a liberative genre of theological reflection remains a distant dream. At its worst it produces a fatalistic outlook redolent of Peel's chilling rhetoric in the wake of the tragic events of 1845-9:

> It has pleased God to afflict us with a great calamity, which may perhaps be improved into a blessing ... let us deeply consider whether out of this nettle, danger, we may not pluck the flower, safety, and convert a griev-ous affliction into a means of future improvement and a source of future security.[21]

Just as the Great Famine had a permanent, irreversible effect on the demo-graphic shape and the sociological spirit of Ireland, it also left an indelible im-print on the religious consciousness of subsequent generations. While it became the catalyst for divisive and often destructive theological reflection, it also cre-ated a religious *cul-de-sac* which strangled the emergence of a productive, dy-namic native theology – which may be a good departure point for gestating a better theology for brighter times.

20 Albert Camus, *The Plague* (New York, 1972), pp. 96-7.
21 *Hansard*, 30 March 1849, civ, pp. 98-101.

Notes on Contributors

THOMAS A. BOYLAN teaches in the Department of Economics at University College Galway. He is a graduate of University College, Dublin and of Trinity College, Dublin. He is the author (with Timothy Foley) of *Political Economy and Colonial Ireland: the Propagation and Ideological Function of Economic Discourse in the Nineteenth Century* (Routledge, 1992).

NEIL BUTTIMER was educated at University College, Cork, the Dublin Institute for Advanced Studies, and Harvard University, from which he holds a doctorate in early Irish literature. He teaches in UCC's Department of Modern Irish, concentrating on pre-Famine Gaelic Ireland.

JAMES J. DONNELLY, JR. is the author of *Landlord and Tenant in Nineteenth-Century Ireland* (1973), *The Land and the People of Nineteenth-Century Cork* (1975), and the chapters on the Great Famine in Volume V, Part I of *A New History of Ireland* (1989). With Samuel Clark he is the co-editor of *Irish Peasants* (1983). He is currently writing a book on Knock Shrine and the cult of Mary in modern Irish Catholicism. A past president of the American Conference for Irish Studies, he is Professor of History at the University of Wisconsin-Madison.

ROBERT DUNLOP has been pastor of the Baptist congregation at Brannockstown, near Kilcullen, Co. Kildare, for over thirty years. A graduate of Trinity College, Dublin, he has a special interest in Irish history and culture, particularly in the areas of theology and church life. He is a regular lecturer, broadcaster and columnist, and he has written a collection of poems and several pieces of local history.

TIMOTHY P. FOLEY teaches in the Department of English at University College, Galway. He is a graduate of University College, Galway and of the University of Oxford. He is the author (with Thomas Boylan) of *Political Economy and Colonial Ireland: the Propagation and Ideological Function of Economic Discourse in the Nineteenth Century* (Routledge, 1992).

LARRY GEARY teaches history at University College, Cork and is also an honorary lecturer in the history of medicine at the Royal College of Surgeons in Ireland. He is currently working on a history of medical charities and the poor law medical service in Ireland between 1765 and 1851.

DONALD JORDAN is Brigham Distinguished Professor of Humanities at Menlo College in California. He holds a Ph.D. from the University of California, Davis, and is the author *of Land and Popular Politics in Ireland: County Mayo from the Plantation to the Land War* (Cambridge University Press, 1994).

MARGARET KELLEHER lectures in English in Mater Dei Institute of Education, Dublin. She has published a number of articles on famine literature. Her study, *The Feminization of Famine*, is forthcoming from Cork University Press in 1996.

ROBERT MAHONY is Associate Professor of English and Director of the Centre for Irish Studies at the Catholic University of America in Washington, D.C. He has also taught in Ireland at Trinity College, Maynooth and Cork, and is the author of *Jonathan Swift: the Irish Identity* (Yale University Press, 1995) and other studies of Irisdh and English writers of the eighteenth century.

CHRIS MORASH is the author of *Writing the Irish Famine* (Oxford University Press, 1995) and has edited a collection of Famine poetry, *The Hungry Voice*. He has published a number of essays on nineteenth-century Irish writing and on Irish theatre, and has contributed to reference works including the *Oxford Companion to Irish Literature*, *Blackwell's Companion to Irish Culture* and the *World Encyclopedia of Contemporary Theatre*. He is a Lecturer with the Department of English in St Patrick's College, Maynooth.

CHARLES E. ORSER, JR. is currently Professor of Anthropology at Illinois State University and Visiting Profesor of Archaeology at University College, Galway. His most recent books are *Historical Archaeology* (co-authored with Brian M. Fagan) and *A Historical Archaeology of the Modern World*. He is the founding editor of a book series, 'Contributions to Global Historical Archeology', and a journal, the *International Journal of Historical Archaeology*. His interests are in global historical archaeology and the archaeology of disenfranchised groups.

SEAN RYDER lectures in the English department of Univerity College, Galway. He has published articles on aspects of Irish cultural nationalism and is currently editing the poems of James Clarence Mangan for Oxford University Press.

MATTHEW STOUT is a cartographer and post-graduate student in the Department of Geography, Trinity College, Dublin. He has published a number of papers on ringforts and is currently researching the historical-geography of early Christian Ireland.

Index

Note: Gaelic names have been indexed under their English equivalents.